W9-CQR-444

THE SHIP IN THE BALLOON

The Story of Boston Scientific and the Development of Less-Invasive Medicine

1983–1995

1995–Present

THE SHIP IN THE BALLOON

IN 1967, DR. CHARLES DOTTER, A PIONEER IN less-invasive medicine, described a ship in a bottle to symbolize the finesse and determination required to reach remote organs through tiny holes.

Boston Scientific's "ship-in-a-balloon" symbol is the medical analogy of the "ship in a bottle." It represents the challenging task of diagnosing and treating damaged organs or vessels through tiny openings from a remote location ... the essence of interventional or minimally invasive procedures. The "balloon" (catheter with a balloon at the tip) is the "Swiss Army knife" of the interventionalist. It is small and maneuverable when deflated. When expanded, it can dilate, occlude, measure, divert flow, retrieve, or sail with blood flow.

The ship in this model is the *Spray*, in which Joshua Slocum completed the first solo circumnavigation of the globe in 1898. Slocum's voyage serves as a model for human enterprise. It embodied hard work, risk taking, perseverance, the quest for knowledge, the testing of uncharted waters, and juxtaposition of self-reliance and trust in others in a world of uncertainty and doubt.

Less-invasive medicine is also a "fantastic voyage" of adventure, exploration, innovation, and constant discovery. Its successful development enhances both patient quality of life and productivity of the health care system by reducing procedural risk, trauma, cost, and recovery time.

THE SHIP IN THE BALLOON

The Story of Boston Scientific and the Development of Less-Invasive Medicine

Jeffrey L. Rodengen

Edited by Jon VanZile
Design and layout by Rachelle Donley and Wendy Iverson

For George Mall,
a man of integrity, sincerity, and courage.

Write Stuff Enterprises, Inc.
1001 South Andrews Avenue, Second Floor
Fort Lauderdale, FL 33316
1-800-900-Book (1-800-900-2665)
(954) 462-6657
www.writestuffbooks.com

Publisher's Cataloging in Publication

Rodengen, Jeffrey L.
The Ship in the Balloon: The Story of Boston Scientific and the Development of Less-Invasive Medicine / Jeffrey L. Rodengen. - 1st ed.
p. cm.
Includes bibliographical references and index.
LCCN 97-062158
ISBN 0-945903-50-2

1. Boston Scientific (Firm) 2. Medical instruments and apparatus industry - United States - History
I. Title.

HD9994.U54B67 2001 388.7'613621'0973
QBI21-74

Library of Congress
Catalog Card Number 97-062158

ISBN 0-945903-50-2

Completely produced in the
United States of America
10 9 8 7 6 5 4 3 2 1

Also by Jeff Rodengen

The Legend of Chris-Craft

IRON FIST: The Lives of Carl Kiekhaefer

Evinrude-Johnson and The Legend of OMC

Serving the Silent Service: The Legend of Electric Boat

The Legend of Dr Pepper/Seven-Up

The Legend of Honeywell

The Legend of Briggs & Stratton

The Legend of Ingersoll-Rand

The Legend of Stanley: 150 Years of The Stanley Works

The MicroAge Way

The Legend of Halliburton

The Legend of York International

The Legend of Nucor Corporation

The Legend of Goodyear: The First 100 Years

The Legend of AMP

The Legend of Cessna

The Legend of VF Corporation

The Spirit of AMD

The Legend of Rowan

New Horizons: The Story of Ashland Inc.

The History of American Standard

The Legend of Mercury Marine

The Legend of Federal-Mogul

Against the Odds: Inter-Tel—The First 30 Years

The Legend of Pfizer

State of the Heart: The Practical Guide to Your Heart and Heart Surgery with Larry W. Stephenson, M.D.

The Legend of Worthington Industries

The Legend of Trinity Industries, Inc.

The Legend of IBP, Inc.

The Legend of Cornelius Vanderbilt Whitney

The Legend of Amdahl

The Legend of Litton Industries

The Legend of Bertram with David A. Patten

The Legend of Gulfstream

The Legend of ALLTEL with David A. Patten

The Legend of Ritchie Bros. Auctioneers

The Yes, you can of Invacare Corporation with Anthony L. Wall

TABLE OF CONTENTS

INTRODUCTION

by

John Abele
Founder Chairman
Boston Scientific Corporation

OVER THE YEARS, WE'VE TALKED with physicians, employees, scientists, business colleagues, and others about how Boston Scientific started and grew, how new products and procedures evolved, and the trials and tribulations of the many individuals and institutions who were part of this revolution in medicine. As the stories continued to grow, various people began to say "You've got to write a book."

It's a daunting task. There are many perspectives from which one can write: medical, business, technical, economic, social, political, and more. Each one influences the other. And it's hard to know where to start. There are multiple histories and multiple beginnings. Each medical society looks at life through the glasses of its specialty, with its heroes, breakthroughs, and tragedies. Each technology has different origins, and its devotees view life through those lenses. Does a "beginning" start with an idea? Or in the implementation of that idea? Even more challenging is the task of determining who and what to include, or leave out. Trying to select from among the thousands of stories and people was extraordinarily frustrating work.

In order to weave all the information into a logical, readable story, but include as much as possible, we employed a strategy that involved three elements. The main text discusses the various factors that led to the development of less-invasive medicine and the creating of the enterprise known as Boston Scientific. Sidebars are used throughout to describe people, events, issues, or stories that are interesting, but tangential to the textual theme. The third component is a three-level time line that runs the length of the book to help the reader keep chronological track of what was going on at BSC, in medicine generally, and in world events.

This book was written primarily for employees, customers, and friends ... people "in the know" or who want to know how this field (if you can call it that) of minimally invasive therapy (it has lots of names) evolved, the role that Boston Scientific played in it, and the story of Boston Scientific's origin

This calligraphy was drawn for John Abele by Princess Kwong Yem Ham, a direct descendant of the 12th century Sung dynasty. The large characters, with "danger" on top and "opportunity" on the bottom, together represent "crisis." The artist's signature and lineage are represented by the smaller characters.

and evolution. Who were these people? What were their dreams, values, experience and philosophies that lead to today's enterprise? How did they think? What were the issues and problems they faced? What were their successes and failures along the way? This is not, nor is it intended to be, either a "tell all" story or a tribute to Boston Scientific. Some parts are pretty critical, other may seem self-serving, but the story is about the revolution in less invasive medicine and one company that drove this revolution and grew during this tumultuous time.

The time period starts in the late 1960s and progresses through today. Tumultuous changes have taken place in all the fields mentioned in the first paragraph. Boston Scientific was influenced by those changes as well as part of influencing the process. The changes were driven by skilled and confident leaders who were able to challenge the establishment and survive. Whether from medicine, business, or science, they were bright, passionate, and committed. They possessed enough knowledge of organizational dynamic and Machiavellian skills to know who to enlist for their cause, how, what to do, and when.

In the 1960s and 1970s, medicine was a steep hierarchy with surgeons at the top. There was a certain noblesse oblige. They made the key decisions, determined how things would happen and who would be anointed. Oratorical skill combined with breadth and depth of experience and knowledge, produced a renaissance man who acted as a beneficent despot for the benefit of society... although they didn't do too badly either.

The giants of the giants were the cardiac surgeons: Michael DeBakey, Dwight Harken, Denton Cooley, the brothers Lillehei, and many others who were as at ease with presidents and kings as they were with doctors, nurses, and patients. As Dwight Harken was said to have commented to a patient after a difficult operation: "You can thank God and Dwight Harken for your life and not necessarily in that order."

Each specialty has its giants, of course. And its priests, cowboys, groupies, inventors, teachers, writers, investigators, entrepreneurs, wheeler dealers, dilettantes, artists, engineers, and the personalities that make up a community.

As medical technology continued to advance, also starting in the 1960s and 1970s, the "service societies" to the surgical specialities, who had been using catheters and endoscopes to provide diagnostic information to their surgical colleagues, began to discover that with a tube in place inside the body they could also provide some therapeutic benefit. Initially, it was limited to helping to make surgery safer or shorter; a radiologist, for example, would embolize a tumor to make it shrink before surgery, or a gastroenterologist would snare a polyp that a surgeon felt was too risky for an operation.

As time wore on, technology improved, imaging got better and physician's skills improved. This led to the exceptional less invasive alternative to a high-risk surgery becoming more common than the surgery itself. And since these new procedures were being performed by nonsurgical specialists in a new environment...the cath lab, the endo suite...tension rose, controversy and turf battles with surgeons became commonplace. This was truly "disruptive technology" at work.

Although Boston Scientific was only one of a number of small companies involved in this new field, we took a different view than the others. Our approach was far more proactive. We adopted a strategy that we should develop technologies that lead to products, that lead to procedures, that reduce risk, trauma, cost, and time. This was our definition of less invasive medicine.

We knew we were taking on the establishment, surgery, and would have a war on our hands. At the risk of being self-righteous, or self-serving, we took the position that what we were doing was fundamentally good for society and we would seek allies throughout medicine to help us develop, evaluate, train others and continually evolve improvements. We asked people to be critical of us and we were critical of ourselves. Our integrity was on the line and we had to be responsible in everything we did. We had to prove that we were safe and effective. Our focus was to be experts in knowledge of disease and procedures to treat it ... as much as, perhaps even more, than the products we made. If something new came along that was proven to be better, we would know about it and be involved.

The development of a company that could do that is what this book is about. It's a complex tale with many ups and downs. We hope we succeeded. We hope you enjoy it.

ACKNOWLEDGMENTS

A GREAT NUMBER OF PEOPLE assisted in the research, preparation, and publication of *The Ship in the Balloon: The Story of Boston Scientific and the Development of Less-Invasive Medicine.*

The list begins with Kathy Koman, the intrepid research assistant who compiled the original narrative time line and poured through thousands of pages of documents.

Primary thanks are also due to John Abele, founder chairman of Boston Scientific. Without his patient assistance and generous donation of hundreds of hours, this book would not have been possible. Mr. Abele provided the philosophical framework and the depth of knowledge that make this story complete.

Thanks also go to Peter Nicholas, chairman of Boston Scientific Corporation. Through his interviews, he provided the "other half" of the story. Similarly, James Tobin, president and CEO, was generous with his time during the research and writing, and Joe Ciffolillo, former president of Medi-Tech and a board member, provided invaluable insight into the company.

Gratitude is also due to Larry Best, chief financial officer, Paul Donovan, vice president, corporate communications, and Paul Sandman, general counsel.

A very warm regard is also extended to Linda Eckard, executive assistant to Mr. Abele. Linda provided a vital link to Boston Scientific and was unfailingly supportive, patient, helpful, and friendly.

Throughout a project of this magnitude, many, many people, both inside and outside of Boston Scientific, contributed their stories and memories. Particular thanks are extended to the men and women who agreed to be interviewed: Lisa Lamb, corporate manager and communications director; Bob Krajeski, former vice president of sales for Microvasive Endoscopy; Paul LaViolette, group president, cardiovascular; Alan Milinazzo, vice president of corporate sales; Al Couvillion, former head of research and development; Don Woods, former president of Medi-Tech; Art Rosenthal, chief scientific officer; H. Axel Schulpf, an outside analyst; Mike Berman, former president of SCIMED; Jim Corbett, former president of BSCI; Larry Jasinski, a former sales and marketing manager with Medi-Tech; Phil LeGoff, former group divisional manager and member of the Executive Committee; Mike Mabrey, former vice president, manufacturing, and member of the Executive Committee; Tim Snyder in the information technology department; Doug Daniels in BSCI; Dave Budreau, former director of corporate sales; Eckhard Lachenauer, former BSC Europe; Ted Feldman, M.D., a pioneer in valvuloplasty; Karen Soltesz, manager of materials; Dale Jackson, former vice president of operations, nonvascular; John Carnuccio, former head of Microvasive Urology; Stephen Moreci, group president, endosurgery; Don Hovey, former manager, strategic planning; Dale Spencer, former president of SCIMED; David Auth, founder of Heart Technology; Bob Brown, former president of BSCI and Medi-Tech's first sales manager; James Vance, founder of Van-Tec; Jerry Lacey, former president of BSCI; Janet Sullivan, former research and regulatory approval manager; Sharon Meyer, formerly in the human resources department; Joe Lacman, head of urology research and development for Microvasive; Wilfredo Casteneda, M.D., a pioneering interventional physician; Harold Coons, M.D., also a pioneering physician; Hal Mardis, M.D., who helped develop less-invasive urology; Joe Dowd, M.D., who helped develop a balloon for less-invasive urology; Bob Arcangeli, an early salesman with Mansfield; Sue Sawyer, director of customer service; Bruce Beauchemin, a 17-year veteran who was involved in the regulatory process; Richard Myler, M.D., a pioneering less-invasive cardiologist; Josh Tolkoff, former head of research and development for Medi-Tech; Dean Harrington in corporate purchasing and Boston Scientific; Lazar Greenfield, M.D., inventor of the Greenfield vena cava filter; and Peter Cotton, M.D., a pioneering gastroenterologist.

As always, special thanks are extended to the dedicated staff at Write Stuff Enterprises. Proofreader Bonnie Freeman and transcriptionist Mary Aaron worked quickly and efficiently. Indexer Erika Orloff assembled the comprehensive index. Particular thanks go to Jon VanZile, executive editor; Melody Maysonet and Heather Cohn, associate editors; Alex Lieber, former editor; Sandy Cruz, senior art director; Jill Apolinario, former art director; Wendy Iverson, Dennis Shockley, and Rachelle Donley, art directors; Bruce Borich, production manager; Marianne Roberts, vice president of administration; Nancy Rackear, former administrative assistant; Bonnie Bratton, former director of marketing, and Sheryl Herdsman, director of marketing; Grace Kurotori, sales and promotions manager; Rory Schmer, logistics specialist; and Karine Rodengen, project coordinator.

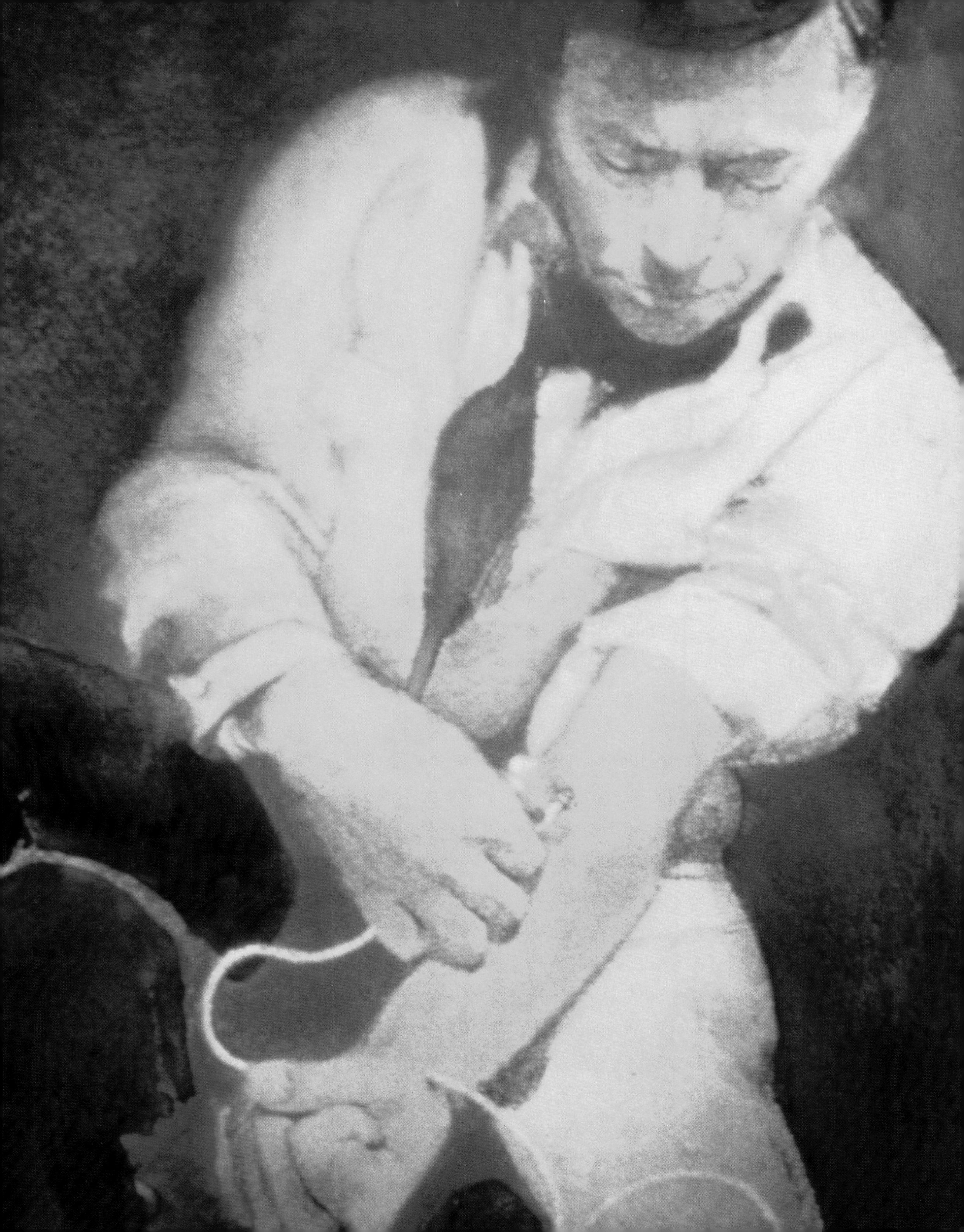

CHAPTER ONE

THE STORY BEGINS

ANCIENT TIMES TO 1964

I had a mirror placed so that by looking over the top of the screen I could see in it my thorax and upper arm. As I'd expected the catheter reached the head of the humerus.... I pushed the catheter in further, almost to the two foot mark. Now the mirror showed the catheter inside the heart, with its tip in the right ventricle, just as I'd envisioned it. I had some X-rays taken as documentary evidence.

—Werner Forssmann, *Experiments on Myself*

MEDICAL TECHNOLOGY. THE PHRASE itself seems like a modern invention, something engineer-doctors might have developed to describe the marriage of medicine with machines, or a kind of advanced cybertherapy on a microscopic level. Yet in its most basic form, medical technology isn't a new concept at all—physicians have been using devices to make medicine less traumatic and more effective since the dawn of recorded history.

In Egypt, archaeologists have discovered evidence that as early as 400 B.C., doctors used hollow reeds and brass pipes as primitive catheters to study heart valve function in cadavers. These same doctors also used long, thin tubes attached to animal-bladder enemas to inject "restorative liquids" into the bowels to harmonize the body's internal spirits. Similarly, in ancient China, an advanced society both medically and technically, doctors used the oiled stalk of an onion to relieve urinary pressure, while ancient Indian doctors used primitive tubes to drain the urinary tract.

Later, in Rome, catheter pipes made of lead, silver, brass, and copper were made in both men's and women's sizes for use in the urinary bladder. Like modern catheters, these were designed to be somewhat flexible to follow the body's natural contours.[1]

These first catheters were used in what would now be called urology, or treatment of the urinary system, as well as in the lower gastrointestinal tract. But it wasn't long before doctors began envisioning catheter-based therapy in the body's circulatory system. Although the catheter's uses were limited in the vascular system, a successful blood transfusion through a catheter was performed in London as early as 1667.[2] The first documented cardiac catheterization was performed on a horse in 1711 by a doctor named Hales, who used a glass tube, brass pipes, and the trachea of a goose. He was able to measure the heart's internal, or intracardiac, pressure.[3]

A century later, a French urologist named Reybard was the first to use a balloon-tipped catheter. In 1803, he used a dual-lumen catheter to compress an engorged prostate gland. The balloon was inflated with water or air that was injected through a syringe. By this time, doctors were using a wide variety of catheters to open various portions of the urinary tract.

Catheter use, manufacture, and acceptance also tended to be very specific geographically, with France the leader in all three areas.[4] French urologists invented a variety of catheters, including devices made of ivory, vulcanized rubber, wire, and even wax-impregnated cloth, which had the misfortune of melting once inside the body.

Early interventional medical technology wasn't limited to catheter-like tubes. In 1805, a physician

Opposite: In 1929, a German doctor named Werner Forssmann made medical history when he catheterized his own heart. It was the first time a catheter had been advanced into a living human heart.

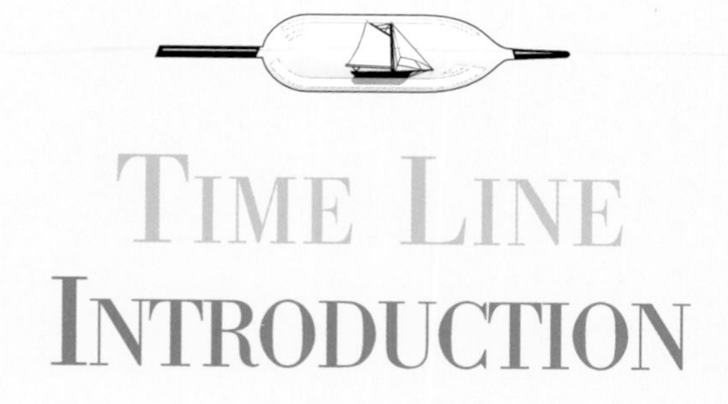

Time Line Introduction

OVER THE LAST CENTURY—*and especially in the last 50 years—a revolution in medical devices has changed the way patients are treated. Patients have generally benefited greatly as devices like catheters and endoscopes, in the right hands, initially improved diagnosis before surgery and, over time, gradually replaced surgery, reducing risk, trauma, cost, and time.*

Like many revolutions, this one has been the product of many brilliant and innovative minds, often practicing outside conventional medicine and scorned by traditional physicians, who thought it unlikely if not impossible that a hollow scope or a flexible tube could be of any practical use. And yet, slowly, these devices improved and gained acceptance, prompting the development of new specialties like therapeutic endoscopy, interventional radiology, interventional cardiology, endourology, endovascular surgery, and endovascular neurosurgery.

Coupled with advances in pharmaceuticals and surgery, this revolution has helped advance medicine far beyond what was considered medically possible even just a few years ago.

This time line traces the evolution of interventional medicine and Boston Scientific within the context of medical and world history.

named Phillip Bozzini invented the rigid endoscope. This inflexible tube, usually about 0.25 inch in diameter, with a magnifying lens, was passed down the throat and allowed physicians to see into the stomach, thus founding the field of gastroscopy. (A gastroscope is simply an endoscope that is used to examine the stomach.)

By the middle of the century, rigid gastroscopes were in wide use in Europe, although American doctors tended to avoid them because of the inherent danger of pushing a rigid tube down the sensitive esophagus and into the stomach. Nevertheless, the concept slowly caught on, and soon other kinds of endoscopes appeared. In 1894, a physician at Johns Hopkins University introduced the sigmoidoscope, which was used to view the sigmoid colon. Although this was an American innovation, almost a century would pass before better, more flexible kinds of endoscopes began to make serious inroads in American medicine.

Artisans and Artists

Around the same time European doctors were using rigid endoscopes to peer into the human body, the term *catheter* (from the Greek word *katheter*, meaning "to send down") came into wide use. The word was first used by a French physiologist named Claude Bernard, who used the long, thin tubes to accurately record intracardiac pressures in animals.[5]

At the time, Bernard was probably using catheters of his own design. Whatever few catheters existed were most likely used in urology, and their manufacture was something of a cottage industry, with doctors

Approximately 1000 B.C.

World Events

Medical Milestones

The Sushruta Samhita, *an early Indian surgical text, describes metal and wood tubes smeared with liquid butter for removal of urine, management of stricture, and installation of medication.*

Boston Scientific

using whatever was available. As science progressed into the twentieth century and catheter use became more widespread, however, their manufacture evolved into a skilled trade. Unlike other manufacturing firms, the typical catheter company wasn't an industrial behemoth churning out thousands of identical devices. Instead, catheter manufacturers tended to work with a particular specialty, sometimes even with a particular doctor, and turned out small numbers of highly personalized devices.

The first major American manufacturer, George Tiemann & Company of New York City, patented a vulcanized curved rubber catheter around the turn of the century. Before long, the company produced a catalog of urological catheters. Around the same time, the J. Elwood Lee Company of Conshohoken, Pennsylvania, began manufacturing catheters that were made of woven cotton, flax, and silk and coated with elasticized varnish.[6]

Nevertheless, there was no sense of a "catheter industry," or for that matter any medical device industry. Instead, all these devices found application among small bands of pioneering medical specialists who hardly ever communicated with each other and had very little or no communication among their various disciplines, even if they used the same basic catheter design. An exception occurred when the x ray was introduced: early radiologists discovered they could obtain better pictures by injecting contrast material into blood vessels, so they often used adapted urological catheters.

With little connection and no unifying force, it was an experimental time in the development of medical devices. At the end of the nineteenth century, "Sanford Kelly of Pennsylvania published a description of 'a novel catheter.' He had used the oiled stalk of a buttercup to relieve a young boy in the country of acute urinary retention, a more formal type of catheter not being readily available."[7]

About 20 years later, Drs. Henry Plummer and Porter Vinson at the Mayo Clinic published a paper on another novel technique, one that would have much longer lasting effects than the oiled stalk of a buttercup. The doctors reported that a patient had entered their office seeking relief from frequent vomiting and cardiospasm. The 45-year-old woman was suffering from esophageal stenosis (a narrowed esophagus) after undergoing an operation for acute appendicitis. Typically, physicians would try forcing the esophagus open with a gastroscope, performing surgery, or even guiding an olive down a wire to push it open.

Plummer and Vinson, however, took a different approach. To treat the condition, they had the patient swallow six yards of strong silk thread, then passed a balloon corseted with a lace doily they had sewn themselves, or "hydrostatic dilator," down the thread to the narrowed point. They inflated the balloon with "very little discomfort," and she returned home a week later completely relieved of her symptoms. "The immediate results are almost spectacular," they later wrote. "One dilatation, provided the cardia has been properly stretched, is sufficient to cure the majority of patients."[8]

Although physicians had been using catgut balloons to open narrowed tubes, this is the first

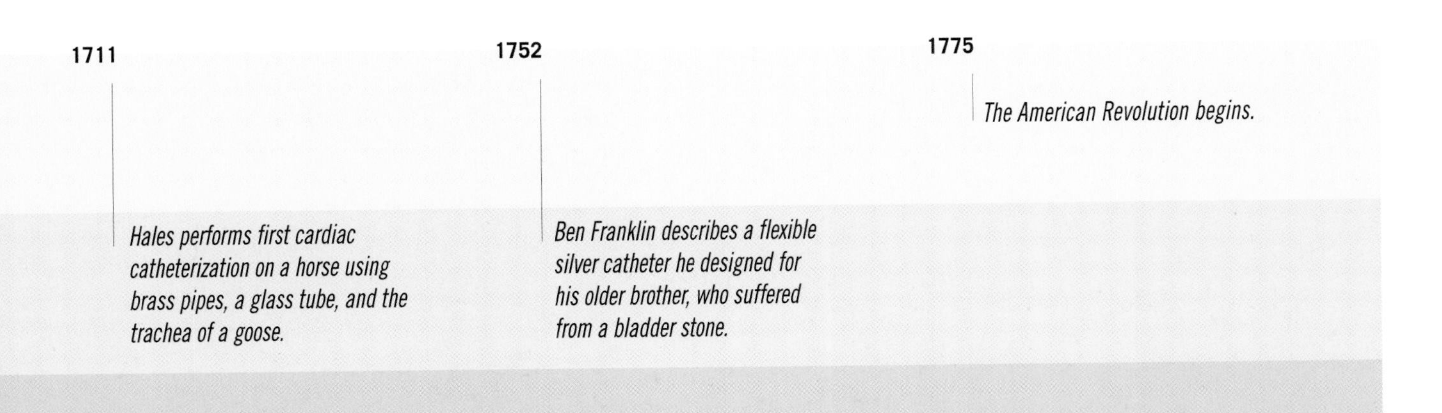

documented use of a guided, limited-expansion balloon used to expand a lumen in the human body. Much later, this same concept would revolutionize the treatment of heart disease.

The Age of Surgeons

Throughout these long, slow decades, medicine developed in many other areas. Doctors were limited by a lack of technological know-how and, more importantly, by infection. Common sicknesses like influenza and bacterial infection killed tens of thousands every year, and other communicable diseases like polio and smallpox also took lives. Even surgeons, considered the highest order of the medical establishment, were able to treat only the most rudimentary internal injuries, and it was dangerous, tricky work. Biological vein grafts, pioneered by the Nobel Prize–winning surgeon Alexis Carrel at the turn of the century, were possible but not a widespread technique. The heart-lung machine, which allowed surgeons to operate on the body's main circulatory systems, didn't appear until 1955, and blood banks were unknown.

By the 1940s, however, the pace of medical innovation had picked up, mostly because of World War II, the greatest medical event of the twentieth century. It represented a dizzying time as doctors and surgeons were confronted with thousands of major injuries to organs, blood vessels, and other tissues. It was during the war that many of the most famous surgeons in U.S. medical history were trained and began their pioneering careers, including cardiovascular surgeons Michael DeBakey, Dwight Harken, John Kirklin, Denton Cooley, Dudley Johnson, and John Gibbon. Perhaps even more importantly, World War II ushered in the age of antibiotics as Alexander Fleming's famous penicillin mold was finally mass produced and became the world's foremost anti-infective.

The development of medical devices also took important steps. Semiflexible endoscopes had been introduced to the United States in the mid-1930s by Dr. Rudolph Schindler, and their use began to spread quickly. By 1941, they were accepted and early gastroenterologists were ready to form the first U.S. medical society devoted to the use of a specific medical device. Thus, the American Gastroscopic Club was chartered and celebrated its first annual meeting in 1942 with just over 100 members.

That same year, Dr. Andre Cournand catheterized the right atrium of a human heart with a radiopaque (visible to x ray) catheter and obtained a blood sample to measure its oxygen content. This was the first time a catheter had been used in a human to measure blood oxygen through direct means. His catheter was manufactured by the United States Catheter & Instrument Corporation (USCI), a small company founded in 1941 as a maker of urological catheters. Cournand, along with Dickinson Richards and Werner Forssmann, later received the Nobel Prize, and their work was recognized as a pivotal step in the founding of cardiology.

At the end of World War II, medicine entered a period that might be called the Golden Age of Surgeons. The physicians who had grown so com-

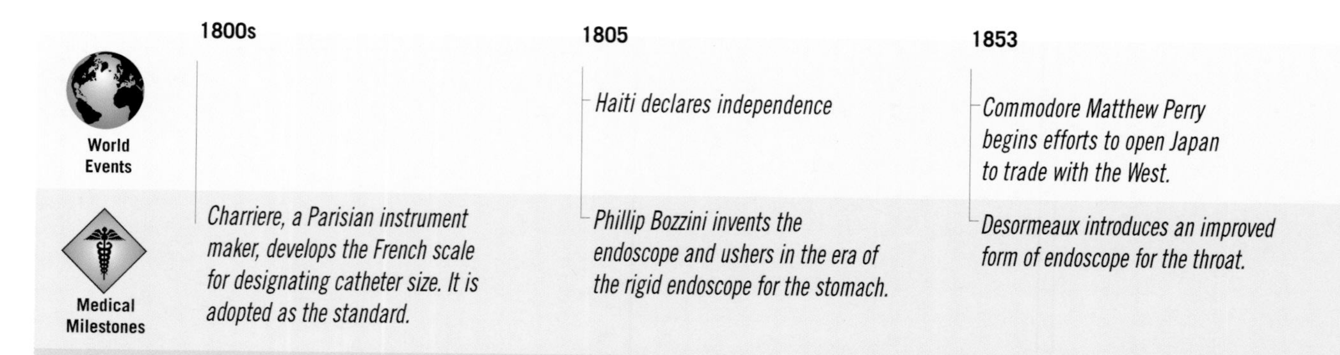

petent during the war turned their attention to new procedures and techniques. In the space of 10 incredible years, the heart-lung machine was developed (a kind of medical device itself), new antibiotics and vaccines all but won the war against many of the known microbes, and artificial vein grafts were introduced. These lifesaving devices were first used to correct dangerous aortic aneurysms. While the credit for developing them is often given to DeBakey, who invented the Dacron arterial graft and went on to become one of the world's most well-known physicians, it is likely that the grafts were introduced almost simultaneously in several different places, including one version by an Armenian rug manufacturer called Meadox. The Meadox graft was created by a renowned heart surgeon named Ormand Julian, who had performed a lifesaving operation on Meadox's owner, Titus Haffa.

DeBakey and many of his peers were the surgeons who introduced the world to a new era of heart surgery, dazzling the traditional medical establishment with complicated open-heart surgeries that attempted to correct the most dreaded congenital heart lesions. As a result, they became superstar doctors whose names turned into household words during the 1950s and remain engraved on the public imagination.

Dr. Michael DeBakey became one of the most well-known cardiovascular surgeons in the world in the 1950s. In addition to his pioneering work in heart surgery, DeBakey is credited with the introduction of the world's first woven Dacron arterial graft.

The Quiet Revolution

Although the decade's advances were dominated by surgeons, less-invasive medicine continued to make important, albeit quiet steps forward. In 1953, a doctor named Sven Seldinger developed the percutaneous ("performed through the skin") method to introduce catheters into the body.[9] With the percutaneous method, doctors used a needle and guidewire to gain entry. No scalpel was needed.

1860

Auguste Nelaton, physician to Napoleon III, introduces a flexible rubber catheter.

1861

The American Civil War begins.

1868

Adolf Kussmaul introduces the gastroscope, a form of rigid endoscope used to view the stomach. He demonstrates with a sword swallower.

1889

U.S. manufacturer George Tiemann & Company's catalog of surgical instruments lists nearly 80 different types of urological catheters.

"I can perform the procedure faster than you can write about it," Seldinger wrote. "Needle in, wire in, needle out, catheter over wire, wire out; that is all."[10] While this innovation was important, it didn't receive much attention at the time, and Seldinger himself published only a few papers on the technique.

Flexible fiber-optic endoscopy "entered the realm of practicality" when, in 1957, Dr. Basil Hirschowitz passed a prototype endoscope down his own throat. The first commercial flexible fiberscope was introduced later that year, representing a major improvement over the conventional gastroscope and forever changing the field of endoscopy.

By the early 1960s, the medical field was firmly established in its patterns. Surgeons sat atop the pyramid of clout in each specialty, supported by a broad network of various other specialists, including pathologists, anesthesiologists, radiologists, and clinical chemists, and at the bottom sat the patients themselves—who had very little or no control over the course of their treatment. Naturally, these surgeons, who favored working in large "open fields," or big openings into their patients, didn't give much thought to a technique that allowed a radiologist to introduce a catheter with a needle. To them, the most important "medical devices" were a scalpel and a steady hand. The idea of patient trauma was less important than the risk associated with small operating fields.

1. 2. 3. 4. 5.

The Seldinger technique of percutaneous catheterization enabled nonsurgical medical specialists to enter the interventional field. In this technique, a catheter was inserted over a guidewire, using a large-bore needle to gain entry. No scalpel was necessary.

In this context, the work of cardiologist Mason Sones had an electrifying effect. In 1958, while a doctor at the Cleveland Clinic, Sones was injecting x-ray contrast material into an aorta when he made a mistake and slid the catheter into the right coronary artery. Doctors had assumed that the coronary arteries could not be catheterized because they were too small and far too sensitive and important. But instead of seeing his patient go into cardiac arrest, Sones was surprised to see the coronary tree glow, under x ray, with the contrast material. This fortunate accident not only earned Sones the nickname Father of Selective Coronary Arteriography but gave doctors a powerful new diagnostic tool and presaged the development of interventional cardiology and even coronary bypass surgery.[11]

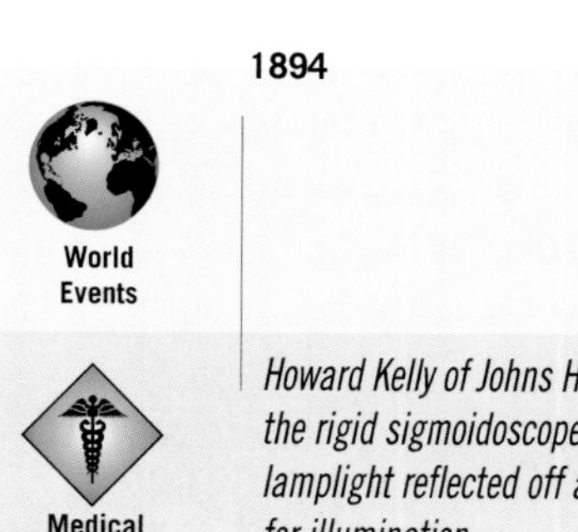

World Events

Medical Milestones

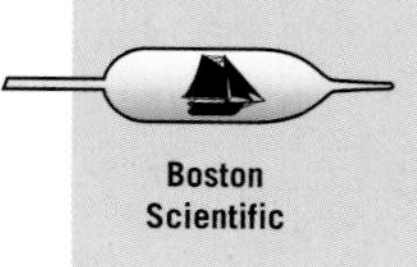

Boston Scientific

1894

Medical Milestones: *Howard Kelly of Johns Hopkins introduces the rigid sigmoidoscope, using ordinary lamplight reflected off a head mirror for illumination.*

1901

Medical Milestones: *Ott, a Russian gynecologist, performs first documented laparoscopy.*

1907

World Events: *Leo Baekeland, a Belgian-born chemist, invents the world's first synthetic plastic.*

By the 1960s and 1970s, medical decision making had evolved into a pyramid with various surgeons on top, supported by a vast network of medical professionals. In the days when patients' rights and cost containment weren't issues, the patients themselves were at the very bottom of the hierarchy.

1916

The first medical specialty board (ophthalmology) is created; 11 specialty boards exist by 1940.

1918

World War I ends with Europe in disarray. The war lasted four years and eventually drew in the United States.

1919

Vinson and Plummer use a corseted, expanding balloon to widen a narrowed esophagus: first use of a limited expansion balloon in a human.

1922

Rudolph Schindler introduces his version of the rigid gastroscope.

In 1958, Mason Sones, a cardiologist at the Cleveland Clinic, accidentally injected contrast material into the coronary tree and obtained a clear image of the coronary arteries. This led to coronary arteriography, which was an important stepping-stone in the development of open-heart surgery.

Like Cournand, Sones was using a catheter made by USCI, which wasn't surprising considering there were still only a few catheter companies in existence. Yet despite the small field of competitors, it's likely that nobody could have accurately described how deeply catheters had penetrated into medicine. Catheterization remained an underground science, practiced by tiny artisan-like companies that made products on demand for specific uses. These early companies were not run by doctors but were totally "physician guided," meaning it was a point of policy that they would not influence a patient's health care decisions. Rather, they positioned themselves as suppliers and hands-on engineers, a sort of hardware store for doctors who wanted to turn their individual visions into actual treatments.

Another of these young start-ups was Cordis Corporation, which in the early 1960s had developed a unique catheter with metal braided into the walls. This development allowed better control of the polyurethane device. Although technically competitors, Cordis and USCI worked in a small universe, so it was not unusual when Robert Stevens of Cordis agreed to let USCI manufacture his catheter in 1963. The partnership failed, however, after USCI could not meet Stevens's specifications. Cordis received patent protection on its stainless steel braided catheters several years later.[12]

A Maverick Pioneer Enters the Scene

One of the companies that would eventually copy Cordis's approach was Cook Incorporated, a small firm founded in 1963 by Bill Cook, a salesman for American Hospital Supply, and his wife, Gayle Cook. They had started their medical device company in their Bloomington, Indiana, apartment, where they produced catheters, guide wires (used in the Seldinger technique to introduce catheters into the vessel), and needles.[13] Like most catheter companies, Cook turned out products that had been designed by doctors for their own use. He did not believe that catheter companies should offer advice to their physician customers.

The Cooks' early manufacturing and quality control were an interesting give-and-take. Bill made the catheters during the day, and after he went to bed at night, Gayle inspected them. She removed any products that did not meet her specifications and hid them in the basement. It wasn't until years

World Events

Medical Milestones

Boston Scientific

1928

British bacteriologist Alexander Fleming discovers penicillin in a petri dish; however, it is not developed for more than a decade.

1929

Birth of Martin Luther King Jr.

Stock market crash precipitates the Great Depression.

Werner Forssmann catheterizes his own heart.

1930s

Takagi pioneers arthroscopy.

Forssmann's Breakthrough

A YOUNG PIONEER NAMED WERNER Forssmann decided in 1929 that he could catheterize a human heart. Although catheters had been used elsewhere in the body, never had a catheter been advanced into a living human heart. Nevertheless, Forssmann, a 25-year-old intern at a small provincial hospital northeast of Berlin, was dissatisfied with the standard methods of cardiac diagnosis, namely percussion, x ray, and electrocardiography, and decided to push ahead.

After studying the writings of Claude Bernard and other nineteenth-century French physiologists, Forssmann pleaded to his superior for permission to experiment with cardiac catheterization on a human patient, but was denied.[1]

Forssmann decided to use himself as a subject. Knowing he would need help to carry out the risky procedure, he befriended a surgical nurse who had access to the necessary sterile instruments. "I let a few days go by and then started to prowl around Nurse Gerda Ditzen like a sweet-toothed cat around the cream jug," Forssmann later wrote.

> *I knew I'd be able to carry out my black deed only during the afternoon siesta while everyone in the hospital was dozing, so I made a point of dawdling in the canteen after lunch, hoping to meet Nurse Gerda as she left the nurses' dining room.... Little by little, I won over my essential disciple. When, about a fortnight after my conversation with Schneider, she said with a sigh, "What a pity we can't do the experiment together!" I decided the time had come.*[2]

Ditzen not only agreed to assist but volunteered to be his subject. Forssmann accepted her offer, though he had no intention of catheterizing the nurse. After obtaining the venesection equipment from Ditzen, Forssmann strapped the nurse to an operating table so she couldn't interfere. Out of her view, he made an incision in his left arm, inserted a needle into the vein, and pushed a rubber ureteral catheter toward his heart. He then released the nurse and asked her to call x ray. "Only then did she realize what had happened," wrote Forssmann. "She started to yell at me for having deceived her."[3]

Though the procedure was a success, Forssmann lost his job after the news of his experiment got out, and he was ostracized by the medical community. It wasn't until 1956 that his work was actually recognized—along with that of fellow pioneers Andre Cournand and Dickinson Richards, who pioneered the use of catheters to measure cardiac output—and he was awarded the Nobel Prize.[4]

1934

Claudette Colbert and Clark Gable win Oscars for It Happened One Night.

Rudolph Schindler arrives in the United States with a semiflexible gastroscope. The procedure begins to spread.

1935

Foley, an American urologist, demonstrates a model of his balloon catheter at the American Urological Association meeting.

1937

The first acceptable color photos inside the stomach are taken.

1939

Adolf Hitler's blitzkrieg overruns Poland, touching off World War II.

later that she revealed where she had been hiding the faulty products.

But quality was paramount since the universe of interventional medicine was so small and fragmented and reputations were so important. One pioneering doctor might be active in several different areas, working with the early gastroscopes, pulling catheters, and experimenting with better diagnostics. In fact, Cook described meeting just such a doctor at the 1963 Radiology Society of North America (RSNA) annual meeting:

I was demonstrating to prospective customers how to pull tips on Teflon catheters when I noticed someone behind me sitting on a box. It was a short, muscular, bald man—I didn't know who he was, but he made me nervous. When there was a lull in business, I turned and asked if I could be of some help, and he said "no"—nothing more—and left.

Just before we closed for the day, he returned and asked if he could use my blowtorch and "borrow" some Teflon tubing. He said he wanted to practice making catheters in his hotel room. Thinking I had a real space cadet on my hands, I said, "Sure, may I have your name?" He answered, "Charles Dotter." The next morning he was waiting for me with ten beautifully made Teflon catheters and my blowtorch. Remember, I had just started my business, and I admit that those ten catheters were sold to someone else for ten dollars each later that day. He was my first production employee.[14]

Like many other radiologists, Dotter had gained experience creating his own catheters because he couldn't find any that satisfied his requirements. "Between the idea and the actual instrument needed to implement the idea," Dotter once remarked, "is a bigger jump than you might think." Thus, he wound his own

Using a blowtorch and lengths of Teflon tubing, Bill Cook fashioned catheters for radiologists at the 1963 RSNA convention in Chicago.

World Events

Medical Milestones

Boston Scientific

1940

Cameron begins making gastroscopes in the United States.

1941

The United States enters World War II.

USCI, an early catheter manufacturer, is founded by Norman Jeckel in New York when WWII shuts off foreign supplies of urological catheters.

Leon Schiff proposes the formation of a gastroscopic society; Schindler proposes and lays the groundwork for the American Gastroscopic Club.

guidewires and made his own catheters with guitar strings and Volkswagen speedometer cables. "It was a crude beginning," he said, "but it worked."[15]

By the time he met Cook, Dotter had already made a name for himself. He had done extensive work with balloon catheters, including measuring pressure, and he was among the first to visualize arteries using a catheter and x ray. He was also one of the first physicians to use the relatively new flexible gastroscopes.

Unquestionably, Dotter was positioned on the rising edge of a wave of futurists, doctors, and technologists who believed that engineering combined with medicine could yield therapeutic miracles. The history of catheterization "is an exciting, instructive testament to the scientific spirit and method," wrote Richard L. Mueller and Timothy A. Sanborn, authors of *The History of Interventional Cardiology: Cardiac Catheterization, Angioplasty, and Related Interventions*. "Like those of most medical discoveries, the stories of the innovations and innovators involved are marked by charismatic and independent personalities, their perseverance despite failure and ridicule, the wise and timely exploitation of serendipitous observations, and several lag periods during which technology and scientific peers caught up slowly with those ahead of their time."[16]

Dotter's Innovation

As 1963 ended, the world was poised for two major medical breakthroughs—one from a leading cardiac surgeon who wouldn't report his success for eight years and one from the eccentric radiologist who made his own devices. In 1964, the world's first confirmed coronary artery bypass graft surgery was performed by a team headed by DeBakey, who kept his achievement a secret.

In contrast, Dotter earned significant notoriety on January 16, 1964, when he used a catheter to dilate an occluded iliac artery of an 82-year-old bedridden woman. She was facing amputation of a foot due to gangrene. Dotter passed a guide wire through the stenotic, or narrowed, portion of the vessel. Then he slipped a tapered, radiopaque (visible to x ray), Teflon dilating catheter (obtained from Cook Incorporated) over the guide and advanced it until it enlarged the lumen of the artery. Dotter completed the procedure within minutes and without difficulty. Eight months later, the woman's foot had healed and she was walking.[17]

With this astonishing success, Dotter founded the field of interventional radiology and began to attract attention. In August 1964, *Life* magazine published several photographs showing him forcing his arterial "snake" through a fatty plug blocking the main artery of a patient's leg, creating a new channel for blood flow and sparing the patient's foot.[18] His public image, however, was forever affected by *Life's* series of photos showing an aproned Dotter in bloody gloves grimacing wildly as he worked the catheter into his patient. Before long, he had earned the nickname "Crazy Charlie."

Dotter himself encouraged this wild image, and may even have been deliberately provoking surgeons

1942

First meeting of the American Gastroscopic Club. The Club issues the first edition of the Bulletin of the American Gastroscopic Club.

1945

World War II ends with the defeat of Japan and Germany.

1946

John Tilden Howard, the Club's secretary, urges gastroenterologists to use esophagoscopy.

1947

American Gastroscopic Club changes its name to American Gastroscopic Society (AGS).

by choosing a pipe and wrench as his trademark—implying that vascular surgeons are simply a form of plumber. "If a plumber can do it to pipes, we can do it to blood vessels," he declared.[19]

In a 1964 article in *Circulation* called "Transluminal Treatment of Arteriosclerotic Obstruction," authors Dotter and his colleague Melvin P. Judkins summed up the effectiveness of transluminal recanalization:

> *However primitive its present state of development and though its application has largely been confined to surgical "cast-offs," transluminal recanalization has proved to be an effective alternative to surgical reconstruction and a safer and otherwise more attractive alternative to amputation. As such, it deserves a serious trial in the hands of competent physicians.*[20]

"Crazy Charlie"

In Europe, doctors quickly adopted transluminal angioplasty, even referring to the procedure as "Dottering."[21] Their enthusiasm, however, was short-lived, and it eventually fell to a German doctor named Eberhard Zeitler to keep the procedure alive. His work helped lay the groundwork for Andreas Gruentzig, who years later would perform the first coronary artery angioplasty.

In the United States, however, the debut of peripheral angioplasty was greeted with scorn and doubt, especially by surgeons, who were suspicious of a radiologist "barging into their territory clutching a catheter."[22] Vascular surgeons regularly refused to refer patients to radiologists for transluminal angioplasty and heaped derision upon the eccentric radiologist who had developed the technique.[23]

Dotter continued to aggravate the tension between himself and the surgeons. Almost two months after his initial angioplasty, he received a request from a surgeon for a radiology consultation for a patient who appeared to have a blockage of the left femoral artery. The surgeon wrote on the requisition form, "Visualize but do not try to fix!!!" Arteriograms confirmed narrowing of both femoral arteries. As ordered, Dotter didn't touch the artery in the left leg. But he couldn't resist dilating the artery in the right leg.[24]

As time went on, Dotter continued to promote transluminal angioplasty. He produced a humorous and educational film featuring Dr. Ward J. White, who suffered from leg pain due to an obstruction of his left superficial femoral artery. Dotter completed the transluminal angioplasty on White in less than

Above: Charles Dotter, who likened his work to that of a plumber, used this image of a crossed pipe and wrench as his trademark.

World Events

1948

An assassin kills Mahatma Mohandas Gandhi.

1953

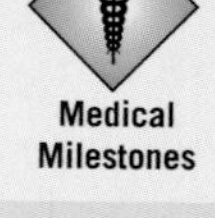
Medical Milestones

AGS distributes a statement on minimum requirements for gastroscope manufacture.

Edward Benedict introduces the operating gastroscope, which incorporates a biopsy forceps and suction tube.

Sven Seldinger develops a percutaneous, or through-the-skin, technique for inserting catheters into blood vessels.

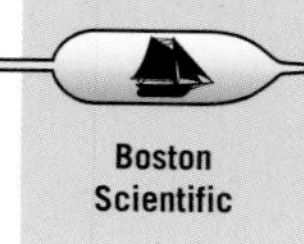
Boston Scientific

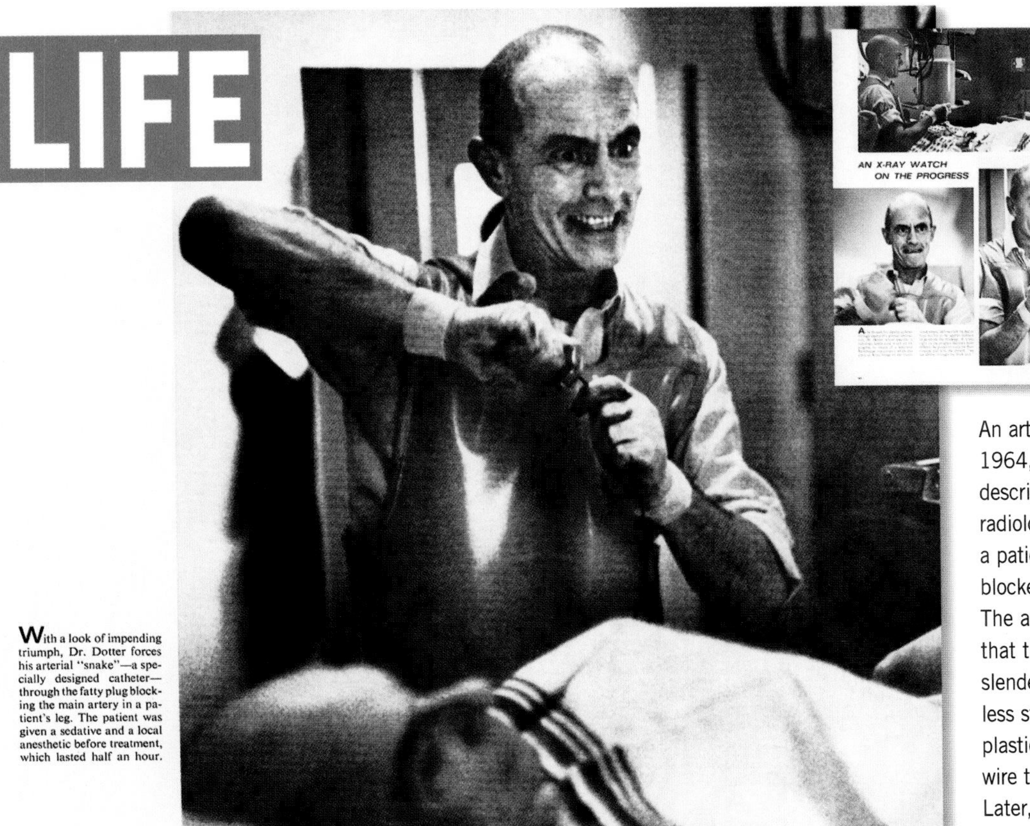

With a look of impending triumph, Dr. Dotter forces his arterial "snake"—a specially designed catheter—through the fatty plug blocking the main artery in a patient's leg. The patient was given a sedative and a local anesthetic before treatment, which lasted half an hour.

Plumbing-style 'snake' restores blocked circulation

CLEARING AN ARTERY

Dr. Charles Dotter, of the University of Oregon Medical School, had every reason to be elated. By applying a bit of know-how straight out of the plumbers' manual, he had Gerhardt, Dr. Dotter had developed—and used successfully on nine other similarly afflicted patients—a new technique employing a miniature device similar to the

An article in the August 14, 1964, issue of *Life* magazine described how pioneering radiologist Charles Dotter saved a patient's leg by clearing a blocked artery using a "snake." The article went on to explain that the snake is actually a slender catheter, "a long stainless steel spring, encased in a plastic sleeve and containing wire to give it some rigidity." Later, Dotter's technique for transluminal angioplasty became known as "Dottering."

1954

USCI and Meadox simultaneously develop the world's first arterial prosthesis for bypassing aneurysms in the trunk and upper legs.

1955

The Mayo-Gibbon heart-lung machine is used successfully by John W. Kirklin. The age of open-heart surgery begins.

1957

The fiber-optic endoscope era begins when Basil Hirschowitz develops a prototype fiberscope and passes it down his own throat.

1958

The best picture of the year is Gigi.

Mason Sones becomes Father of Selective Coronary Arteriography after he discovers he can inject media into coronaries and get good pictures.

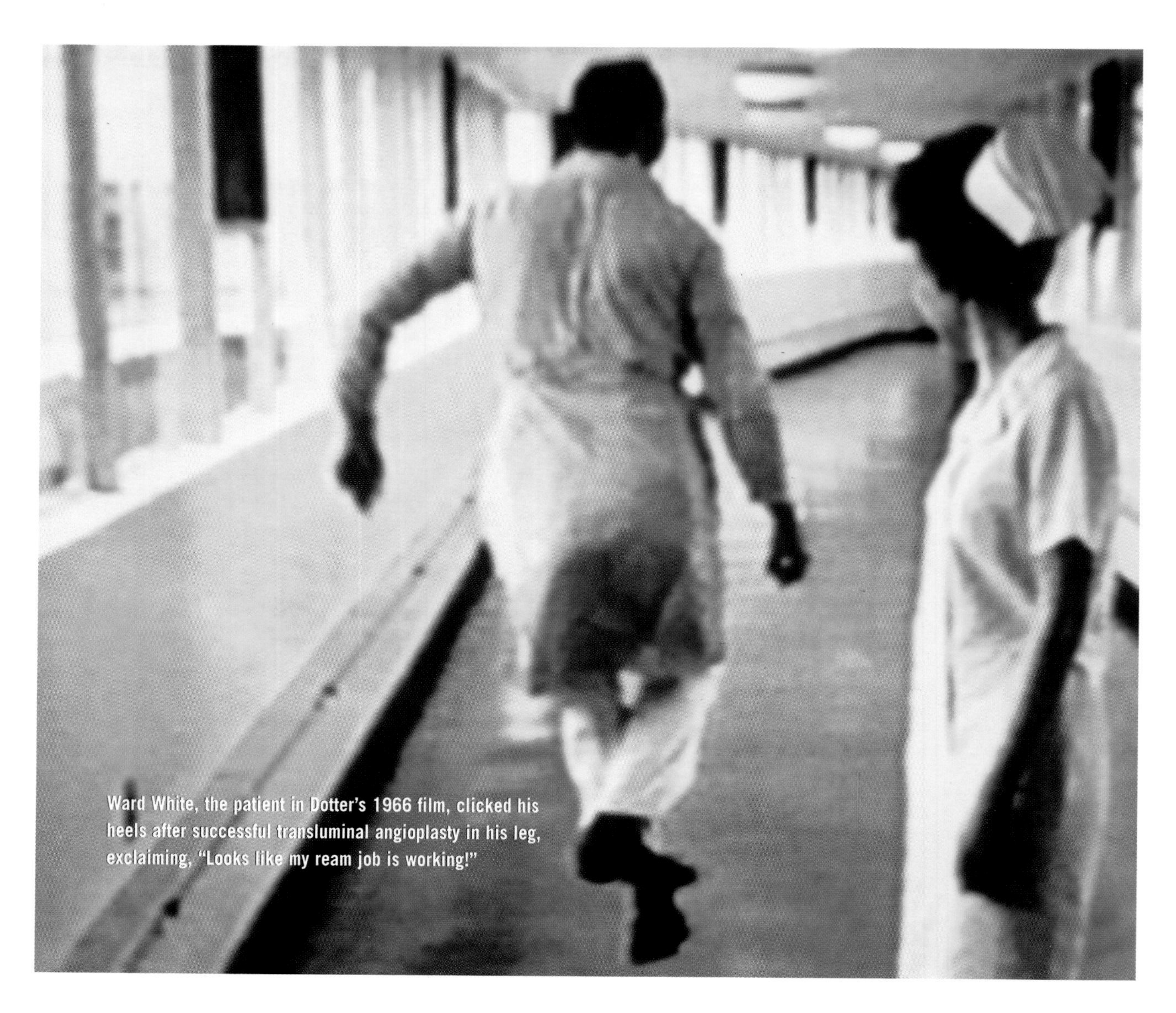

Ward White, the patient in Dotter's 1966 film, clicked his heels after successful transluminal angioplasty in his leg, exclaiming, "Looks like my ream job is working!"

World Events

Medical Milestones

Boston Scientific

Late 1950s

Charles Dotter introduces angiographic catherization into the United States.

AGS members fear a "retreat from the patient and his disease with a new emphasis on technique, optics, instruments and suction machines."

Early 1960s

Robert Stevens of Cordis Corporation develops a more modern catheter using metal braided into the walls to withstand high torque and pressure.

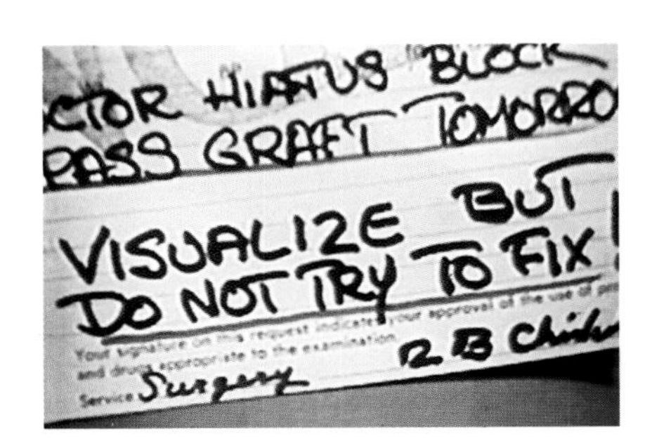

In 1964, Dotter received this radiology consultation request from a vascular surgeon who clearly was aware of Dotter's talents but warned him to "Visualize but do not try to fix!!!"

45 minutes, and the next day the patient was clicking his heels as he walked down the hospital corridor. The film showed White turning to a nurse and saying, "Looks like my ream job is working!"

However, as Dotter illustrated with images of an atomic bomb explosion, a jackhammer, the Wile E. Coyote cartoon character, and an exotic dancer, the procedure involved "no reaming, or drilling or anything like Roto Rooting. Nothing's blasted, nothing's blown out or broken up. The intima isn't plowed up. There's no stripping. Instead, in transluminal angioplasty, the narrowed, irregular lumen is dilated from within by a system consisting of a guide and two catheters.... The mechanism is like a nail hole, like ski tracks pressed into, not dug out of, snow."

Compared with vascular surgery, said Dotter, transluminal angioplasty "involves no incision, no operative exposure, no arteriotomy, no sutures, much less vascular trauma, not to mention wound healing."[25]

But with Charles Dotter as its chief spokesman, transluminal angioplasty had about as much respect in the medical community as did telepathy: It was an intriguing concept, but not applicable to real-world medicine.[26] Its very existence, however, made a valuable point: using medical technology and catheters, doctors could achieve amazing results for their patients with less cost, less trauma, less risk, and less time spent in the hospital.

1961

The Berlin Wall is constructed in East Germany.

AGS again changes its name, this time to the American Society of Gastrointestinal Endoscopy.

1963

Popular movies include Lilies of the Field *and* Hud.

Cook Inc. founded in bedroom of Bloomington, Indiana, apartment. Bill Cook meets Charles Dotter at RSNA annual meeting.

1964

The first coronary artery bypass surgery is performed. The event is not publicized for another eight years for fear of backlash from the medical community.

Dotter performs first percutaneous transluminal angioplasty (PTA) on a woman facing amputation, thus founding the field of interventional radiology.

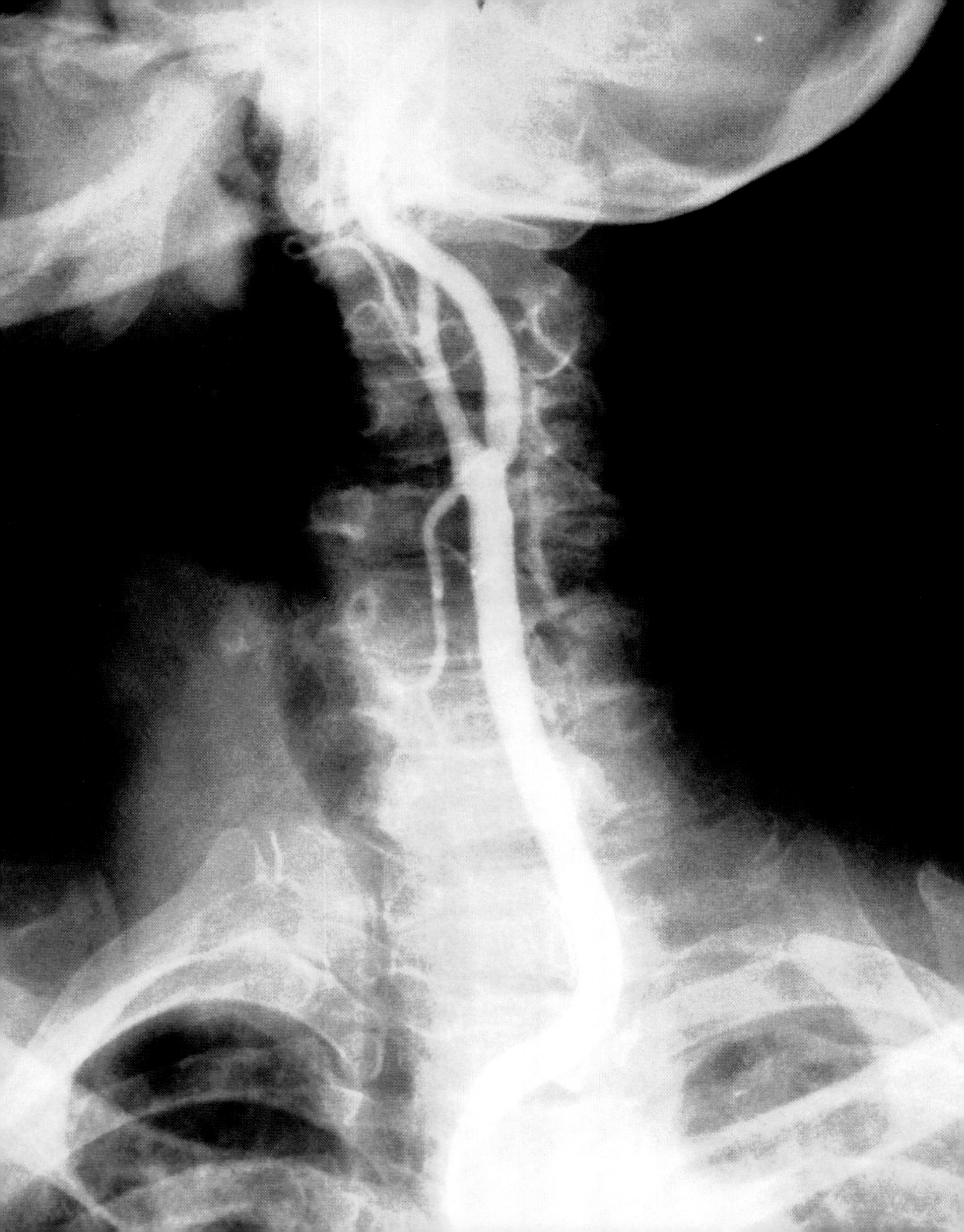

CHAPTER TWO

LAYING THE GROUNDWORK

1965–1969

In the Medi-Tech steerable catheter, I saw a platform on which to build a business.

—John Abele, 1997

CATHETER DEVELOPMENT AND TECHnology remained a bedroom science into the mid-1960s. The companies that were producing catheters acted at the behest of innovative doctors who supplied them with designs and therapeutic objectives. Most catheters were designed by physicians, who often oversaw their manufacture and heavily modified the final product to suit their unique and particular needs.

But a transition was already in progress, one that would reduce the artisan-like nature of the business. Some inventors and physicians were working toward a more generic catheter that anybody could use, or even trying to develop one that could be steered within the vessel and used for many purposes.

One of these early innovators was Melvin Judkins, who in 1967 developed a more reliable method of coronary arteriography using precurved catheters of his own design and a percutaneous transfemoral approach (insertion of the catheter via a groin puncture).

At the time, coronary arteriography was still a rare procedure. Moreover, it required great skill. Perhaps a few thousand arteriograms had been performed, and about half had been done by Mason Sones, the inventor of the technique. Sones used USCI catheters with a braided Dacron tip that were made to his specifications.

Hoping to make this procedure more intuitive and widespread, Judkins had developed a system that used a family of preshaped catheters molded to easily enter the right coronary artery and others for the left coronary. Since no companies were making preformed catheters, Judkins formed his own by slipping polyurethane tubing over a wire bent to mimic the blood vessel and softening the polyurethane in boiling water. These catheters were introduced in 1972 by Cordis Corporation.

According to the book *The Catheter Introducers*, "The coronary-seeking catheters greatly simplified selective coronary arteriography and increased the ease and confidence with which angiographers could place catheters. Judkins himself commented in 1985, 'The catheters know where to go if not thwarted by the operator!'"[1]

At the same time, other catheter companies—including USCI, maker of the braided Dacron tip, and Cook, which was working from a Cordis design—were working toward their own simplified catheters. One of these early catheters was kept straight with a guide wire in the lumen until it reached a curve in the vessel. As the wire was withdrawn, the catheter bent into the desired shape. An adaptation, called a catheter tip deflector, relied on a helically wound wire guide that could be bent in one direction only, by means of a lighter-gauge wire strung through the center of the coil. To direct this catheter, physicians rotated the entire assembly

Opposite: X-ray film showing a selective catheterization of a left carotid artery made with a Medi-Tech steerable catheter.

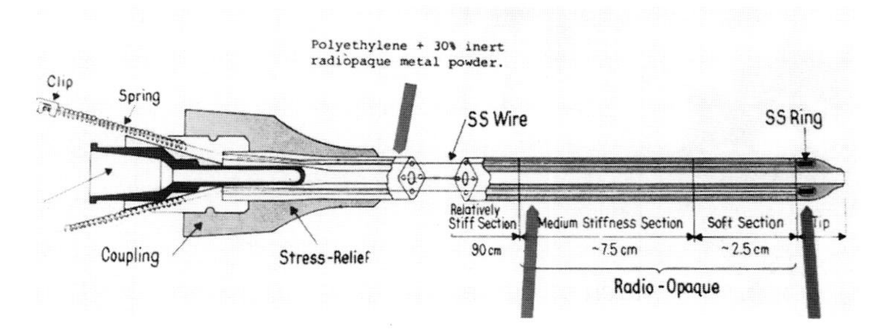

Bentov's original schematic for his steerable catheter. The device was designed with a deflecting tip that physicians could manipulate in any direction and degree without rotating the catheter.

and, once it was in position, worked around the obstructing guide wire.

These two crudely steerable devices were limited in their ability to be controlled, and they required that the lumen of the catheter be occluded during manipulation.[2]

Nevertheless, they represented a changing mind-set: catheter development was shifting away from the total customization of products by individuals to families of products designed for specific uses by any qualified physician.

Steering Their Course

Around this time, radiologists Keith Rabinov and Morris Simon, both of Beth Israel Hospital in Boston, began a search for a new type of catheter that could be steered from outside the patient's body and did not have a wire obstructing the lumen.[3] In 1967, they were referred to Itzhak Bentov, an eccentric inventor who ran a small contract research company called Medi-Tech from the basement and porch of his rented house in Belmont, Massachusetts. The two radiologists asked Bentov if he could design a remotely controllable catheter. Three days later, Bentov presented them with a working prototype.[4]

Unfortunately, tests proved the first prototype to be unstable. The device had wires going through three tubes that connected to a ring at the tip of a central and larger tube. By pulling on the wires, the tip of the larger tube, or main body of the catheter, could be deflected, much like a marionette.

When this first system proved inadequate, Bentov began to refine his thinking. He spent the next six months developing a four-wire system that had the controlling wires embedded directly into the walls of the catheter itself. To do this, Bentov had to invent a way to extrude a plastic tube with multiple lumens.[5] His final version measured 100 centimeters in length and was made of several progressively softer sections of polyethylene and ethylene vinyl acetate tubing. It was tipped with a flexible, radiopaque tip that measured 10 centimeters. At the control end, the wires connected to a plastic clip for attachment to the catheter handle. The handle was mounted on a ball joint and controlled by a lever that could swivel in all directions, much like early mechanical joysticks used to steer aircraft.[6]

Bentov's invention, officially released in 1969, was hailed by customers and competitors as an

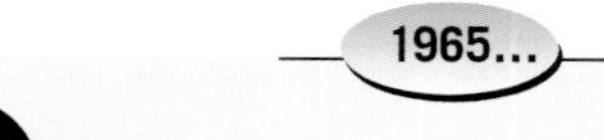

World Events

Lyndon B. Johnson is inaugurated.

Popular films include Dr. Zhivago *and* The Sound of Music.

Medical Milestones

Charles Dotter describes corkscrew action liver biopsy catheter, used in dogs.

Bill Cook develops Safe-T-J wire guide.

Wire-guided, catheter-technique percutaneous nephrostomy for drainage is introduced.

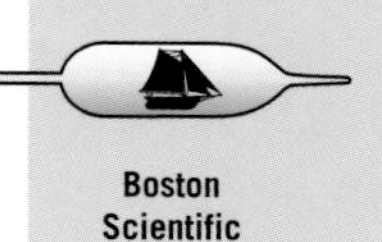

Boston Scientific

extraordinary piece of engineering.[7] In September 1969, a profile of Bentov's steerable catheter appeared in *Product Engineering*:

> *A new steerable angiography catheter, guided by a doctor's thumb on a miniature joy stick, will soon take much of the tedium and hazard out of hospital procedure for probing the human circulatory system. The new instrument ... is expected to expand the physician's ability to examine, diagnose, and treat areas of the body cavity that are now not accessible to him except through surgery.*[8]

In an article in the journal *Radiology*, Rabinov and Simon described the steerable catheter as a device that "has proved particularly useful in catheterization of branches of the aortic arch, the abdominal aorta, and the iliac artery. It is also useful in venous catheterization, notably of the renal, ovarian, and adrenal veins. Applications of the instrument to other hollow-organ systems such as the airway and bowel are being explored."[9]

The catheters were made in different sizes, ranging from 5 French, which is a little under two millimeters, to 13 French, which is a little over four millimeters. Doctors could easily guide the catheter into different areas of the body—including arteries, veins, the lungs, and the bowels—with great precision, then advance instruments or inject contrast medium through the open central lumen.

Above: At the time Medi-Tech introduced its steerable catheter, the company was able to get both a technical write-up in *Product Engineering* and a clinical write-up in the journal *Radiology*.

Inset: Itzhak Bentov was a multitalented inventor who produced the first steerable catheter. His multipurpose device provided the foundation for Medi-Tech.

Malcolm X is killed.

Winston Churchill dies.

The Association for the Advancement of Medical Instrumentation is founded. The first issue of Gastrointestinal Endoscopy *is published.*

Machida and Olympus introduce fiber-optic colonoscope.

Provenzale and Revignas perform first total colonoscopy.

Itzhak Bentov founds Medi-Tech as contract R&D company.

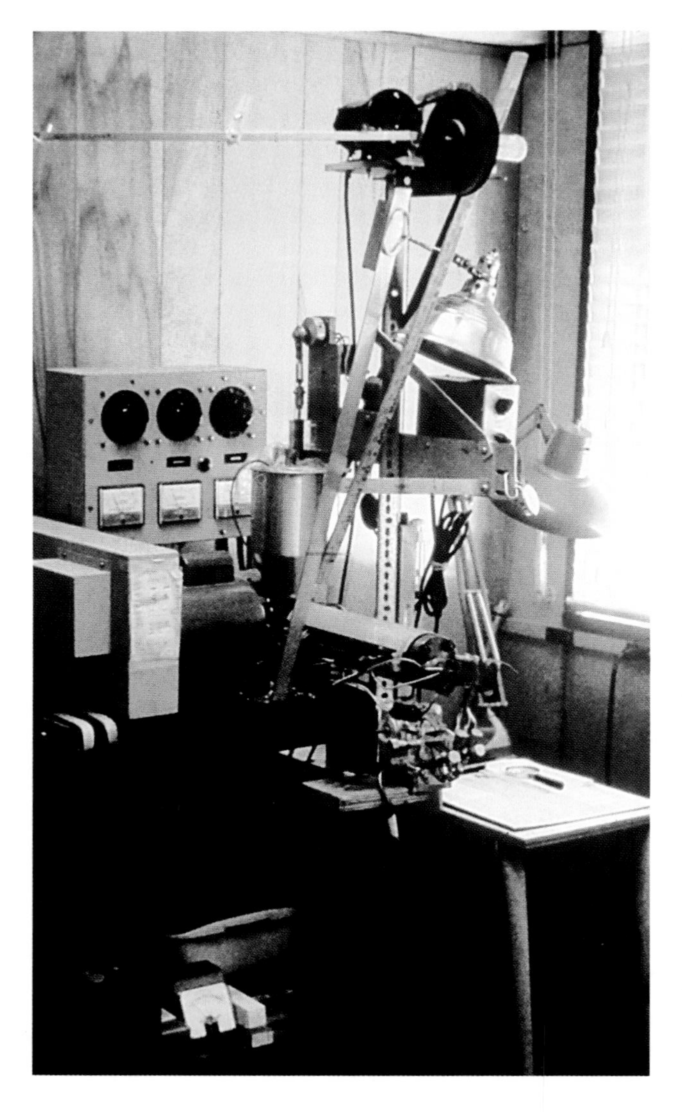

Truly a multipurpose device, the steerable catheter could open up holes that had been closed or close holes that had been open. It could remove debris or take tissue for biopsies. A hollow model of the abdominal aorta was provided for training.

A Latter-Day Tesla

Bentov himself was as much a marvel as his catheter. Born in Czechoslovakia in 1924, he escaped to Palestine in 1941 after his family was murdered in the Holocaust. There he joined the Hagannah underground movement as a freedom fighter against the British.[10]

While designing and building weapons in Israel, Bentov enrolled as a part-time student at Haifa Technion but did not complete his formal engineering education.[11] In 1954 he emigrated to the United States and later worked in the Arthur D. Little think tank in Cambridge, Massachusetts.[12] At night and on weekends, he conducted biomedical research in the basement of his Belmont home.

Bentov and Dan Singer, a business friend, formed Medi-Tech Inc. in 1965 to provide medical development services to companies that knew of them. Bentov liked to refer to his enterprise as IB Development—the initials representing both "in basement" and Itzhak Bentov—and he didn't bother

This extruder was modified by Bentov to make very small multilumen tubing that had been considered impossible to make.

1966...

World Events

Fuel injection for auto engines is developed in United Kingdom.

Miniskirts and color TV are popular.

Medical Milestones

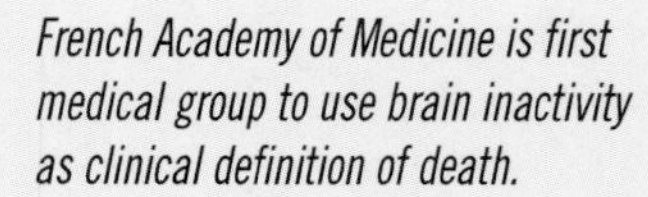

French Academy of Medicine is first medical group to use brain inactivity as clinical definition of death.

John Abele testifies before U.S. Senate regarding medical devices.

Boston Scientific

Bentov's worktable was a study in commonsense engineering. The inventor had developed most of the machinery himself. Later, when Medi-Tech replaced it with more "professional" apparatus, it didn't work as well.

with advertising.[13] Sales for his company never exceeded $15,000 in the 1960s.

Bentov, however, wasn't particularly concerned with money. His friends called him a "modern day Leonardo da Vinci."[14] He spoke 11 languages, including a Bedouin dialect, and was the inventor for a number of patents on a wide variety of products including the first pacemaker electrode, the first disposable ECG electrode, brake shoes, and diet spaghetti ("Slenderoni"). His basement workshop included a collection of "mini-labs" for electronics, optics, chemistry, machining, and plastics.[15] The basement also housed some sculpting equipment belonging to his wife, Mirtala.[16]

To most who knew him, Itzhak was called Ben. "He had a tremendous sense of humor and a capacity to explain very complex ideas in a very simple and understandable way," Mirtala said. "Ben called himself a nuts and bolts man, a plumber. He was informally trained as a mechanical engineer, and somewhere along the way, he started meditating, and his consciousness opened up."[17]

Bentov's spiritualism was a central element of his personality. He spent a significant amount of his time trying to establish a link between science and mysticism, and in 1977 he published a book

Isaac Asimov, author of Fantastic Voyage, *is keynote speaker at the first meeting of the AAMI in Boston, where the movie was premiered at MIT.*

Popular films include Alfie *and* The Bible.

C. R. Bard acquires USCI. Erik Boijsen devises hook-tail close-end catheter.

titled *Stalking the Wild Pendulum: The Mechanics of Consciousness*.[18]

People were attracted to Bentov as a psychic healer and clairvoyant. One woman swore that his touch cured her of migraine headaches, and a scientist claimed to have witnessed the moment when Bentov foresaw his own death. Paul Nardella, an electrical engineer who worked with Bentov, was cautious when interviewed for a 1980 newspaper article about the inventor. "Many strange things have happened to people who were associated with him," he said. Nardella also admitted that he was skeptical of such psychic phenomena when he first met Bentov. "I didn't believe in meditation or any of that gobbledygook," Nardella said.[19]

Bentov died on May 25, 1979, in a DC-10 jetliner crash outside Chicago, 10 years after his catheter had been introduced. According to an article in the *Middlesex News*, "Hours after his death, a medium in Hawaii claimed to have made contact with a stranger named Itzhak Bentov, who by an act of will forced a crippled airplane to cartwheel away from a trailer park as it crashed."[20] At the time of his death, he had nothing more than advisory contact with the company he founded.

John Abele Finds Medi-Tech

In 1969, the same year the steerable catheter was introduced, John Abele joined Medi-Tech with an option to buy the company. At the time, the company's employee roster was a short one, and Medi-Tech reported only $12,000 in contract research and development revenue for the year. Dan Singer, who worked at Arthur D. Little, was the company's part-time business agent and was partially responsible for bringing Abele to the company. Prototype catheters were made by Louisa Miller in Bentov's basement laboratory.

Although he did not hold a medical degree, Abele focused on learning everything he could about medical devices and the challenges facing the new discipline. The situation with the steerable catheter was complicated because, unlike most of the single-purpose devices on the market, the steerable catheter could be used in a variety of disciplines. In a sense, it was a mind-set more than a single device, a system of multiple catheters that could be used in many medical disciplines to treat a variety of conditions.

"The technology was multilumen extrusion, the use of polymers, the use of wires," Abele remembered. "It was a very elegant, sophisticated way of developing microassemblies that would operate in concert with one another to provide guidance and direction to the user in order to get this tube to wherever they wanted it to go."[21]

Building the Business

John Abele was comfortable with both the advanced technology of his new company and the missionary-like challenge of converting doctors to the use of new medical devices—or in the terminology more common to the business world, creating markets.

1967...

World Events

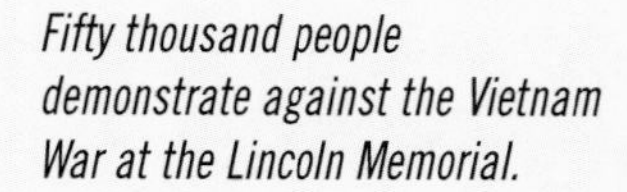

Fifty thousand people demonstrate against the Vietnam War at the Lincoln Memorial.

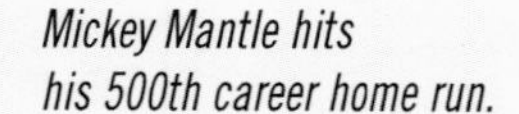

Mickey Mantle hits his 500th career home run.

Medical Milestones

Schneider is founded and begins manufacturing medical accessories; the three-employee company is managed by Hugo Schneider.

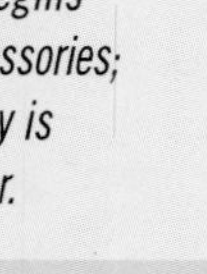

Cleveland surgeon Rene Favaloro develops coronary bypass operation.

Boston Scientific

JOHN ABELE

As a boy, John Abele fell ill with osteomyelitis and underwent debilitating treatment. He is pictured in his wheelchair.

JOHN ABELE, WHO WOULD COFOUND Boston Scientific Corporation with Pete Nicholas, was born in New London, Connecticut, to a submarine commander whose ship, the *Grunion*, disappeared in 1942 off the Aleutian Islands. A World War II destroyer, the *M. L. Abele*, was named after John's father. It was sunk by Japanese kamikaze pilots shortly after its launch.

After losing her husband, Abele's mother moved her family to Newton, Massachusetts, where she taught violin and school orchestra. John and his two brothers spent these early summers with their uncle and three cousins in Rhode Island. The boys worked on a farm, planting and harvesting crops.

During his childhood, Abele suffered from a staph infection called osteomyelitis. Between the ages of five and eight, he underwent three operations and was among the early patients who were treated with penicillin during surgery. Between the last two operations, Abele entered a rigorous program of 1,200 injections to cure the disease. He finally recovered—but learned an important lesson about medicine that he carried into his future career. He saw that doctors are frequently "experimenting" on their patients, constantly learning and evolving their approach to improve their results.

During high school, he worked in an old-fashioned hardware store among the myriad nuts and bolts and tools of construction. He graduated from Amherst College in 1959, with a major in physics and philosophy. Abele felt he needed to work a little before committing to a career, and a bad physics professor in college had soured him on physics—although gadgets and inventions remained a central focus of his life. So instead of going on for a master's degree in physics, he began looking for a job. This first job hunt led him to an Ohio company, where he went to work selling lighting fixtures.

Twiggy takes Western fashion by storm.

Computer keyboards are put into use.

Popular films include Bonnie & Clyde *and* Guess Who's Coming to Dinner.

Mammography for detecting breast cancer is introduced.

Dr. Christiaan Barnard performs world's first human heart transplant.

"Dottering" is reported in Europe.

Two Boston radiologists ask Bentov to design catheter with steerable tip.

He had gained sales experience while selling lighting equipment for an Ohio company, where he developed another trait he would carry into his career: close relationships with customers. Yet this career had remained undecided until 1960, when he called on a small medical device firm called Advanced Instruments, which made an osmometer to test concentrations of fluids. It was at Advanced Instruments that "Abele had found his calling," according to a profile in *Forbes* magazine. "Here were people that were saving lives, not turning on lights."[22]

John Abele, left, in his first office on Main Street in Watertown, bottom, complete with zigzag tile floor and metal desks. Sue Sawyer, inset, one of Medi-Tech's first employees, helped with everything from sales and billing to human resources.

Abele began working for Advanced Instruments, creating a market for osmometry, cryoscopy, and blood gas instruments and selling early Medtronic pacemakers. To help his customers better understand the products he was selling, Abele sought out a retired Massachusetts Institute of Technology (MIT) chemistry professor to learn more about the physical chemistry of solutions. That experience presaged the courses Abele would one day teach to hundreds of physicians around the world. Abele's approach to his career was now established—it was a combination of invention, education, and customer relationships.

By 1965, he had risen to become the general manager of Advanced Instruments and was ready for a new challenge. The

1968...

World Events

Richard Nixon is elected president.

The Vietcong attack Saigon in the Tet offensive.

Medical Milestones

Melvin Judkins develops pigtail catheter with multiple sideports.

Boston Scientific

Medi-Tech exhibits steerable catheter at RSNA meeting; the device is enthusiastically received.

owner of the company didn't want to grow, so Abele decided he wanted to run his own company, where he could control the growth. He left Advanced Instruments and began looking for a company to buy.

These were very educational years for Abele. He realized the key to selling medical devices was communication across professions and industries that traditionally held each other at a distance. In 1965, he was a founder of the Association for the Advancement of Medical Instrumentation (AAMI), a society that challenged doctors, engineers, and manufacturers to develop standards, improve communication, and organize education.[23] A year later, he published an article in *Industry* magazine highlighting the lack of communication in the design, purchase, application, and service of medical devices.[24]

In 1966, he addressed this problem in testimony before the U.S. Senate.

> *All too often a manufacturer tends to say, "Tell me what you want, doctor, and we'll build it for you. From then on it's your responsibility." Clinical medicine tends to remain sacrosanct to the instruments builder. The designer-manufacturer relies too heavily on and passes too much responsibility to the physician for the proper use and operation of the instrument.*[25]

This mind-set was radically different from that of the existing medical device manufacturers, who preferred to leave clinical and design decisions to physicians.

In 1967, while he continued looking for a business to buy, Abele joined the Technical Education Research Center in Cambridge as a consultant for the biomedical field. There, he helped develop training programs for technicians who repaired and maintained medical equipment.[26]

A Model Patient

After two years at the Technical Education Research Center, Abele discovered Medi-Tech in 1969. The steerable catheter was a young product, but it had potential and appealed to his sense of possibility. Furthermore, in its range of uses, it had the potential to unite branches of medicine.

Abele was not alone in his quest. During his search for companies to buy, he had maintained a partnership with Pat Alessi, whom he met at Advanced Instruments. Because Alessi still worked at Advanced Instruments full-time, Abele conducted the legwork and the two met at night to discuss their plans.

Abele joined the company that year with an option to buy it. Alessi joined a year later, when Abele's purchase option was exercised.

"The technology was a classic entrepreneur's dream," Abele said.

> *It was technically sophisticated, it was easy to understand just by looking at, and it was almost impossible to duplicate. You could take it apart but you couldn't reverse engineer it. The catheters were semidisposable and easily attached or detached from the reusable control handle. It was like the camera and film. Because the steering*

Martin Luther King Jr. and Robert F. Kennedy are assassinated.

Figure skater Peggy Fleming wins the only U.S. gold medal at winter Olympics in Grenoble.

Popular films include 2001: A Space Odyssey *and* Funny Girl.

Cook Inc. grows to 20 employees.

Olympus fiber-optic esophagoscope displaces the gastrocamera.

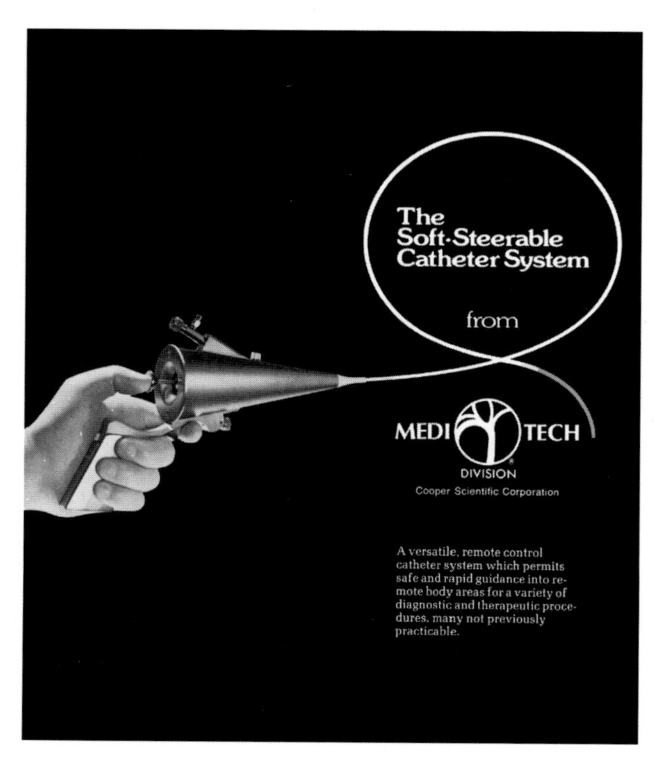

Above: The steerable catheter was marketed as a complete platform or system. At one point, Andreas Gruentzig was interested in it for coronary applications, although its greatest success lay with interventional radiologists, who used it to remove retained gallstones.

Right: During his frequent presentations to physicians' groups, John Abele used slides to illustrate the emerging field of minimally invasive medicine. The Swiss Army knife represented the multifunctionality of the steerable catheter. It was a popular metaphor that was often borrowed by physicians for their presentations.

wires were in the wall, the central lumen remained open for passage of wires, tools, fluids, or other materials, unlike the numerous earlier steering devices.

The catheter could be made in different lengths or diameters to accommodate the needs of many potential applications. Everybody who saw it would come up with a new idea.[27]

As bypass surgery gained more publicity, the steerable catheter seemed like an ideal tool for radiologists and cardiologists who wanted to help surgeons image the arteries before surgery. After its introduction, numerous papers appeared in peer-reviewed journals describing different uses for the novel device.

1969...

World Events

Neil Armstrong walks on the moon.

Medical Milestones

Boston Scientific

John Abele joins Medi-Tech with option to buy the company.

John Abele meets cardiologist Dick Myler. They discover a mutual interest in developing a catheter-based coronary endarterectomy tool.

This road sign for Artery Cleaners, a dry-cleaning company in Massachusetts, was used to depict minimally invasive therapy's goal of cleaning arteries of obstructing plaque and lesions without the debilitating ordeal of surgery.

Medi-Tech wanted to expand the steerable catheter into gastroenterology, urology, and pulmonary medicine, finding that each specialty had uses for a steerable catheter and that each discipline required a different approach. Thus Medi-Tech became one of the few device companies to sell across the medical professions, giving it a unique overall view of the development of minimally invasive medicine.[28]

"In the Medi-Tech steerable catheter, I saw a platform on which to build a business," Abele later said.[29] "Doctors would look at it and say, 'Gee, if you could only do this, then I could apply it this way.' So the steerable catheter was a platform for development."[30]

But not everyone was as receptive as Abele had hoped. Some physicians argued they didn't need Medi-Tech's catheter because they could perform

The first U.S. troops are withdrawn from Vietnam.

The first artificial heart is used in a human.

Itzhak Bentov works in his basement laboratory on his invention, the steerable catheter.

the same functions with precurved tubing and guide wires. Others argued that major surgery was actually easier than learning how to use catheters.

"But the steerable catheter could do more complex procedures, and it gave them the ability to change their minds when they were well into the procedure," said Abele. "Most everyone who was doing angiography at that time, which wasn't many people, bought one. But success wasn't having them buy one. Success was having them use it as an integral part of their practice. And initially that was a very small percentage."[31]

This "small percentage" of doctors, comprised mostly of radiologists who used the catheter to inject contrast material, helped make the steerable catheter a one-time hit—and made it painfully obvious how much education was needed before catheter-based therapies gained wide acceptance. "We have to help the radiologists and others who will be using our catheter to 'unlearn' the techniques they have always used," Bentov said in a 1969 article.

To help angiographers train to use the catheter, Medi-Tech began to market a life-size transparent

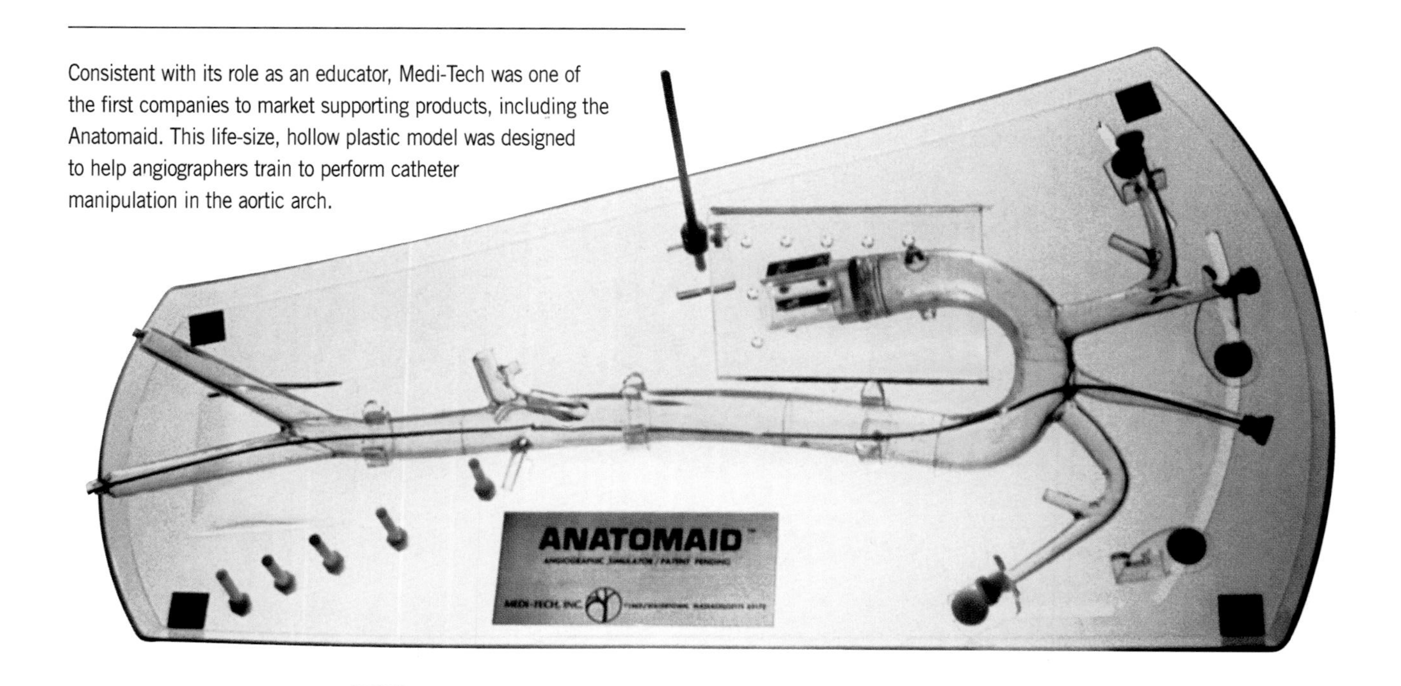

Consistent with its role as an educator, Medi-Tech was one of the first companies to market supporting products, including the Anatomaid. This life-size, hollow plastic model was designed to help angiographers train to perform catheter manipulation in the aortic arch.

1969...

World Events

A giant "love-in" occurs at Woodstock in New York.

Inflation becomes a worldwide problem.

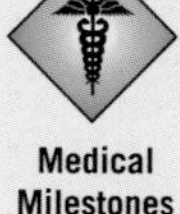

Medical Milestones

The scanning electron microscope is put into practical use.

Boston Scientific

plastic model of the aorta and its major branches, which had been designed by Bentov and a physician. A smaller version of the model was included with each initial shipment of catheters.[32] Although the model was too expensive for individual users, Medi-Tech had great success selling it to medical schools as a training tool.

The aorta model, called the Anatomaid, was described in detail by Morris Simon and Keith Rabinov in the *British Journal of Radiology*:

> *A new flexible and hollow model of the aorta and its major branches has been developed for demonstrating, teaching, and practicing the various techniques of angiography, particularly the newer methods of selective and superselective catheterization.*[33]

In its first press release, issued on June 24, 1969, Medi-Tech announced its Selector Catheter System, which included catheters (available in three different lengths), a control handle, and a small aorta model.[34] Every component of the system was sterilizable, hence reusable, unlike some other catheters. The complete kit sold for $465.

Shortly after introducing its new catheter system, Medi-Tech announced a new goal: "To expand applications of the catheter by designing associated instruments and accessories, including pressure transducers, microphones, fiber optics, photography, calorimetric and tissue sampling devices."[35]

Exercising His Options

Immediately after joining Medi-Tech, Abele began searching for a financial partner to help him buy the company from Bentov. He first presented his idea to banks, investment companies, and wealthy families—even going so far as to hold a presentation in the living room of one prominent family.

Some of the potential investors turned him down, and several made proposals that were unacceptable. Abele approached Parker Montgomery, the chairman of Cooper Laboratories, a small but growing pharmaceutical firm that wanted to get into medical devices. Abele remembered Montgomery's reaction:

> *When I first proposed that Cooper Labs fund my purchase of Medi-Tech, Parker Montgomery smiled and said, "Come back a bit later, show me that you can do something here." That was a great lesson for me because I instantly understood and respected that he saw something that could be valuable but he was waiting to find out if I knew how to make it valuable.*[36]

Popular films include Midnight Cowboy *and* Easy Rider.

Medi-Tech moves to basement of 372 Main Street, Watertown; the company has a four-woman production and testing line.

CHAPTER THREE

FIXING ORGANS THROUGH SMALL HOLES

1970–1978

Medi-Tech was in this tiny, stand-alone building with production in the basement. In those days, a lot of doctors made their own catheters, and the whole concept of putting a catheter into a vein wasn't that old.

—Bob Brown, former vice president of sales

IT DIDN'T TAKE LONG FOR MEDI-TECH TO prove its value. During the first year of John Abele and Pat Alessi's running the company, sales rose from $16,000 to $70,000. Although Medi-Tech was still a small company, the growth in sales was important psychologically. Medi-Tech was successfully creating a market for its steerable catheter and was one of only a few companies in the world marketing catheters at all.

This success was important for another reason as well: When John Abele approached Parker Montgomery again in 1970, he had irrefutable evidence that Medi-Tech was a viable investment. Montgomery agreed, and a deal was struck between Cooper Labs and Medi-Tech partners John Abele and Pat Alessi. Under the agreement, Cooper owned a majority interest; Abele stayed on as president, focusing on marketing and sales; and Alessi handled operations.[1]

After the acquisition, the company's official name, and the one that appeared on employees' paychecks, was changed to Cooper Scientific, which operated as a holding company for Medi-Tech. But because so many customers already recognized the company as Medi-Tech, that name was kept on the sign, company products, and literature and was used when answering the phones.[2]

The contract with Cooper was "a Russian roulette agreement. It was simple, almost a handshake," Abele later remembered. "One person sets the price and terms and the other person decides whether they will be a buyer."

Although Cooper was the partner with all the money, Abele wasn't worried that the company would dominate the partnership. "In a small company, the knowledge of the person running it is probably the most valuable asset," he said. "The interest that Cooper Labs had in this is that they were a pharmaceutical company and they were interested in expanding into the device business. They were intrigued with the potential and opportunity of these devices and obviously bought into that."[3]

Down on Main Street

Medi-Tech was soon ready to take advantage of other opportunities. With the steerable catheter enjoying moderate success and production increasing, the company was ready to grow. In 1969, Medi-Tech moved from Bentov's basement into the basement of a building at 372 Main Street in Watertown, Massachusetts. At the time of the move, the company's entire production line was comprised of Claire Arena, who joined Medi-Tech in March 1969 as a part-time assembler and packager, Marion Taverna, and Louisa Miller.

Opposite: Medi-Tech technician working on the assembly of a steerable catheter at the Watertown facility in the mid-1970s. The steerable catheter carried the company through the early part of the decade.

"Bentov was a pleasure to work for," recalled Arena. "He could talk to you for hours on what he was doing and how he would test things out on himself, like hypodermic needles."[4] Later that year, Sue Sawyer joined Medi-Tech as a customer service representative and the seventh employee.

As Medi-Tech set up shop on Main Street, only one person was left behind: Bentov himself. "He was a loner," Abele recalled. "It would never make sense for him to have a lab that was far from his bed. He kept odd hours. He didn't sleep a lot, probably four hours a night."

Early catheter production was simple. Bentov extruded the tubes in his basement and sent the unfinished products to Main Street for assembly and packaging.[5] Bentov's assembly equipment was "eloquent common sense. It was frequently made of wood and sometimes cardboard," Abele recalled. "Later on, when we had engineers come in and professionalize it by making it with brushed aluminum and lucite, it didn't work as well."[6]

Abele handled the sales and marketing end, while Sue Sawyer fielded customer phone calls and did a little of everything else. "It was a very close-knit group of people," Sawyer remembered.

Everybody helped everybody else, which was absolutely required in order to survive. John was on the road most of the time. The production people did their thing. I answered all the phones. I did all of John's business, his letters and communications and correspondence. I talked to all the customers. I typed all the orders, then got them together to ship out the door, and extended the invoices. And it was all done by hand. My original desk was a kitchen table with a big old IBM typewriter on it.[7]

Sawyer also functioned as Medi-Tech's intercom, alerting Abele by screaming, "John, telephone!"[8] Over the years, Sawyer—described by Abele as "the mother of the company"[9]—took personal responsibility for making sure that employees' and customers' needs were met.

Extended Family

Over the next five years, Medi-Tech slowly expanded from its 800-square-foot basement at 372 Main Street into the entire 11,000-square-foot building.[10] The growing company took over offices formerly occupied by a dentist, a bookseller, and a consulting agency.

Abele moved into a new office featuring a floor with black and white zigzag tiles and old metal desks. "The floor drove me crazy," Abele remembered, "but I loved those desks." In one of the workrooms, all of the tables were doors propped up with store-bought legs. "It was very inexpensive," said Abele. "We gradually got more sophisticated."[11]

In 1971, Bob Brown joined the company as sales manager. Before coming to Medi-Tech, he had been a salesman at Baxter Laboratories, a medical supply company that provided intravenous solutions and anesthesiology trays. "Medi-Tech was in this tiny,

1970...

World Events

National Guard kills four Kent State University students protesting Vietnam War.

First of the jumbo jets, the Boeing 747, goes into service across the Atlantic.

Medical Milestones

In Europe, nuclear-powered heart pacemakers are implanted in three patients to correct heart blockage.

Orthopedists begin to perform arthroscopy widely.

Hospital care costs in the United States average $81 per patient per day.

Boston Scientific

Cooper Scientific is founded by John Abele and Cooper Labs and acquires Medi-Tech; sales are $10,000 per month.

Medi-Tech moves from 800 square feet to entire building (11,000 square feet) over the next five years.

Sue Sawyer joins Medi-Tech as customer service representative and the 7th employee.

stand-alone building with production in the basement," Brown said. "In those days, a lot of doctors made their own catheters, and the whole concept of putting a catheter into a vein wasn't that old. Cooper owned us, but we didn't make any money for them. They kind of left us alone. We'd go down to headquarters once a year and give a report, and that was it."[12]

The atmosphere in the office was hard-working but friendly and close—so close, in fact, that employees on the phone found themselves competing with each other to hear. And Bob Brown usually came out the loser. Brown had suffered high frequency hearing loss in the Vietnam War and couldn't focus his hearing when Abele, Sawyer, and Alessi were all on the phone at the same time.

> *So I told John about my problem. I said, "John, I just can't hear while all of this is going on." And he said, "Okay. I'll take care of that." The next day, he brought in a big garbage pail with foam on the inside. He turned it over, punched a hole in the bottom, and put an eyebolt in it, then ran a rope through the eye and hoisted it up over my desk. He said, "When they get too noisy, just lower it down." Sure enough, I'd lower it over my head and I'm in this cone of silence. The really funny thing is when I was hiring people, some of them would look up and say, "What the hell is that thing?" Some people would have the nerve to ask. Others wouldn't. But it worked.*[13]

On Wednesday nights, the group would often venture to a bowling alley across the street, remembered Bob Arcangeli, who was hired as a salesman in the mid-1970s. "Everyone would come, have a beer, pull a couple of strings, and do that kind of stuff," he said. "It was like that in those days. I remember in the blizzard of 1978, something like three feet of snow fell in a 24-hour period and there were 60- to 70-mile-an-hour winds blowing. It closed the city for about five days. But we worked every day. John came in his Jeep and picked me up at my house and drove me to work."[14]

Medi-Tech's Early Products

With the steerable catheter slow to catch on, Medi-Tech needed other products to feed its early growth. As a result, the company developed several bread-and-butter products in the early 1970s: a Cooper Labs depilatory (hair removal cream) called Surgex, used to prepare patients for surgery; the Zavala Lung Model, a popular product that was developed to help doctors train for bronchoscopies; and a lung cytology brush and microbiology brush.

The cytology brush, used to obtain cell samples from the lung, was an early Medi-Tech product. John Abele and Bob Brown shared a patent on a variation of the product for collecting microbiological samples.

The floppy disk is introduced for storing data.

Films include Catch-22 *and* True Grit.

Five hundred thousand die in Pakistani cyclone.

University of Wisconsin scientists announce first complete synthesis of a gene.

Medi-Tech's tabletop exhibit at the RSNA meeting in Chicago in 1970. The Anatomaid arterial model is displayed on the screen.

At the 1972 College of Surgeons, Cooper Scientific salesman Bob Brown demonstrates to a crowd of customers. Medical meetings were a primary way for the company to reach and teach physician customers.

The Surgex cream was designed to remove hair preoperatively. Compared with shaving, the depilatory resulted in a lower incidence of postoperative wound infection.[15] Sales of this Cooper product provided revenue until Medi-Tech's other products gained a following. Although Surgex was created for use in hospitals, some customers ignored the product guidelines and tried the depilatory on themselves at home. Abele addressed some of these cases in the following letters:

[To Rene Luks of Cooper Cosmetics SA, Switzerland] As you know, our major bad public relations have come from doctors' wives using samples to remove facial hair. It sometimes works the first time, but then the skin becomes sensitized and they get severe irritation, rash, etc.[16]

[To Aaron J. Ball, football player with the Buffalo Bills] Thank you very much for your kind letter about Surgex received here September 27th. Surgex was not designed as a substitute for regular shaving, however, because as with all depilatories, if you use it often enough, your skin will become sensitized and begin to irritate. Frankly, I would think you would prefer a beard for the psychological effect it would have on your opponents. Nevertheless, I am enclosing a couple of tubes for you to reevaluate. Just make sure to wash it off thoroughly if it starts to irritate. A shower is the best method.[17]

The Zavala Lung Model, meanwhile, was a life-size, anatomically correct, flexible, translucent, hollow model of the bronchial tree. Developed in cooperation with Dr. Donald C. Zavala of the Department of Medicine at the University of Iowa Hospitals, the model facilitated the teaching and practice of bronchoscopy and bronchial catheterization.[18] Like the aorta model, this product was designed to provide an educational tool for physician customers. At the time, Medi-Tech may have been the only catheter company actively educating physicians about its products—a trait which became a defining quality of the growing company.

The two brushes were actually accessories to be used with the steerable catheter, although most

1971...

World Events

Direct phone dialing on a regular basis begins between the U.S. and Europe.

Diamond-bladed scalpel is introduced in U.K.

Niklaus Wirth develops Pascal, a popular language used on home computers.

Texas Instruments introduces first pocket calculator (weighs 2.5 pounds, costs $150).

Intel introduces first microprocessor.

Medical Milestones

Kurt Amplatz develops a simple method of rendering polyvinyl plastic surfaces antithrombogenic.

Hiromi Shinya introduces the polypectomy procedure and snare.

SCIMED founded by six entrepreneurs from Litton Industries; specializes in oxygenators and other devices for cardiovascular surgery.

Boston Scientific

The American Heart Association meeting in 1971. The screen shows Medi-Tech catheter manipulation in the aortic arch.

of the products were sold to bronchoscopists. The lung cytology brush was a tiny brush that was used to take samples of lung tissue to detect cancer. It was a simple procedure with one complication: as the device was withdrawn from the lungs, the cell culture became contaminated. Abele designed a Teflon sheath to help the brush slide through catheters and bronchoscopes. This innovation, which allowed physicians to collect uncontaminated cell cultures, became the industry standard. Similarly, Abele and Brown developed a removable, sealed tube for the microbiology brush and were issued a patent in both their names.

In 1976, Medi-Tech hired its first full-time research and development engineer other than Abele himself. Josh Tolkoff, a Harvard/MIT-educated engineer, with experience in anesthesiology research at Massachusetts General and Instrumentation Laboratories joined Medi-Tech. "There were about 20 people in the company when I joined, including four salesmen," Tolkoff remembered.

> *My first office at Medi-Tech was in a five-sided building that did not look at all like a pentagon. They cleared out a little storage closet in the basement that literally looked like a bunker. It had a giant cement pillar in the middle of it. On my second day, the only technician came into my office and said, "Well, I've been waiting for somebody to arrive so I could pass along this information. Here's my notebook. I'm going to Hungary." ... My first project when I got here was taking a bunch of stuff that he had sitting on the shelf, and that must have been 100 projects in some level of completion, and finishing them.*[19]

The first project Tolkoff actually completed was an improved microbiology brush. Tolkoff implemented a better way to keep lung tissue from collecting in the end of the catheter as it moved down the throat. To do that, he needed to find a material that could be used as a biocompatible plug in the end of the catheter. Once the catheter was in place, the plug would be pushed from it and left to dissolve harmlessly in the body.

While selling these products, Medi-Tech continued to develop the medical relationships that would be valuable later. In 1974, Abele met Lazar Greenfield, a cardiovascular surgeon with an interest in preventing pulmonary embolism.

Greenfield, chairman of the Department of Surgery at the University of Oklahoma and later chairman of the Department of Surgery at the University of Michigan, had several ideas and had already helped develop a novel vena cava filter. In a later interview, Greenfield said he collaborated

One of the early Medi-Tech products, the Zavala Lung Model, was used to train doctors to use bronchial catheters and bronchoscopes. The life-size model sold very well to medical schools and training hospitals.

Nixon orders a 90-day freeze on wages and prices and announces other measures to curb domestic inflation.

U.S. conducts large-scale bombing raids against North Vietnam.

Wolff and Shinya introduce removal of colonic polyps with wire loop snare in the biopsy channel of a fiber-optic colonoscope.

Bob Brown joins Medi-Tech as the sales manager.

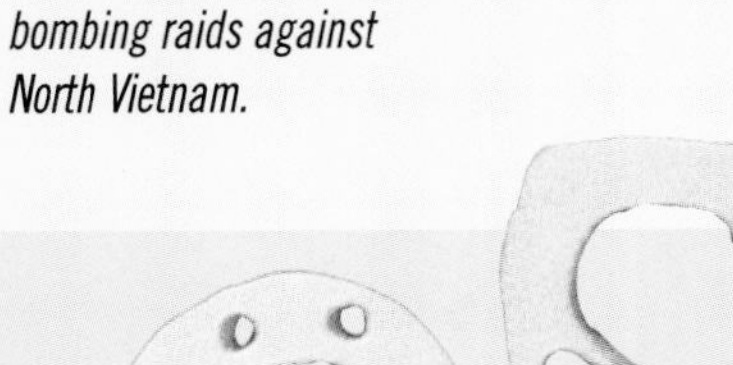

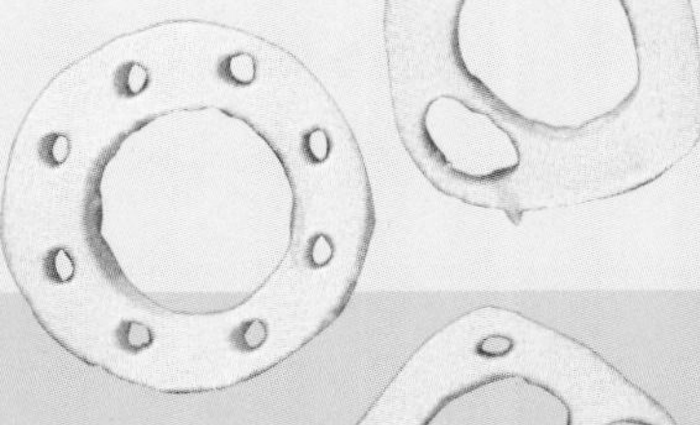

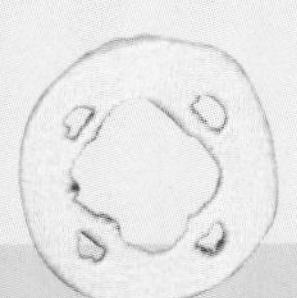

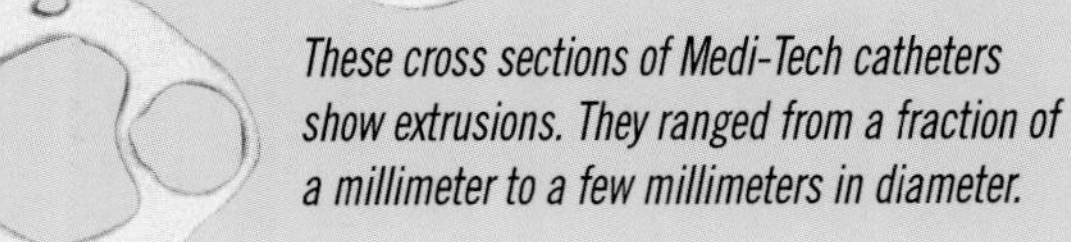

These cross sections of Medi-Tech catheters show extrusions. They ranged from a fraction of a millimeter to a few millimeters in diameter.

with an oil industry engineer to create his vena cava filter.

At the time, the accepted surgical method to protect patients was to open them up and clip the vena cava with a gap-toothed clip that collapsed the vein, turning it into a natural filter. This procedure had drawbacks, however, because the vena cava is one of the body's two major veins and is responsible for transporting blood back into the heart before it is pumped into the lungs. Clipping it had the effect of reducing one large, open-flowing tube into several smaller conduits. The procedure had other drawbacks as well. First, the patient underwent major surgery, which added risk to an already unstable patient. Second, Greenfield's first two patients died of pulmonary embolism while still in surgery.

"I told this to Garmin Kimmel, a petroleum engineer, and he said that sounded a lot like the problem they had in the oil field with sludge in the pipelines that would gum up valves," Greenfield recalled. "They used to have to dig down and clean out the valves until they discovered the value of using a cone-shaped trap that would trap the sludge. So I sat down with him and we came up with a design."[20]

Greenfield conducted several successful tests of the filter in animals, then switched to human patients in 1972. The filters went into small-scale distribution in 1973 (this was before the days when the FDA approval process slowed product introductions). The early filters were made by an oil field mechanic and demonstrated that clots could be trapped and dissolved before they reached the lungs.

The next step, Greenfield saw, was to discover a way to remove existing clots. "I was working with Kimmel, who was a very innovative person himself," Greenfield said.

> *He had worked on a cardiac valve and on a heart/lung machine. So I told him I wanted to work on a device to pull blood clots from the lungs. I had the concept of putting a cup device on the end of a catheter and using that to grab the clot and pull it out. We were able to do that on some patients, but those who had successful extractions were still susceptible to additional embolic events.*[21]

A year later, when Greenfield saw the steerable catheter, he approached Abele about developing a steerable catheter with a suction cup on the end. This device would be able to retrieve clots once they had already traveled to the lungs. In 1975, Medi-Tech introduced the steerable pulmonary embolectomy catheter.[22]

The Burhenne Technique

This kind of give-and-take relationship and ability to attract attention was critical to Medi-Tech's success. Unafraid to educate physicians and promote change, Medi-Tech was a target for innovative physicians with ideas. And yet the steerable catheter was still a novelty item. Before it could support Medi-Tech, it needed to find an application

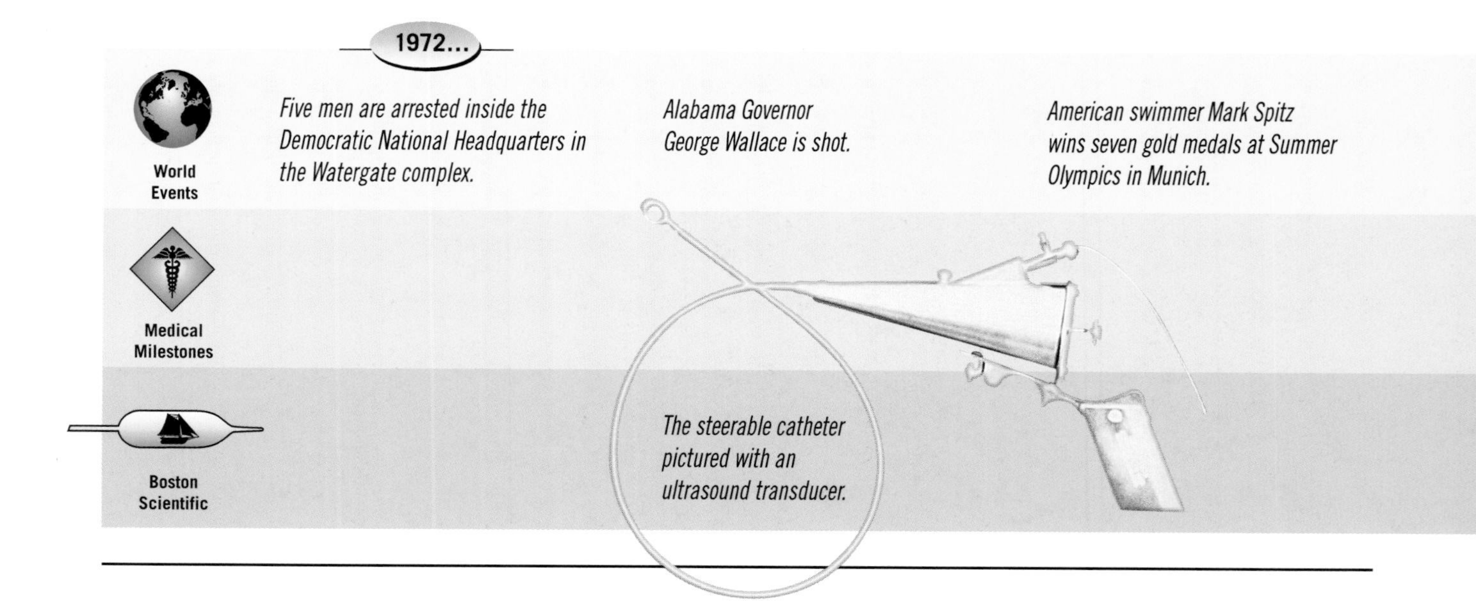

The steerable catheter pictured with an ultrasound transducer.

THE COWBOY DAYS AND THE FDA

THERE ARE A LOT OF WORDS THAT MIGHT be used to describe the medical device companies of the late 1960s and the doctors who helped develop techniques and equipment. They might have been described as the cowboys, prophets, visionaries, and sometimes even the quacks of the medical world.

Everybody, it seemed, had some opinion on medical devices except for the federal government—which had little oversight into their use or manufacture.

The need for some kind of regulation had been recognized in 1969 during a two-day conference on medical devices in Bethesda, Maryland. The conference was sponsored by the Association for the Advancement of Medical Instrumentation. In the subsequent conference report, Dr. Harry Lipscomb, editor of the *Journal of the Association for the Advancement of Medical Instrumentation*, noted that doctors had access to 5,000 types of devices produced by 1,300 manufacturers.

Another conference attendee, Herbert Ley Jr., then the commissioner of the FDA, had this to say about government regulation of the medical device industry: "The need is urgent for the development of a system of standards and premarket clearance procedures for medical devices."[1]

Seven years later, the FDA announced that it was finally ready to regulate medical devices. In 1976, the agency passed amendments to the Food, Drug and Cosmetic Act. The Medical Device Act of 1976 was designed to ensure, through clinical trials before the devices were marketed, that new devices were safe and effective.

New devices were required to go through a two-step approval process. Companies like Medi-Tech had to notify the FDA at least 90 days in advance of their intent to market a medical device. If the device didn't closely resemble an existing one, the agency required a Pre-Market Approval, or PMA, before the device could be released.[2]

The FDA's presence in the medical device industry set off howls of protest, but in reality it was clear that some government oversight was necessary to maintain high standards and to protect the credibility of medical devices. For the first several years, the FDA was concerned with classifying existing products, registering device manufacturers, and developing a sound PMA process. This era, nicknamed the "Era of Cooperation" by John Abele, lasted into the early 1980s, when a more confident FDA began a broad effort to educate the industry and develop guidelines for the various classes of products.

Arab terrorists shoot 11 Israelis in Olympic Village.

Nixon is reelected president.

U.S. airports institute strict antihijacking measures.

In the U.K., the first CAT scan imager is introduced.

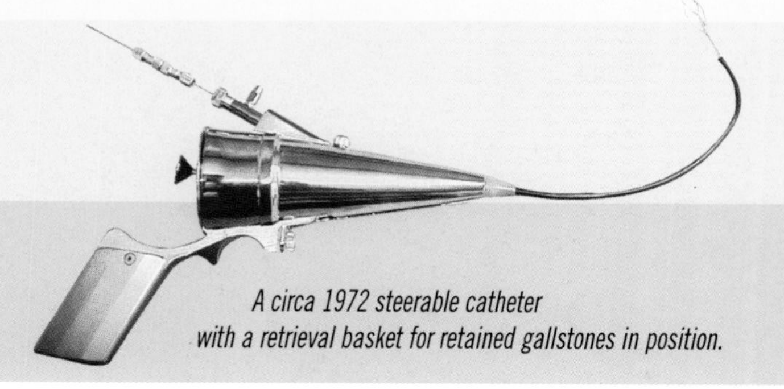

A circa 1972 steerable catheter with a retrieval basket for retained gallstones in position.

that capitalized on its unique versatility and opened up whole new therapeutic fields. Unlike the huge majority of other catheters on the market, which were diagnostic in function and used for imaging, varieties of the steerable catheter were being developed as therapeutic tools.

In the early 1970s, an interventional pioneer named Joachim Burhenne, a German-born physician who became chair of radiology at San Francisco Children's Hospital and later professor of radiology/chairman of Vancouver General Hospital, finally developed a successful therapeutic use for the steerable catheter. Burhenne had found a technique for nonoperative removal of retained gallstones.[23]

At that time, an estimated half-million people annually underwent cholecystectomy (surgery to remove gallstones). However, in approximately 20 percent of these patients, a postoperative x ray indicated that one or more stones were retained. These retained stones eventually wound up in the common duct and required repeat surgery in about seven percent of the patients. The Burhenne technique, which used Medi-Tech's catheters, tiny baskets, and other accessories, eliminated the need for general anesthesia and a long and painful second operation.[24]

With the Burhenne technique, a physician advanced a steerable catheter through a tract of scar tissue that was formed by a drainage catheter left in the patient after surgery. After maneuvering the catheter tip into position, the physician injected contrast media in order to visualize stones. The physician then passed a wire basket to the site and used it to dislodge, reposition, and secure the stone. Finally, the stone was withdrawn. The procedure took about 20 minutes and was virtually painless.[25]

In 1972, Burhenne demonstrated his technique to an audience of 2,000 surgeons at the American College of Surgeons meeting and received a rare and lengthy standing ovation. Using a 16-millimeter film, he showed how easy it was to manipulate a stone in the biliary tree with a catheter. One physician in the audience compared the movement of the retained gallstone to that of "a hockey puck gliding on ice."[26]

At various meetings of the American College of Surgeons in the early 1970s, crowds flocked to Medi-Tech booths to see demonstrations of the steerable catheter removing retained stones. Interestingly, many of the surgeons who asked about the device wouldn't admit they wanted it for themselves. After all, a retained stone meant the surgeon had performed an incomplete operation. Instead, they said, "I have a *friend* who has this problem."[27]

Nevertheless, Burhenne continued to attract attention. He had developed an interactive scientific exhibit complete with a model mounted on a frame so users could actually try the technique. This novel exhibit about nonoperative removal of retained gallstones won a gold medal at the American College of Surgeons and, in Abele's opinion, became the first successful less-invasive therapeutic technique in the interventional field.[28] Burhenne's technique foreshadowed the development of laparoscopic cholecystectomy.

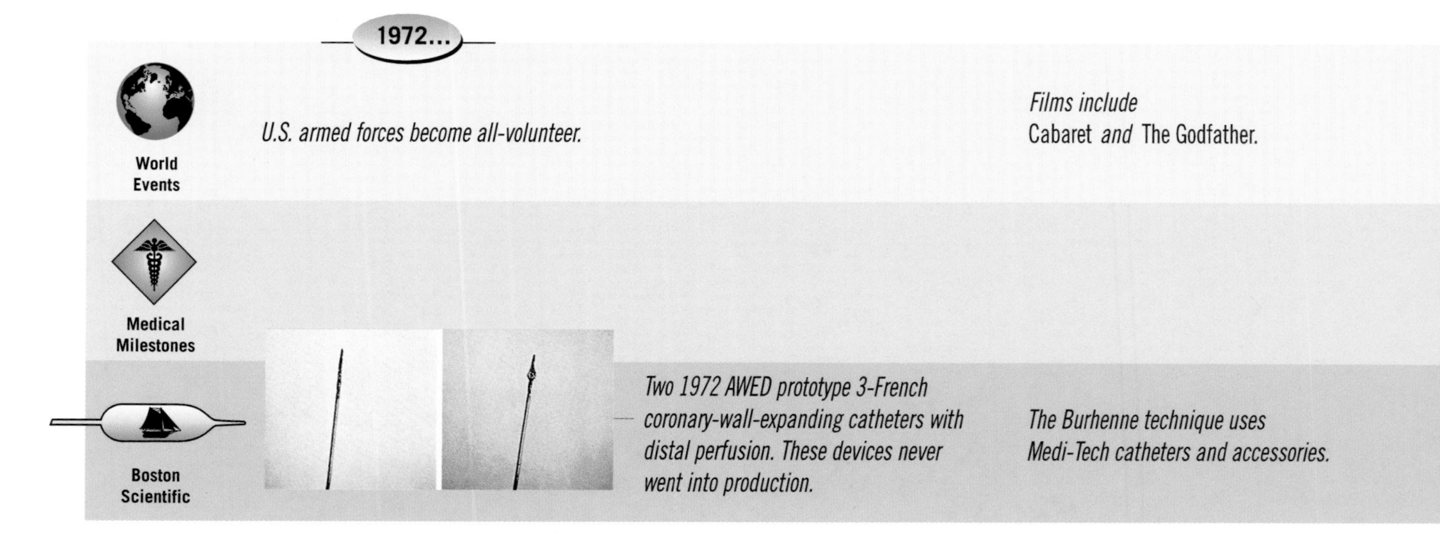

U.S. armed forces become all-volunteer.

Films include Cabaret *and* The Godfather.

Two 1972 AWED prototype 3-French coronary-wall-expanding catheters with distal perfusion. These devices never went into production.

The Burhenne technique uses Medi-Tech catheters and accessories.

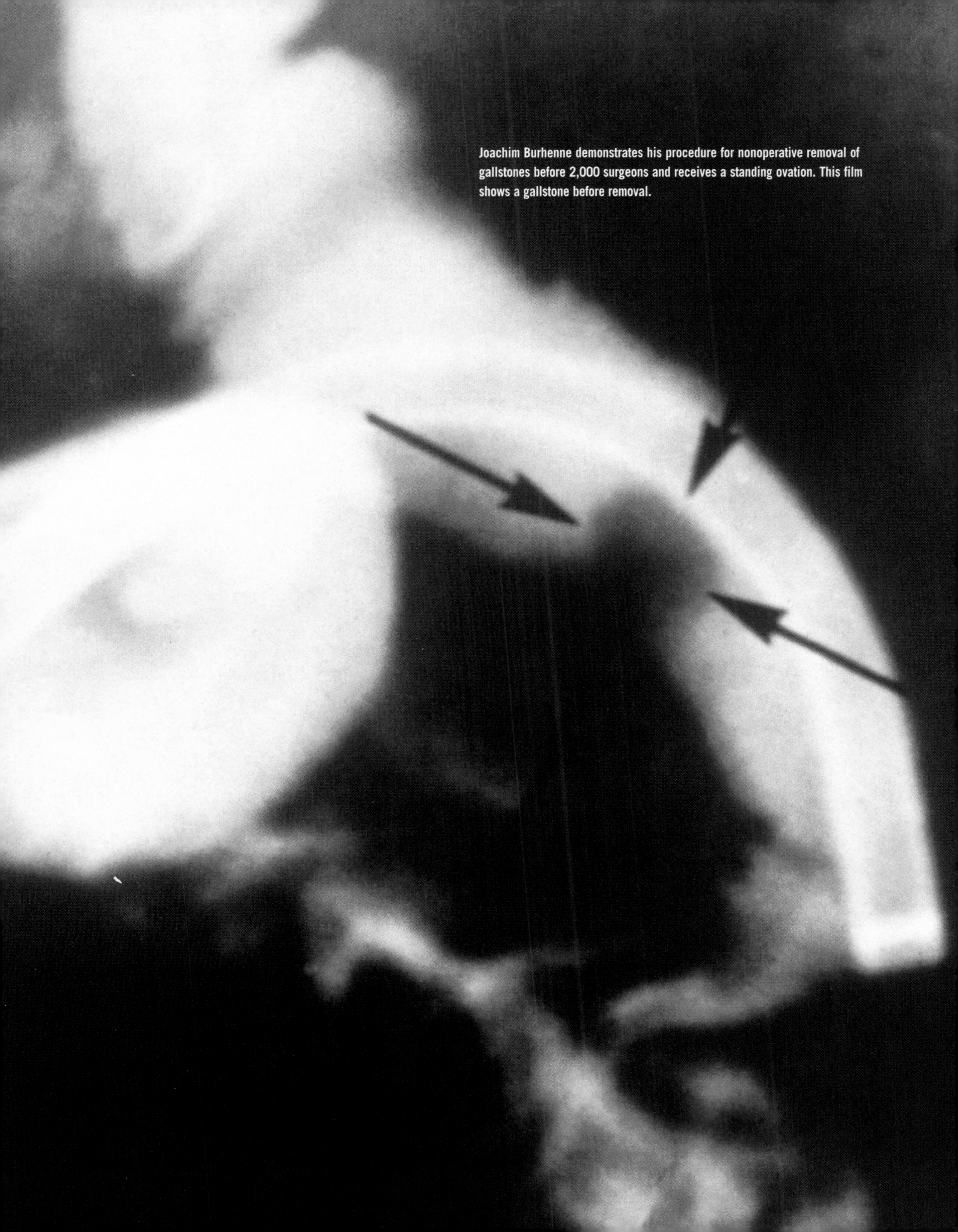

Joachim Burhenne demonstrates his procedure for nonoperative removal of gallstones before 2,000 surgeons and receives a standing ovation. This film shows a gallstone before removal.

Joachim Burhenne in Poland performing the technique he pioneered with a steerable catheter. The Burhenne technique, used to remove postoperative kidney stones, found a ready audience overseas, where doctors were more open to interventional medicine than were doctors in the United States.

1973...

World Events

Vice President Spiro Agnew resigns.

Energy crisis begins, due to Arab oil embargo and shortage of petroleum.

Drought in Ethiopia kills fifty thousand.

Billie Jean King defeats Bobby Riggs in "battle of the sexes" tennis match.

Medical Milestones

Andreas Gruentzig uses balloons of his own design to dilate human peripheral arteries.

Boston Scientific

The Medi-Tech booth at the meeting of the International College of Surgeons in Barcelona, Spain.

People in Glass Houses ...

No matter how successful a device might be, the whole idea of selling something that corrected a surgical mistake, as opposed to selling a diagnostic instrument, was fraught with political landmines. "Before we could really even develop the product, I had to find out how common these retained biliary stones were," Brown remembered. Naturally he wanted medical opinions, so he went to the Georgetown University Hospital to ask the operating room supervisor for the doctor who did the most biliary surgery in the hospital. At 5:30 that evening, he was standing in the surgeon's office with his provocative question.

I told him I was doing some research and there's a radiologist on the West Coast who has developed this product for nonsurgical retrieval of retained biliary stones, and I don't know anything about them. "I've been doing biliary surgery for 20 years," the surgeon said, "and I've never left a stone!" I think he probably had one that day. He threw me out of his office. But there was something in his voice that told me he had problems too.[29]

Overseas, surgeons were also ambivalent about embracing the Burhenne Technique. In 1975, Abele and Burhenne traveled to Moscow, where they presented the Burhenne Technique to a group of surgeons and radiologists. Abele described what happened:

In the mid-1970s, Abele and Burhenne traveled to Moscow to spread the word about an interventional treatment for retained gallstones. This picture, showing Dr. Josef Rabkin wearing the Gold State Prize Medal, was taken by Abele during that trip.

Our host was a radiologist who complimented Dr. Burhenne on his extraordinary technique but explained that in the Soviet Union surgeons were very competent and never left retained gallstones in patients. "The technique is good for the United States, but not useful for the Soviet Union," the radiologist decreed through a Russian translator. An older and obviously important Soviet surgeon then commented, "I beg to differ with my young colleague. We do leave stones, and this is a very

Scientists at Bell Labs invent a tunable, continuous-wave laser.

The push-through tab on soda and beer cans is introduced.

Werner Forssmann invents a caged balloon dilator, which is a precursor to modern angioplasty balloons.

A calf is produced from a frozen embryo.

U.K. scientists introduce the nuclear magnetic resonance scanner for medical diagnosis.

valuable technique." An honest and respected leader had spoken.[30]

On the second leg of their trip, Abele and Burhenne stopped in Poland, where at 6:00 in the morning they used the steerable catheter to remove a retained stone from a former surgeon who was also the father of the chief of neurosurgery at a Warsaw hospital. The patient was so delighted to be spared a second operation that he leaped off the table and kissed both Burhenne and Abele.[31]

Less than a year later, in England, Abele and Albert Reddihough, Medi-Tech's dealer there, staged a remarkable demonstration that may have been the first of its kind anywhere in medicine. At the time, Dr. Peter Cotton, the chief of gastroenterology at Middlesex Hospital in London, was working to develop a similar technique using an endoscope. Like their counterparts in the Soviet Union, English doctors were more open to new techniques and experimentation than was the U.S. medical establishment. In fact, Cotton himself had developed a technique to remove retained gallstones using a duodenoscope inserted through the mouth to reach the duodenum. He then slid a smaller scope through the opening of the duodenoscope and out through a side port into the common duct, and removed retained stones.

Cotton and Burhenne agreed to participate in a meeting called "Surgery without Scars," in which both doctors performed their technique on four patients before a live audience of about 70 surgeons and held an informal competition to see who could remove a retained gallstone faster. An Internet tribute to Dr. Burhenne described what happened:

> *When it was Dr. Burhenne's turn, he turned to the local radiologist and posed the question, "Have you ever seen this equipment before?" When the radiologist responded "No," Dr. Burhenne said, "To show you how simple it is to use, and knowing you have no experience with it, I am going to train you to use it right now, on this patient, in front of this audience." The radiologist proceeded to quickly,*

In honor of the first live, televised, gallbladder surgery competition, John Abele, left, presented this award to Albert Reddihough, Medi-Tech's dealer in England. Programs like this helped Medi-Tech become established as an educational innovator.

1974...

World Events

President Nixon resigns in connection with Watergate.

Gerald Ford becomes president and pardons Nixon.

Medical Milestones

The Society of Cardiovascular Radiology is formed.

Boston Scientific

Abele meets Gruentzig, leading to Medi-Tech's role in development of peripheral and coronary angioplasty.

Ahead of Its Time

After losing his 58-year-old father to a heart attack, cardiologist Richard Myler had made treating coronary artery disease his life's work. Myler was attending the 1969 meeting of the American Heart Association (AHA) when he first heard about the practice of widening obstructed arteries with a catheter. Although the technique described at the AHA meeting, transluminal angioplasty, dealt with peripheral arteries instead of the coronary arteries, Myler later remembered that "it felt like my heart was going to burst out of my chest with excitement."[1]

After that meeting, he called John Abele at Medi-Tech, and the two began work on a way to use the steerable catheter to clear obstructed coronary arteries. They discussed their ideas at length. Eventually, Abele came up with the idea of using a guide wire with a reversing Chinese finger-puzzle design to dilate and remove debris from coronary arteries. With help from a technician at Medi-Tech, he created the AWED, or Arterial Wall Expanding Device. Abele's idea for the AWED stemmed from his youth, when he worked in a hardware store and saw the braids that go over electrical wires. His hollow guide wire was designed to pass through the obstructing lesion in the unexpanded state, expand, and then pull back. The braid would not only dilate the artery but remove some of the obstructing material as well. Abele didn't intend for the AWED to remove all of the arterial debris, just enough to let some blood pass through. He wanted his device to simply buy a little more time for patients who had suffered an acute myocardial infarct, or heart attack. Like Andreas Gruentzig, who later performed the first successful coronary artery dilatations, Abele believed percutaneous therapies should do just enough to let the patients heal themselves.[2]

Myler was intrigued when he first saw the AWED. In 1972 and 1973, he and Abele exchanged many letters in which they listed and sketched improvements to the original prototype. Ultimately, however, Myler hesitated to use the device because he was concerned that it would be too traumatic, abrading the blood vessel. As a result, Abele abandoned the AWED.[3] Ironically, about 15 years later, a stent device appeared in Europe featuring a metallic skeletal framework to keep blood vessels open—with the same Chinese finger-puzzle design as the AWED.[4]

Smallpox epidemic kills ten thousand to twenty thousand in India.

Worldwide inflation causes dramatic increases in cost of fuel, food, and materials; economic growth slows to near zero in most industrialized nations.

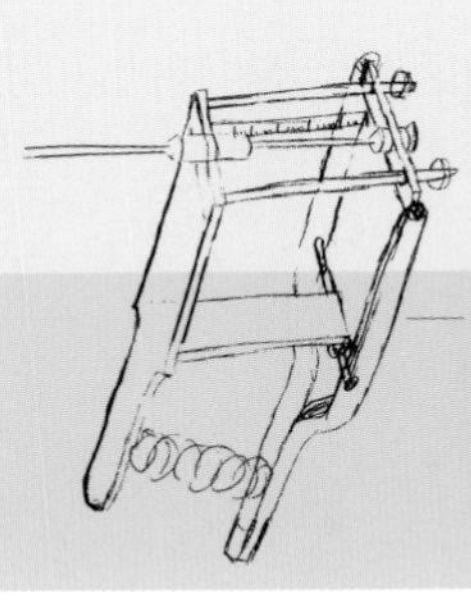

John Abele and Richard Myler refine the AWED device, at one point making this rough sketch of its control handle.

safely, and successfully remove the retained gallstone. "The audience of physicians insisted it was the best medical demonstration they had ever witnessed," said Abele. "To my knowledge, a competition of this sort has never been held since."[32]

"It wasn't as if we were doing anything wrong," Cotton later said of the televised demonstration. "We were just demonstrating that there were new ways of removing gallstones. Anyway, I think it was a tie."[33]

At the end of the decade, Burhenne's technique was used to remove retained gallstones from the Shah of Iran. This procedure was carried out under the strictest security, and the steerable catheter didn't receive any publicity as a result. The grateful Shah, however, sent Burhenne a massive 60-foot-by-60-foot Persian rug, which proved to be so large that Burhenne had to build his house around the rug.

Throughout these critical years, the Burhenne technique "marked a milestone in the basically uncharted territory of less-invasive medicine," said Abele. It helped make the steerable catheter a viable interventional therapy and, by extension, gave Medi-Tech a reputation for quality and innovation.

Burhenne's prize-winning interactive display for the removal of retained gallstones, pictured at the 1972 American College of Surgeons. This display, which Medi-Tech helped design, let physicians practice.

A Can-Do Culture

As the steerable-catheter method for removing retained biliary stones became accepted, Medi-Tech began to grow more quickly, remembered Dean Harrington, who joined as an accountant in 1971. "The growth was rapid and steady, but not too dramatic," Harrington said. "We hired people on an as-needed basis, so you found people who were more jack-of-all-trades types, where the person who was responsible for shipping and receiving had all kinds of warehouse and inventory management responsibility."[34]

At the center of this growth was John Abele, who was earning respect in medical circles as an

World Events

Streaking becomes a fad in the United States.

Medical Milestones

L. Demling and associates convert surgical technique of transduodenal sphincterotomy at laparotomy to an endoscopic technique.

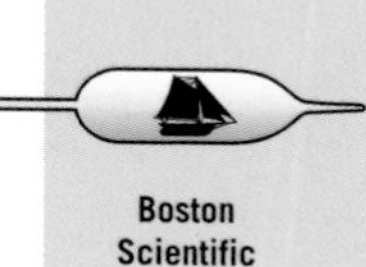

Boston Scientific

advocate for less-invasive medicine and the unique "can-do" culture of his small company.

"He was a pretty quiet guy except when he had something to say," Brown remembered.

> *He had a talk that he gave at radiology meetings. Very few nonphysicians were ever asked to talk at a medical convention, but he had slide presentations that explained how everything worked....*
>
> *Just to give an example of John's clever ability, one time we were flying from Boston to L.A., and there was an Alfred Hitchcock movie on the plane. In those days, the movies were reels. They were playing one of his classic movies, and the damn projector breaks down in the middle of the movie. Stewardesses can't do anything about it. Engineer-copilot comes back and he couldn't do anything about it. John always carried a Swiss Army knife hooked to a lanyard on his belt. He got up there and fixed it. The plane landed in L.A. with the projector in the down position and running. The plane taxied to the gate with the film running. The doors opened with the film running, and no one got off. He can fix anything.*[35]

Andreas Gruentzig

Throughout the 1970s, developments in less-invasive medicine took place across a deep cross section of the medical world with a variety of instruments, including catheters and endoscopes. A medical revolution was taking place, but it was a quiet one that had yet to burst into the public consciousness (with the exception of Charles Dotter and his wildly eccentric *Life* magazine spread). That changed when a charismatic European doctor named Andreas Gruentzig made history by treating heart disease with a catheter and became a highly visible spokesperson.

The movement of less-invasive techniques into the treatment of heart disease was not a surprise to many—indeed, it had been imagined since the devices first appeared on the medical scene. Doctors who watched Charles Dotter open a clogged artery in the leg imagined the day when a catheter could open a clogged coronary artery. The social implications of a procedure like this were enormous. Heart disease was (and remains) the leading cause of death in the industrialized world. The coronary bypass operation, which itself was less than 15 years old in the 1970s, offered the first real therapy for this dreaded disease, but it was a traumatic technique that involved cracking open the chest and stopping the heart.

Naturally, people like Abele and the pioneering interventional doctors were eager to extend the diagnostic use of catheters in the heart and find a way to treat coronary artery disease through minimally invasive techniques. From the work of Dr. Mason Sones, who pioneered coronary angiography and even into the 1970s performed almost half of the coronary angiograms, it was known that catheters could probe into the coronary arteries. The next step was devising a therapeutic approach.

Scientists call for halt of genetic engineering research until its implications are better understood.

AT&T bans discrimination against its gay and lesbian employees.

King and Mills report on closure of atrial septal defect (ASD) with a catheter-delivered double umbrella.

The challenge led a young German-born physician named Andreas Gruentzig to begin experimenting with ways to open blocked coronary arteries with catheters. His story is one of the most important in the history of interventional medicine.

Following the Heart

Gruentzig was often described as a handsome man with a dashing presence. According to cardiologist Richard Myler, a friend of John Abele's who later became involved in Gruentzig's pursuit, "He was a tall, nice-looking fellow with a moustache, and he looked a little Bohemian in the way he dressed."[36]

After graduating from medical school in Heidelberg in 1964, Gruentzig received an internship and research fellowship in epidemiology, during which he studied coronary artery disease. He later received training in peripheral vascular disease at the Ratchow Clinic in Darmstadt, Germany, where he was exposed to the Dotter technique:

> *My chief invited me to attend an afternoon meeting in Frankfurt. For the first time, I heard Dr. Eberhart Zeitler speaking about peripheral recanalization using Dotter's method. I recall that my chief was very upset that someone would try to attack diseased arteries by forcing catheters into areas of narrowing. He made it clear that he never wanted such a treatment to take place in his hospital.*[37]

After his training at the Ratchow Clinic, Gruentzig became a resident in radiology at the University of Zurich. Here he was granted permission to visit Zeitler and observe the Dotter method.[38] He first saw the technique demonstrated at a clinic near Cologne and was greatly impressed with its potential. Immediately, he began thinking of a way to treat the heart.

In a biography of Gruentzig, author Sheila Stavish described him as a "cautious innovator" and detailed his passion for improved treatments.

> *He promptly tried the [Dotter] method on his own patients, but he was dissatisfied with the crude coaxial catheter that reamed its way through plaque. So he worked at transforming it into a device with a distensible sausage-shaped segment [balloon] that pressed plaque against the arterial wall. It was gratifying to have a new technique for opening up leg vessels, but that wasn't what really excited young Dr. Gruentzig. "The legs were only my testing ground. From the very beginning, I had the heart in mind."*[39]

The Balloon Breakthrough

As Gruentzig worked toward his goal, he became increasingly unsatisfied with Dotter's method of sliding catheters through the occluded part of the artery. His search for solutions soon led him to balloon-tipped catheters. This kind of catheter was originally used in the field of urology in the 1800s,[40] but it was not strong enough

World Events

The U.S. ends two decades of military involvement in Vietnam.

Medical Milestones

Andreas Gruentzig practices dilating coronary arteries in dogs and cadavers using catheters he built in his kitchen.

Boston Scientific

Burhenne and Abele demonstrate Burhenne technique in Moscow and Poland.

to dilate blood vessels. In 1964, Charles Dotter and Melvin Judkins introduced the concept of a telescoping angioplasty catheter system, which used catheters of gradually increasing size, sliding one over another to mash arterial plaque against vessel walls.

In 1972, Werner Forssmann, an interventional practitioner in East Germany, collaborated with Dotter to invent a rubber balloon surrounded by a Teflon cage, or "corset." This was an improvement over the telescoping catheters because it didn't carry the same risk of embolism.[41] Medi-Tech, in fact, began a research program to make balloons in the mid-1970s.

Gruentzig wanted to try the balloon dilatation method in the coronary artery and began to fabricate his own balloon catheters in 1972,[42] as described in an article in the medical journal *Circulation*:

> *Gruentzig worked evenings in his kitchen with his assistant, Maria Schlumpf, her husband, Walter, and Michaela, Andreas's wife, and during those sessions, many versions of the balloon catheter were designed and built with tiny bits of rubber, thread, and epoxy glue. The problem was always the same: when distended in a constriction, the balloon always took on an hourglass appearance without opening the lesion. The concept evolved to use a sausage-shaped distensible segment that would not expand over a predetermined size and would accommodate high pressure.*[43]

Charles Dotter pictured at a percutaneous transluminal angioplasty (PTA) symposium in Nuremberg in 1982. He is holding an original PTA catheter from 1964. Although Dotter's work was groundbreaking in PTA, it took an effort from many pioneering doctors and companies to establish PTA as an accepted treatment.

Unemployment rate in U.S. reaches 9.2 percent, its highest since 1941.

The Suez Canal reopens.

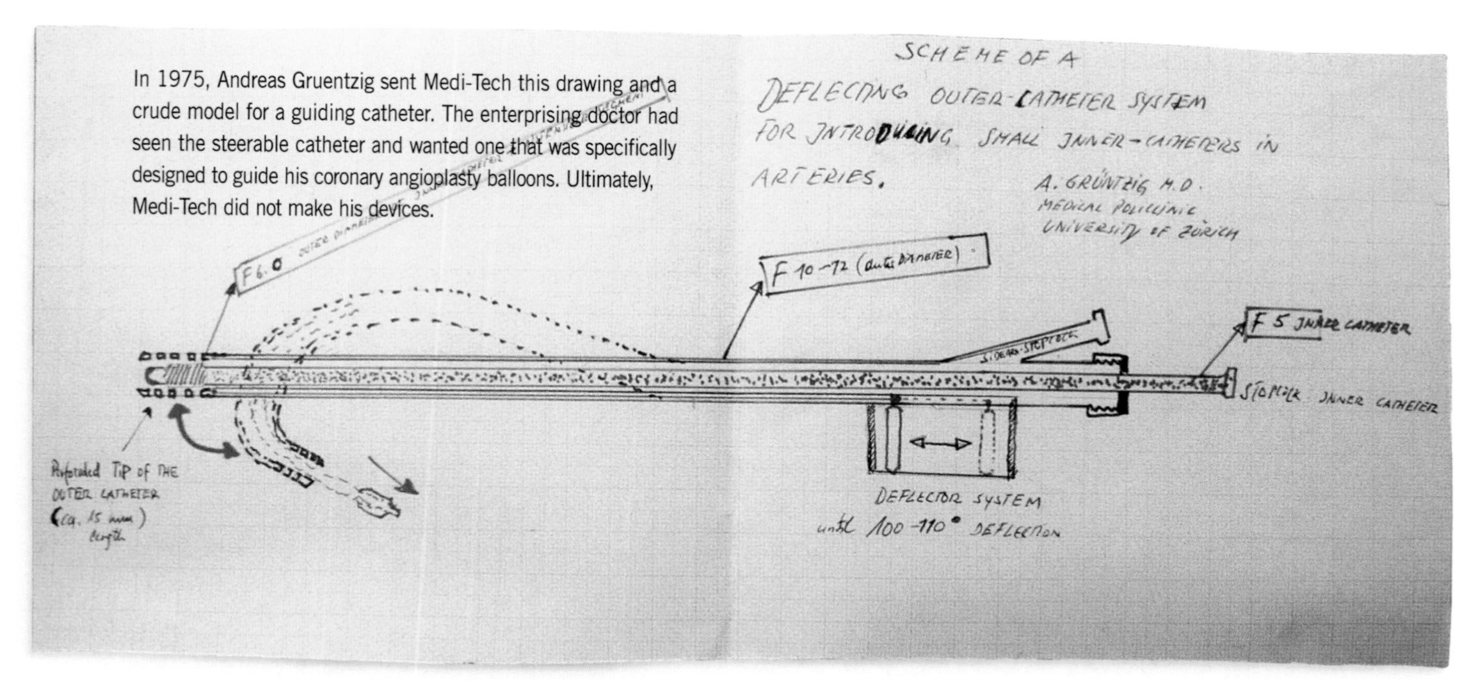

In 1975, Andreas Gruentzig sent Medi-Tech this drawing and a crude model for a guiding catheter. The enterprising doctor had seen the steerable catheter and wanted one that was specifically designed to guide his coronary angioplasty balloons. Ultimately, Medi-Tech did not make his devices.

In 1973, Gruentzig began a residency in cardiology at the University of Zurich. During the day, he practiced orthodox medicine at the hospital. But at night, he worked in the animal lab and hospital morgue, where he practiced dilating the arteries of dogs and cadavers using catheters that he had built in his own kitchen. Knowing that his research would be greeted with skepticism, Gruentzig kept his experiments to himself. "I found it was an advantage that my colleagues laughed at Dotter," he said. "I laughed along with them. Then I just went about my work quietly."[44]

Gruentzig believed that balloons were the answer to successful coronary angioplasty, but he had trouble fabricating devices that performed well. In 1974, he contacted Medi-Tech, saying he was very interested in obtaining a steerable catheter that could reliably guide a balloon into the coronary artery. "Gruentzig had sent me a model of a guiding catheter made out of Teflon with a wire attached," Abele recalled, "and when he saw our steerable catheter where the wires were neatly built into the wall, he said, 'This is clearly the sort of thing that we need.' " Abele not only sent him the

steerable catheters but also visited him in Zurich in 1975.[45]

In Gruentzig's apartment kitchen, Abele marveled at the young doctor's method for making catheters:

He took single lumen tubing, and in order to get two lumens into the catheter, he would put a sheath over the outside. The first lumen was on the inner tube, and the second lumen was in that space in between. The problem had been, if he applied suction, it would tend to collapse the outer sheath. In order to prevent that sheath from collapsing, he took a razor blade and went all the way down the catheter twice, making a "V" groove—which is, if you've ever tried that, more tricky to do than brain surgery, to say the least.

I said, "Andreas, don't you know that you can get two-lumen catheters?" ... He said he had asked about them, and people said they didn't exist. So I said, "Well, we make them!"

As a result of that, Andreas came over and visited us in Watertown, near Boston, and we actually spent time on the extruder. In fact, Andreas ran the extruder. He was a very hands-on sort of person.[46]

Spreading the Word

Gruentzig was a quick study when it came to work and when it came to play, noted Abele, who taught his new friend how to windsurf during a weekend on Cape Cod in 1975. "He just basically learned in about 30 minutes and was up sailing in 20-knot winds—just incredible!" said Abele.[47]

In 1976, Gruentzig prepared to come to the United States to present his canine coronary experiments in a poster session at the American Heart Association meeting in Miami. Dr. Spencer B. King, who would later head the Andreas Gruentzig Cardiovascular Center at Emory University, was one of many skeptical observers at that poster session. He recalled the event in a 1996 article in the medical journal *Circulation*:

Andreas stood in the center of a small group. His bushy mustache and ascot telegraphed his European roots even before he began to speak. He clearly was convinced that the method would work. Armed with some knowledge of the pathology of atherosclerosis, I said, "This will never work," and we parted.[48]

Despite negative responses like this, there were others at the AHA meeting who saw the potential of Gruentzig's work. Abele, who had called Gruentzig to come to the session, was one of them, and so was Dr. Richard Myler, a cardiologist who had been waiting for exactly such a development ever since hearing Charles Dotter talk about transluminal angioplasty in 1969. Abele later recalled the poster meeting:

I'd actually called up Dick Myler beforehand and said, "Hey, Dick! Remember that work we did some years ago in the coronary artery? I think

Films include Jaws *and* The Sunshine Boys.

Hospice movement (end-of-life care) starts in the United States.

Patty Hearst is apprehended by FBI.

First meeting of the Society of Cardiovascular Radiology; 24 members present; membership limit of 75.

First strike by doctors in the U.S. takes place.

First endoscopic sphincterotomy is performed in U.S.

this guy's figured it out. He's somebody you gotta meet!"

And so Dick came down and we met together. I stayed by the booth with Andreas to give him some guidance on who was coming up and who was asking questions. And Bob Hall—he was a cardiologist-in-chief at the Texas Heart Institute—came up and in his marvelous style asked him a series of questions, but kind of setup questions. And Gruentzig was just incredibly well prepared and in his very ingenuous and humble way answered every question and then asked some questions that Hall hadn't thought of. And it was the sort of thing that even the most cynical of people, looking at this very significant and provocative new procedure, had to be impressed by.[49]

In 1972, Gruentzig had begun experimenting with his balloons to expand peripheral arteries in humans. In early 1977, Myler and his wife flew to a meeting in Nuremberg to attend a demonstration. When he arrived, Myler was surprised to learn that only 15 doctors from around the world were in attendance and "was amazed at how few Americans were there," he said.

Dotter was there, and the others were European, some from even behind the Iron Curtain. After we left Nuremberg, I went to Zurich, and I actually scrubbed in with Gruentzig and did some peripheral work. I thought, "Gee, this is interesting." It was kind of a Rube Goldberg setup. The catheters were great, but in order to inflate the balloon, he had to build this huge thing to inflate and deflate the balloon. Andreas never necessarily wanted things to be simple. In fact, sometimes the more complicated the technology was, the more he liked it.[50]

Shortly after that demonstration, Gruentzig traveled back to the United States, where Myler helped him "put a stake in the ground" for U.S. angioplasty. In San Francisco in May 1977, Gruentzig performed the first intraoperative coronary angioplasty in a human, with assistance from Myler and his surgical colleague, Elias Hanna,[51] dilating an artery during the course of a conventional bypass operation.[52] The procedure encouraged the doctors to continue their work, said Myler.

We used a smaller, shorter version of the balloon catheter in the operating room just before the

This cross-sectional diagram of arterial dilatation was drawn by Dr. Wilfredo Casteneda and appeared in the journal *Radiology*. The landmark article described the mechanics of balloon angioplasty.

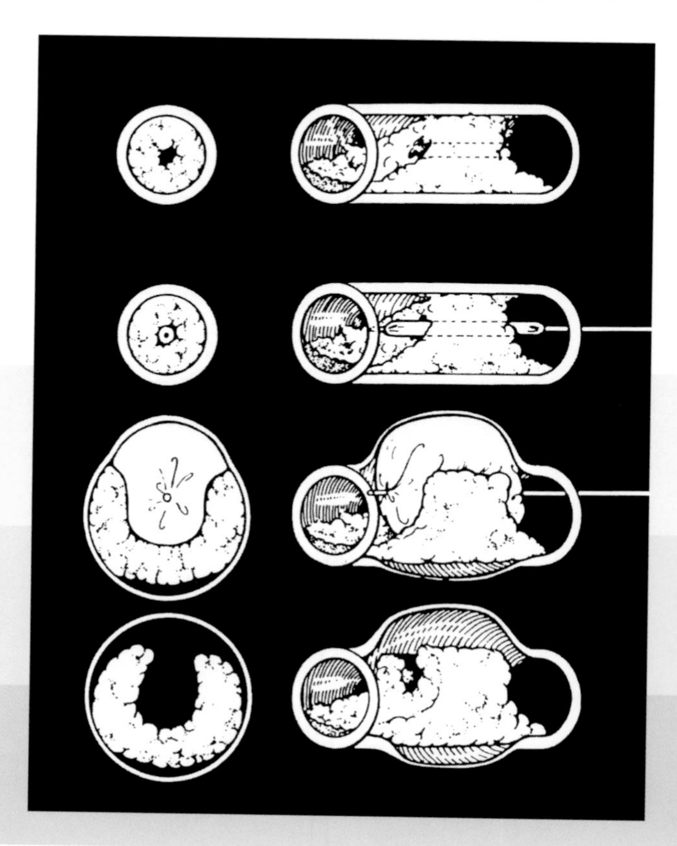

1975...

World Events

Jimmy Carter is elected U.S. president.

Medical Milestones

ASGE membership approaches 1,200.

Boston Scientific

bypass grafts were placed. We wanted to know, one, what would the vessels look like a week or so after surgery, and second, when we put this balloon catheter in the areas of the narrowing and inflated and then deflated the balloon, would any pieces of the plaque be knocked off? We never found any emboli during tests, so that was very heartening to us.[53]

By the end of the year, Gruentzig was ready for the next step. On September 16, 1977, Gruentzig performed the first coronary angioplasty on a conscious human in a catheterization lab in Zurich. His patient was a 37-year-old insurance salesman, who was eager to be the first to undergo the new procedure. Upon successful completion of the angioplasty, the patient wanted to notify the newspapers, but Gruentzig stopped him, for he was concerned that if his procedure had already been covered in the mainstream news, scientific publications would not want to highlight it. On the other hand, Gruentzig felt anxious that others would copy what he had done and displace him if the results of his successful coronary angioplasty were not published quickly.[54]

A few months later, after performing the procedure on four additional patients (all in Europe), Gruentzig shared his results with the medical world in a short letter to the British journal *Lancet*.[55] In November 1977, he presented his human cases at the AHA meeting, where he received a standing ovation from the small audience of doctors. Mason Sones

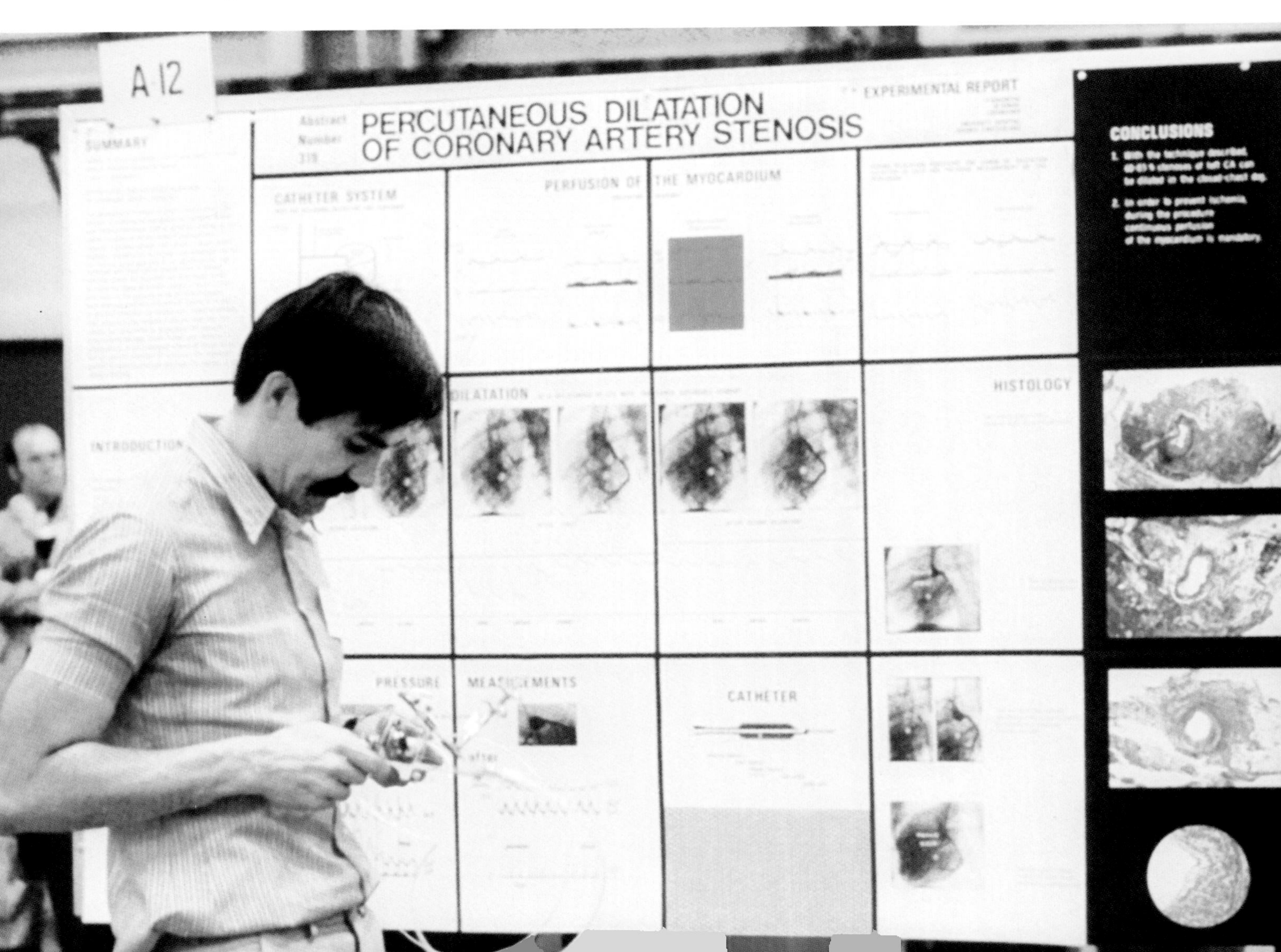

In 1976, Gruentzig came to a poster session of the American Heart Association to demonstrate balloon angioplasty. He is pictured here holding a Medi-Tech steerable catheter.

PETE NICHOLAS

PETE NICHOLAS AND JOHN Abele had a lot in common, but more important than what they shared was what they didn't share.

Peter Nicholas had gone to Duke University for his undergraduate degree, where he met and married Ruth Virginia Lilly, described as "a pretty, hazel-eyed blonde debutante—and pharmaceutical magnate Eli Lilly's great-great-granddaughter."[1] After graduation, Nicholas went into the military and later returned to graduate school at the Wharton School of Business for his MBA. After graduating, it seemed natural that he work for his wife's company, where her grandfather was chairman emeritus. After five years in sales, marketing, and other positions in the U.S. organizations, the couple was sent to Europe, where Nicholas, still in his thirties, took over as general manager of the Northern Europe office.

It was an exhilarating experience to go out and run something, and a great opportunity to be selected to run an overseas division of a Fortune 500 *company. But after I was almost ten years at Lilly, maybe in 1975, Eli died. I probably didn't appreciate the extent to which people were treating me with kid gloves because of Eli's presence in the company. Life became a little more difficult. At the same time, I began to realize that I had ambitions for the company that the company, at the level I was, couldn't embrace. I was always someone who thought we could do more.*[2]

The year Eli Lilly died, Nicholas was selected to attend Harvard University's advanced management program in Switzerland. "It was the first time I'd really had an opportunity to step out of an operational job and into an environment that was much more focused on broader issues of management," Nicholas said. "I really got excited about it. I think when I was there for only two or three days, I called my wife up and said, 'Honey, I'm quitting the company.'"[3]

World Events

North and South Vietnam reunite.

During a raid on Entebbe, Israeli hostages are freed.

Medical Milestones

The Medical Device Act of 1976 is passed, creating regulation for the manufacture and design of medical devices.

Boston Scientific

A London hospital hosts an unprecedented contest for the better technique in removing retained gallstones (the use of a flexible endoscope versus the Burhenne technique).

It was a momentous decision. Nicholas turned his back on a comfortable career at one of the world's largest pharmaceutical companies. Moreover, he had no idea what to do next, except that he probably wanted to join a smaller company and move back to the United States. He launched an intensive search for the right atmosphere and networked with executive search firms and old contacts in New York, studying the flow of executive talent through American industry. In the course of this self-education, he became a student of small enterprise and realized, "That's what I wanted to do. I wanted to lead something."[4]

He was looking for an opportunity to build a company but hadn't identified any particular industry in which he wanted to work. If nothing else, his employment at Eli Lilly had given him experience in health care, but he was more interested in guiding a growing enterprise than staying in health care.

Around the same time, he began to realize the tremendous "paper weight" of his résumé. He built a data base of companies and contacts and was recruited by Millipore, a maker of high-technology filter systems.

Shortly after joining Millipore, however, he realized he had made a dreadful error: "I felt the company didn't seem to have an established set of values, at least compared to where I had been for the past ten years. I realized it was a huge mistake. And then serendipity stepped in."[5]

The Nicholases lived next door to a Duke graduate, who arranged a dinner party to help the family meet some of their new neighbors. This same neighbor also knew the Abeles and "was vaguely aware" that the two men shared some background in terms of military fathers and careers in the health care industry.

"We went to this party, and I met John," Nicholas remembered. "We gravitated toward one another and I was intrigued instantly."

John doesn't seem to be a business person, but he is a guy who has a sixth sense about how things happen, and I think in some sense, I do as well. It clicked. He could imagine how plastics and tubes could profoundly change the way treatment occurred, and so could I. But his interest was in conceptual, theoretical and developmental. Mine was in the part that said, "Let's do something with it that makes a difference to people's lives."

Now, John had befriended somebody at Cooper to invest in a place where John had become the caretaker. I said, "Let's get together." A month later, I went to his office in Watertown, where he had all these neat little inventions. We discovered many, many common threads between us, but the most aligning one was that I suggested to him that we try to acquire this company and build a business.[6]

The ink jet printer is developed.

Hank Aaron retires from baseball.

The Society of Cardiovascular Radiology has 48 active members.

was in the audience and after the meeting said the percutaneous transluminal coronary angioplasty was the realization of a dream that had taken root almost 20 years previously.[56] He had, in fact, been experimenting with a kind of roto-rooter catheter since the late 1960s but never published for fear of recrimination from the medical community.

"That session led to an avalanche of people ... going over and visiting Gruentzig in Zurich," said Abele. "He was kind of a lowly person in the hospital, and having visitors come to the hospital all the time and crowd the cath lab was not looked upon favorably by his bosses. So he had sort of run out of his favors he could ask, and the solution was 'Why don't I invite them all here at once?'"[57]

The result was the first live demonstration course, in which Gruentzig brought together cardiologists, radiologists, and surgeons.[58]

Mission Accomplished

The first percutaneous transluminal coronary angioplasty (PTCA) procedures, or balloon angioplasties, in America were performed in March 1978 by Myler in San Francisco and Simon Stertzer in New York. Stertzer was an effective self-promoter who was later featured in *Time* magazine and took credit for the procedure.[59]

In 1980, Gruentzig emigrated from Zurich to Atlanta, where he became professor of medicine (cardiology) and radiology and the director of interventional cardiovascular medicine at Emory University.[60]

Choosing a Distributor

Although Medi-Tech made some two-lumen catheters for Gruentzig, the devices never satisfied the criteria for human use. In 1977, Gruentzig contracted with Schneider, a needle manufacturing company in Zurich, to begin making his angioplasty balloon catheters.[61] In an interview, Schneider President Heliane Canepa described the early days of balloon angioplasty:

> *We started in a garage. We had a production team of 10 people. And, of course, there was no cleanroom. We made about five catheters a week. And we were not allowed to sell one catheter to a doctor who didn't show us a training certificate from Andreas Gruentzig.... Andreas was really a very cautious man.... He trained all doctors on live cases. He was a very good teacher. And he didn't allow us to sell [catheters] freely to everybody. He had absolute control over what was going on, about all patients in every country. They were all reporting to him. They were all giving him the data. So he was the best clinical regulatory department we could ask for.*[62]

Gruentzig asked Medi-Tech to be distributors for Schneider's PTCA catheters, which was an agreement Abele was interested in for the short-term. Schneider, however, stipulated that Medi-Tech could distribute the balloon but wasn't allowed to manufacture competitive balloons or, far more importantly, continue the product development

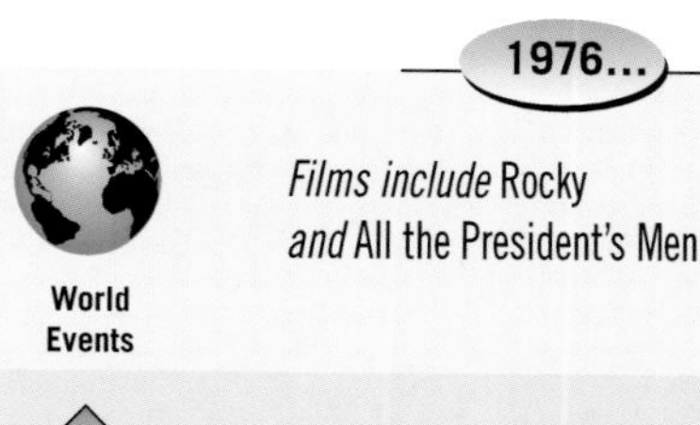

World Events

Films include Rocky *and* All the President's Men

Medical Milestones

Gruentzig presents his canine coronary experiments at an AHA meeting in Miami.

A viral cause of multiple sclerosis is discovered.

Boston Scientific

CLOGOLOGY

ONE OF THE MORE INTERESTING aspects of minimally invasive therapy in the 1970s is that there wasn't any such thing. It was known by many names and across a spectrum of specialties that seemed hardly related. A partial list of the specialties and their terms for the discipline shows how confusion results:

- **Radiology:** *Interventional radiology*
- **Cardiology:** *Interventional cardiology*
- **Surgery:** *Less-invasive surgery, Minimally invasive therapy, Minimal access surgery, or keyhole surgery*
- **Vascular Surgery:** *Endovascular surgery*
- **Neurosurgery:** *Neuroendovascular therapy*
- **Urology:** *Endourology*
- **Orthopedic Surgery:** *Arthroscopy*
- **Gastroenterology:** *Therapeutic endoscopy*

More than a quirky chapter in the development of interventional medicine, this naming schism pointed out the profound chasms that separated people in the field.

David Fleischer, a gastroenterologist at Georgetown University Medical Center, wrote an editorial in 1990 for the Mayo Clinic journal that nicely captured the emerging spirit of interventional medicine:

> *In the past, the distinction among surgeons, internists and radiologists was precise. Surgeons cut. Internists diagnosed and prescribed medications. Radiologists took X-ray films. No longer are the divisions so black and white.*[1]

In many cases, Fleischer pointed out, the new medical specialties had more in common with each other than with related specialties in their field. Yet the practitioners coined their own descriptions, calling themselves gastrointestinal endoscopists, endourologists, interventional radiologists, cardiac angiographers, interventional cardiologists, and more.[2]

In the late 1970s, however, the term "less-invasive surgery" was coined by Channing, Weinberg & Company, a medical consulting firm, to describe the use of catheters and endoscopes in general. Although the terminology would shift, Boston Scientific was an early advocate and had been using the term "alternative to surgery" for a number of years before Channing, Weinberg came up with "less invasive." Unlike other companies, Boston Scientific worked to transfer findings from one specialty to another. Gradually, interventional medicine began to emerge as a cohesive theory that united many different kinds of doctors.

The United States celebrates its bicentennial.

Genentech, the first commercial company aimed at developing products through genetic engineering, is established in San Francisco.

Medi-Tech hires its first full-time R&D engineer, Josh Tolkoff.

with iterative improvements. After only six months, Abele elected not to continue the contract.

> *I thought it was necessary that we should drop out of the cardiology business, so I actually returned the rights to distribute the Schneider balloon products back to Schneider at a time when people said, "You gave away a chance of a lifetime." I did it because I saw that activity totally devouring us. It would require 100 percent effort; it would have dragged us in over our head, over our ability to perform. Our greatest opportunities were in radiology and peripheral vascular.*
>
> *The cardiac business was much more expensive to get involved in and required a lot more resources, and I thought that would have been more difficult for us and that a larger company would have been more appropriate. I recommended that they go to USCI/Bard, which they did.*[63]

United States Catheter & Instrument Corporation (USCI) picked up the contract and soon established itself as the leading marketer and later manufacturer of coronary angioplasty balloons. Medi-Tech's balloon development program, meanwhile, focused on larger peripheral angioplasty catheters.[64]

The Bridge to an Emerging Field

Gruentzig's breakthrough had a profound effect on the fledgling science of interventional medicine. Not only was he the perfect spokesman (intelligent, well-spoken, careful, meticulous, and understated), he proved that the impossible could be done and went on to teach others how to do it. He was an excellent experimenter who could design an experiment that would answer his question, then communicate his results clearly. Moreover, instead of focusing only on like-minded physicians, Gruentzig sought out cardiac surgeons, his biggest critics, and convinced them of coronary angioplasty's potential.

This acceptance, and Gruentzig's effective method of spreading a new interventional therapeutic technique, coincided with the development of techniques across many fields of medicine.

Arthroscopes, used by orthopedic surgeons for less-invasive joint surgery, came into wide use in the 1970s as new advances in optical technology made the devices more practical. The first arthroscopes had appeared in the 1930s, invented by a Japanese student named Masaki Watanabe. These devices were a kind of internal spotlight, or camera, that doctors inserted into the knees and other joints to obtain a good image of damaged tissue. Once the injured area was under vision, the doctor used a shaver to remove the excess scar tissue and allow the joint a wider range of motion. This valuable surgery was accomplished through an incision that was only a few millimeters long, as opposed to one that opened up the whole knee.

Endoscopes also found application in gastroenterology, where doctors found they were able to use the device for injecting contrast material and even

World Events

President Carter issues warnings about energy crisis, urges Americans to make significant changes in their oil consumption.

The Apple II, the first preassembled personal computer, is introduced.

Medical Milestones

Schneider Medintag AG is founded in Switzerland.

Boston Scientific

Itzhak Bentov publishes his book Stalking the Wild Pendulum, *which explains his views on the mechanics of consciousness.*

for removing polyps in the colon. This polypectomy was a blessing for patients, who could undergo the relatively simple procedure instead of a painful and traumatic operation on the colon.

Medi-Tech was in the midst of this small world, and its influence was profound as it worked to tie together all the various disciplines. In 1976, the company released a long-range plan that insisted that its products be proprietary or unique and that they save money, time, patient risk, trauma, or a combination of all these.

> *The opportunities for our technology seem almost limitless, and it appears to make most sense at this time, therefore, that we should dedicate ourselves to grow through product development rather than by acquisition.... Our selling philosophy has been and will continue to be to concentrate on applications as solutions to problems rather than trying to sell the product itself....*
>
> *Products that represent alternatives to surgery deprive income to surgeons. They also improve the status of the particular specialty that inherits the procedure. Because surgeons are traditionally father figures in hospitals and the most dominant politically, it has been and will be difficult to win over surgeons to allow radiologists, cardiologists, pulmonary internists, etc., to perform procedures which were heretofore sacrosanct properties of the surgeon. We are seeing in some places, however, that surgeons are beginning to be interested in manipulating catheters and using endoscopes, so we regard that as a sign that they see the handwriting on the wall and will accept these new techniques.*[65]

With words like this, Medi-Tech was treading on dangerous ground and therefore walked a careful line. The company had no interest in antagonizing surgeons, but there was no denying that Medi-Tech was a unique kind of device company. Whereas the other device manufacturers voluntarily stepped aside during the development of their products, letting doctors make the decisions and mold their uses, Medi-Tech was actively involved in the development and use of its products—even going so far as to help medical societies organize around interventional medicine and to sponsor programs instructing doctors how to use the new technology and build a practice around it. No other company would have attempted this. At Medi-Tech, John Abele handled that role, setting himself up as a bridge between the medical profession and his company, and between the medical specialties themselves.

Internal imaging was an early goal of interventional medicine. This Medi-Tech steerable catheter, circa 1974, is shown with a modular fiber-optic endoscope. Adaptations like this made Medi-Tech a technology leader.

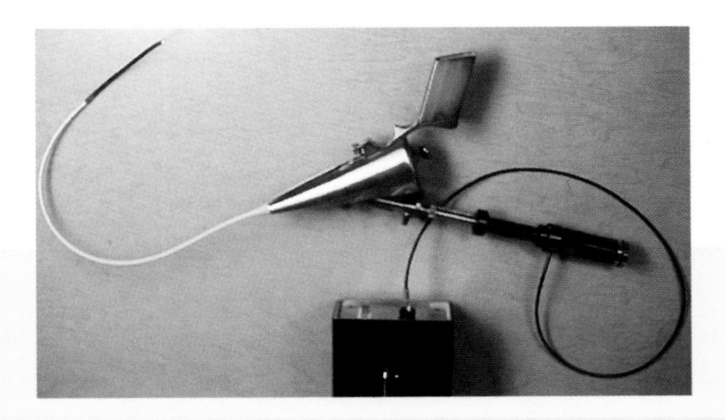

The U.S. Department of Energy is established.

British scientists determine the complete genetic structure of a living organism.

Medi-Tech has 35 employees.

Gruentzig arranges for Medi-Tech to distribute Schneider's PTA and PTCA catheters.

DOTTER'S CRYING TOWEL

EVEN FOR MEDICAL PIONEERS, THE best medicine is still sometimes laughter—especially when it comes to treating indignation. In 1977, Medi-Tech made a steerable pulmonary embolectomy catheter, the tip of which had removable cups available in different sizes, to be used for blood vessels of different sizes. Famed radiologist Charles Dotter ordered a spare cup, for which he was billed $40. To protest what he considered to be an outrageous price for the cup, Dotter sent Abele a copy of the invoice after circling the $40 with a magic marker and adding an enormous exclamation point and question mark.[1]

Rather than let the matter rest, Abele fired back a three-page letter that justified the expense by way of a rather elaborate analysis of capitalism. "I think you know me well enough to know that we're not out to rape the public and, therefore, an explanation is appropriate," the letter began.

> *The prices we establish for our products are based on a number of factors: 1. Direct labor 2. Direct material 3. Yield 4. Amortization of "front end" expenses (mold costs, set-up charges) 5. Amortization of engineering and development costs 6. Manufacturing overhead.*
>
> *We then have to multiply the resulting costs by a factor which enables that product to contribute to General Overhead (operating expenses). This includes marketing, general and administrative (that includes me, and I don't take a big salary) and R&D (we have to provide for all those specials and prototypes we don't get paid for, too). We have to provide for a marketing discount to distributors. And, of course, we have to provide for a profit.*
>
> *What makes the numbers seem absurdly high in this case is product volume. We originally thought that the concept of catheter pulmonary embolectomy would be more widely applicable than we now know to be the case....*
>
> *If we hadn't made it, NIH [National Institutes of Health] would probably have spent $100,000 developing a model that wouldn't work, so there's been a net savings to society.... If we price it so low that we lose money on the product then we won't be able to stay in business so we couldn't make all the specials we do, or our other products. Nor could we pay taxes to the Government so they can support all their extravagant and non-productive research (over $100 million to date on the artificial heart).*[2]

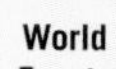

World Events

Films include Star Wars *and* Annie Hall.

DEC founder Kenneth Olson says, "There is no reason for any individual to have a computer in his home."

Medical Milestones

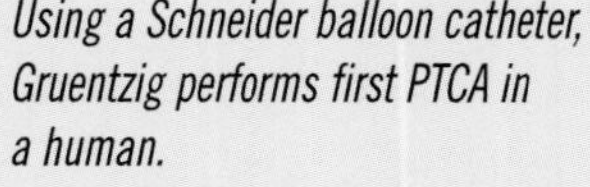

Using a Schneider balloon catheter, Gruentzig performs first PTCA in a human.

Two homosexual men in New York City are diagnosed with Kaposi's sarcoma and are probably the first known AIDS victims in New York.

Boston Scientific

Abele rejects Schneider contract; Medi-Tech focuses on larger-size peripheral angioplasty catheters instead.

Dotter's response to the letter was equally emphatic. He sent Abele a "crying towel" imprinted with a University of Oregon Health Sciences stamp.

Not to be outdone, Abele shot back another letter, explaining that he was reluctantly going to inform the university administration that he had located the source of their missing towels.

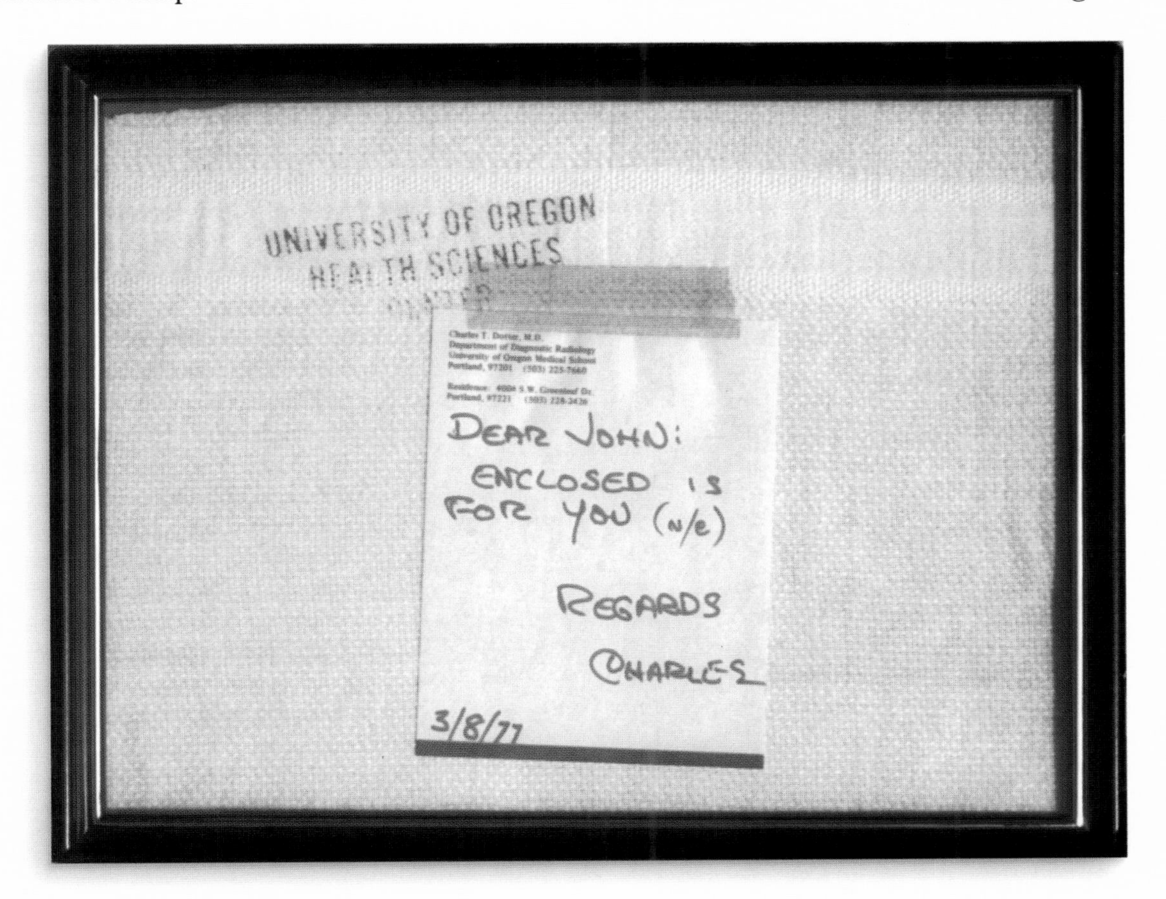

Apple introduces the first disk drive for personal computers.

Rashkind and Cuaso present data on a hooked, single umbrella for closure of ASD.

Abele lectures on early balloon catheters at Harvard Medical School.

The show floor of the American College of Chest Physicians in 1976. In contrast to later years, after big money had moved into the development of medical technology, booths at this time were still relatively small and simple.

The Patient Speaks

From the outside, the field appeared to be chaotic, with multiple developments across many medical specialties and an almost tribal sense of ownership among the companies and groups of doctors performing procedures. There wasn't a "school of thought" focused on minimally invasive medicine or even an agreed term to describe these innovative, device-based therapies. Nevertheless, the concept of less-invasive medicine was beginning to form, binding together all the companies and doctors with one common thread: less trauma, less risk, and less cost for the patient.

It was a new role for the patient but certainly not a ridiculous one. Traditionally, both the public and doctors had been trained to think that only established medical authorities could make treatment decisions, and these decisions were accepted without question. It was assumed that the patients themselves did not have the necessary information and were possibly psychologically unable to make decisions regarding their own treatment.

By the late 1970s, however, people were beginning to research their conditions and were making informed decisions about their own treatment. They became empowered. If a medically sound interventional treatment was available, people were likely to demand it because the surgical alternative was so much more painful, disruptive, and expensive.

"The trend towards informed patient consent as well as the invasion by the media into the heretofore private sanctum of medical procedures has a very positive effect on our business," Medi-Tech stated in its long-range plan. "The informed prospective patient will always vastly prefer a procedure which costs less, keeps him in the hospi-

1978...

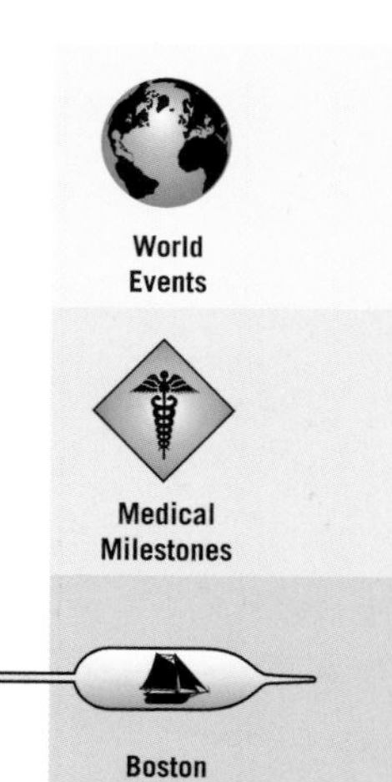

Trading on NYSE hits record single-day volume of 63.5 million shares.

Hank Prikken, the European sales manager for Medi-Tech.

tal for less time (if at all), has less risk associated with it, is less disfiguring, etc."[66]

At the same time, another patient-oriented movement was forming in U.S. medicine. Hospices, or end-of-life care facilities, began to appear. The National Hospice Organization was founded in 1974. In a frank acceptance of death, something the medical profession was not always comfortable with, hospice organizers designed their facilities to make patients' final days and weeks as comfortable as possible but not to artificially prolong life.

This movement presaged a rumbling debate in medicine. As the level of medical expertise began to rise, thanks to innovations like respirators, it became theoretically possible to keep comatose and other terminally ill patients alive almost indefinitely. Since doctors were trained to keep their patients alive at all costs, the hospice movement presented an uncomfortable situation for the medical establishment. This debate promised to continue into the future.

These important changes in medicine were accelerated by the media, which covered emerging medical technology from a positive angle and played an ever larger role in the public's perception of health care. One of the first major media pieces

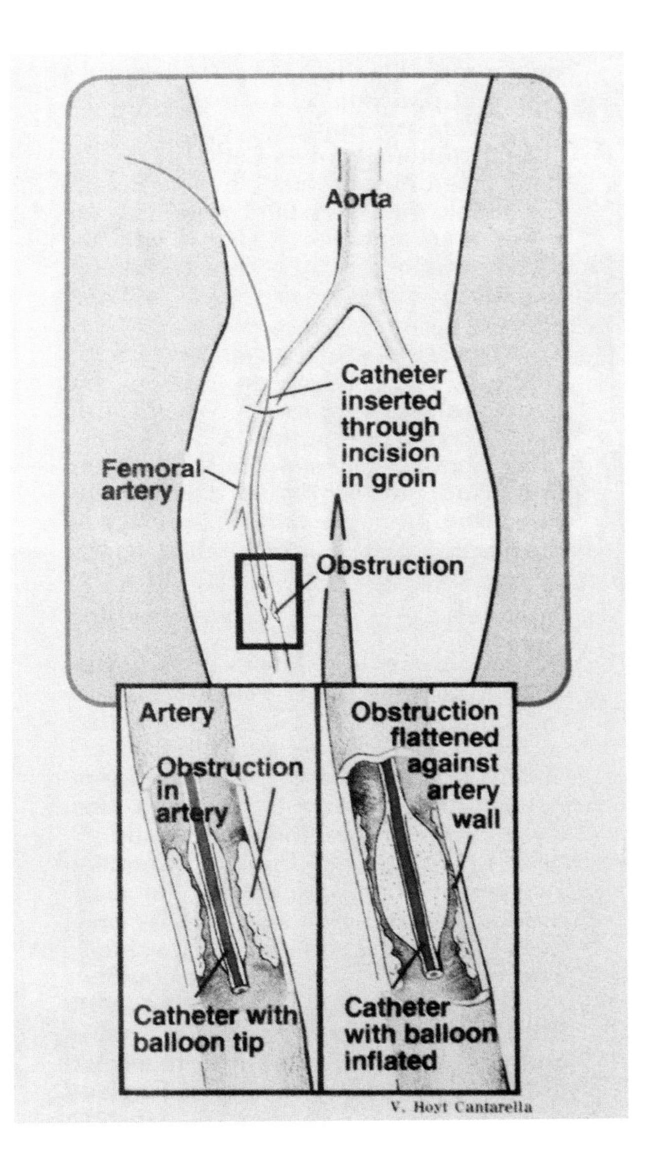

Illustration from a 1978 *Newsweek* article titled "Substitute Scalpel," one of the first major news magazine articles that described the emerging field of less-invasive therapy, including angioplasty, stone removal, stopping hemorrhages, and other applications.

The first "test tube baby" is born in England.

Newsweek *prints article that discusses catheter as substitute scalpel, almost summarizing Medi-Tech's product line.*

Peter Nicholas meets John Abele at a party in Concord, Massachusetts. The two form a partnership to acquire and grow Medi-Tech.

Cooper Scientific Corporation's presence at trade shows, which reached an audience of physicians, complemented any positive media coverage, which influenced the general public.

to address interventional medicine appeared in *Newsweek* on October 30, 1978. Titled "Substitute Scalpel," the article seemed to pit catheterization against conventional surgery—and surgery was the clear loser. Without mentioning the company's name, the article basically summarized Medi-Tech's product line:

> *The 62-year-old New York stockbroker arrived at the emergency room, doubled over with massively bleeding ulcers. Surgeons normally would have performed radical surgery to remove part of his stomach. But the patient had suffered several heart attacks, and his doctors feared he might not survive a long operation. Fortunately, they had a simpler and safer treatment. Using a local anesthetic, they inserted a flexible catheter through a small incision in his groin and pushed it upward to the bleeding gastric artery. Then, by injecting liquid plastic through the slender tube, they plugged the blood vessel. In two days, the broker was back home and doing well.*
>
> *The case illustrates just one way in which the catheter is replacing the scalpel. As a surgical tool, it is also effective in removing gallstones, unplugging arteries blocked by atherosclerosis, and even shrinking tumors deep within the body. By eliminating more traumatic surgery, the catheter may also spare patients prolonged hospital visits, cut the cost of medical care and reduce the surgical death rate to near zero.*[67]

A Meeting of Minds

In 1978, Medi-Tech was nearing its 10th anniversary. It was a small company with a tight familial atmosphere, but it was a highly influential company. John Abele, who traveled the world meeting with interventional pioneers in all disciplines, had set his company up as a kind of independent think tank within Cooper Labs. Although Medi-Tech's growth rate hovered somewhere around 30 percent annually, the company was chiefly concerned with creating new markets and spreading the word about its innovative products.

1978...

World Events

Anwar Sadat and Menachem Begin win the Nobel Peace Prize.

Medical Milestones

The first PTCA cases in America performed simultaneously by Myler in San Francisco and Stertzer in New York.

Boston Scientific

Abele writes letter to Andreas Gruentzig and Richard Myler regarding PTCA and how to evaluate new technology; the letter becomes an early version of the device procedure registry.

But external influences would soon shake Medi-Tech out of its comfortable relationship with Cooper. By the end of the 1970s, bankers were becoming concerned that Parker Montgomery, Cooper Laboratories' chairman, had overextended the company. They believed that companies like Medi-Tech were diluting Cooper's focus, and they urged Montgomery to get out of the device business. As a result, he put Medi-Tech on the market.[68]

Abele talked with a number of organizations that were interested in acquiring Medi-Tech. "But I didn't find any of them consistent with what I wanted to do, and it would have been hard for them to buy the company unless I went along with it," he said.[69]

While he was still looking for solutions, a chance 1978 encounter took Abele in an entirely new direction. John Abele and his wife were living in Concord, Massachusetts, in the same neighborhood as Pete Nicholas, who had recently moved into the area after accepting a position as manager of the medical division of a scientific instrument company called Millipore.

Besides being neighbors, the two men had much in common. They both had grade-school-age children, two sons and a daughter, and all their kids went to the same school. Both men were sons of World War II submarine commanders, both worked in fields related to health care, and both were unsatisfied with their careers.

After some discussion, the two became convinced that a partnership would work because of their complementary talents and personalities. "He's more interested in the creation of building of an enterprise," Abele said. "I'm more interested in the vision, if you will—what could happen, what it might become."[70]

Disco is popular.

Scientists propose that DNA sequencing can be used to develop gene markers for diseases.

Orthopedic salesman operates on patients. The medical community warns the public about "Salesmen Surgeons."

Abele conducts a strategic session at Cape Cod in which managers rate each other.

SPRAY
BOSTO

CHAPTER FOUR

BOSTON SCIENTIFIC IS BORN

1979–1982

We were simply going to run our business on the basis of what we agreed to agree about and what we agreed to disagree about, and that's it.

—Pete Nicholas

THE NEW PARTNERS' FIRST ORDER OF business was to gain control of Medi-Tech. Since Cooper had announced that Medi-Tech was for sale, interested parties had come forward with offers to buy the company. In April 1979, Bill Cook, president of Cook Inc., wrote a letter to the executive vice president of Cooper Laboratories to express his interest in acquiring the company. His offer of $400,000 in cash for assets of the business, exclusive of cash and accounts receivable, was conditional upon Abele staying on as president of Medi-Tech for two years.[1]

But John Abele and Pete Nicholas weren't interested. Instead, they continued to lay the groundwork for a relationship and planned their own acquisition of Medi-Tech. "We were going to develop a partnership. We were going to create a 50/50 enterprise," Nicholas said. "We made a commitment to make this little enterprise the sole focus of our careers."[2]

Many of their early discussions focused on the driving principles behind a business. Abele, who was devoted to minimally invasive medicine almost as a religion, was worried that Nicholas was "too much of a deal maker," while Nicholas fretted that Abele might not have interest in supporting the business activity necessary to build an enterprise. Nonetheless, the two men soon discovered they agreed on many of the "soft principles" of a corporation. The vision they ultimately shaped was so consistent that employees often remarked that they used exactly the same words to describe the same concept.

They believed in the idea of clarity and accountability in a corporate structure that was designed to push decision making deeper into the organization and wouldn't hinder the free flow of information between departments, yet would be responsive to management.

As the discussion progressed, their model began to assume a more defined shape. The pair believed in shared goals and risks across an organization and in "giving people a lot of rope." This kind of "loose/tight" organization enabled control and involvement at all levels, while giving managers the necessary authority to carry out their job functions.

Also, they understood that organizations of different sizes have different managerial needs, and this belief would become increasingly critical if their new partnership was to grow into a large corporation. Their ideal was a "transparent" company, or one in which every employee understood his or her position and how it affected both the ultimate success of the company and personal financial and career success.

Opposite: The Boston Scientific ship-in-a-balloon logo was modeled after Joshua Slocum's *Spray*, which is depicted in this painting. The *Spray* was used for the first solo circumnavigation of the globe in 1895. The logo (inset, upper) and a model of the *Spray* in a glass balloon (inset, lower) are enduring symbols.

Each partner would be able to bring something unique to this vision. Nicholas, with extensive managerial and finance experience, would be responsible for the business decisions. He would work with the banks to raise money, he would orchestrate acquisitions and recruit managers, and he would handle the day-to-day management of the company. Abele, with his enduring interest in the medical revolution that was slowly gaining ground, would advance the cause of minimally invasive therapy and guard the soul of the enterprise. He would build the company's early relationships and, with Nicholas, identify trends, opportunities, and technologies.

With this partnership in place, Abele and Nicholas were ready to make a bid for Medi-Tech. In 1979, Abele wrote a letter to Cooper Laboratories' executive vice president in which he made a proposal to acquire Medi-Tech:

> *Until now, the only other parties who were interested in Medi-Tech were interested in it only with me, and only if it were operated as a development group. I am not interested in that arrangement....*
>
> *The only reason I am in a position to make any offer is that a gentleman by the name of Pete Nicholas has agreed to work with me on a partnership basis. He brings not only financial backing and expertise, but the critically needed administrative, strategic and people skills that complement my technical and market strengths. He is motivated by the same desire for equity and independence as I am. He is not interested in working for Cooper. He was employed by Millipore and has recently resigned from his position. He has been looking at a number of possible ventures in which he can take an equity position. Although this one is the most likely, he naturally won't be available indefinitely.*[3]

Cook's offer had established a benchmark for the value of the company, enabling Nicholas and Abele to come up with a reasonable bid. "I'm not sure if Cook knew

1979...

World Events

President Jimmy Carter persuades Egypt and Israel to end their 30-year war.

Medical Milestones

Joachim Burhenne uses his technique of nonoperative removal of gallstones on the Shah of Iran, an event that inflames anti-U.S. sentiment.

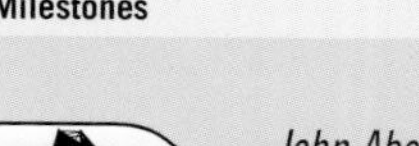
Boston Scientific

John Abele and Pete Nicholas form Boston Scientific to buy Cooper Labs' interest in Medi-Tech.

BSC medical device sales (not including Surgex) reach $1.8 million.

The steerable catheter accounts for 30 percent of sales.

exactly what he was doing in this case, but he did us a favor," said Abele.[4] The price they arrived at was figured as a multiple of earnings, which although ridiculously low by later methods of valuation was standard practice at the time.

John Abele, left, and Pete Nicholas, right, in Paris in 1979. During the early fall fashion season, all the city's hotel rooms were booked, so the partners rented a hotel conference room and had cots wheeled in.

On June 29, 1979, Abele and Nicholas formed Boston Scientific as a holding company to buy Cooper Laboratories' interest in Medi-Tech.[5] For the leveraged buyout, Nicholas persuaded some Boston bankers to put up $500,000, and the partners scraped up an additional $300,000. "We hocked ourselves to the limit," Abele recalled.[6] But it was consistent with their goal of keeping Boston Scientific a private company. In fact, they even turned away several investors and investment firms.

The negotiations for acquiring Medi-Tech were long and complex, partly because the people at Cooper Laboratories were suspicious that Medi-Tech had some hidden value. They believed that the minute Abele and Nicholas were on their own, the partners would unveil a $100 million secret invention. "We had great difficulty convincing them otherwise," said Abele. "And I think after the deal was closed, one of the Cooper people talked to Pete and said, 'Okay, now you can tell us what we just sold you and John.' "[7]

In fact, the hidden value of the company was the partnership between Abele and Nicholas. Almost immediately, Nicholas moved to reorganize. One condition of the buyout was the removal of all minority shareholders, including Pat Alessi.

The timing for this was right. In the year before the sale, Abele's partnership with Pat Alessi had become strained. As senior partner and president, Abele had the authority to fire Alessi but instead decided to offer him a choice. One of them had to leave the company, and Abele would leave it up to his

A nuclear disaster is narrowly averted at Three Mile Island in Pennsylvania.

Patty Hearst is released from prison.

Itzhak Bentov dies in a plane crash. His American Airlines DC-10 crashes outside Chicago; some people report seeing a halo around the plane as it crashes.

Medi-Tech grows to four salespeople in the United States and one in Europe.

Bob DePasqua becomes Medi-Tech's production manager.

partner. Alessi opted to move on, clearing the way for Abele and Nicholas to buy his shares of Cooper Scientific and fold it into the new company: Boston Scientific Corporation. Both Pete and John believed that long-term success demanded that ownership of the company be 100 percent aligned with the strategic intent of the company. Boston Scientific was on its way.

Their 50/50 Future

Not everybody thought that Abele and Nicholas could pull it off. From the outset, many people couldn't understand the foundation of a relationship in which one partner would build a business while the other fought a crusade. Moreover, from the outside, the two men appeared as different as night and day. Abele was more of a scientist philosopher, more at home in the realm of ideas and technology. Nicholas was a "plain vanilla, business suit guy." In later years (1992), local media seized on the superficial differences and painted the partners as strange bedfellows, which in many respects they were.

"But those are superficial observations that are irrelevant," Nicholas said. "What was important was truth. And how that truth operated around what we were trying to do. That's the essence of the beginning of the enterprise."[8]

In some ways, it might be accurate to say that the Boston Scientific enterprise was founded in a local Greek diner where many of these early discussions between Abele and Nicholas took place. This is where the partners got together and discussed issues such as company ownership and how much equity they should make available to employees (10 percent). Like so many of these early decisions, these would also have lasting implications. When Boston Scientific went public in 1992, more stock had become available to employees as a reward for their loyalty and as an incentive to grow the company.

The diner is also where Abele and Nicholas discussed their personal lives. The two men were very different socially and came to the mutual understanding that they wouldn't become involved in each other's lives outside of work. Instead, they would remain completely committed to developing the partnership.

In a very revealing anecdote, Nicholas remembered how he at first thought he should have a controlling interest in the company. "Then, as he and I talked and talked and he expressed his views and I thought about mine, I realized I wasn't thinking about this right," Nicholas remembered. "I was thinking about ownership from a control point of view only because I didn't know him. As I got to know him, it became clear to me that company control was not the issue. We were so close in philosophy that he would almost always agree with what I wanted to do."[9]

This tacit understanding that the two men had different strengths, and that each would be allowed to capitalize on his own strengths, formed the backbone of the company. "It was a remarkable period of change for both of us," Nicholas said.

Margaret Thatcher becomes the first woman prime minister in Britain.

BSC moves to 480 Pleasant Street in Watertown.

Not long after we bought the company, we flew over to England to talk to some of our European dealers, and we flew across the English Channel in a tiny plane with the owner of our U.K. dealer, our largest, and his partner. These two said they had great enthusiasm for our partnership but that someone had to make decisions. Someone had to be responsible at the end of the day because you cannot own things 50/50. I told them we were not going to weigh or count votes at all. We were simply going to run our business on the basis of what we agreed to agree about and what we agreed to disagree about, and that's it. They didn't understand that, and at the end of the plane ride, they told me it wasn't going to work. We said it would.

Ten years later, when we went public, the owner sent us a pair of silver goblets arranged end-to-end in the shape of a balloon catheter that said, "Congratulations on a 50/50 success. I was proud to be associated."[10]

The Nature of the Business

As it turned out, Bill Cook really did do the partners a favor. The $800,000 that Abele and Nicholas spent on Medi-Tech was less than half of the company's annual sales of $2 million[11] (this was before the days when companies were valued on multiples of sales). Steerable catheter systems, the company's oldest product line, accounted for approximately 30 percent of sales, a testament to how hard Abele and his sales force had worked to create a market for the specialized catheter. Cytology brushes made up another 45 percent,[12] while Surgex, the Cooper Laboratories depilatory, accounted for about 12 percent of sales. When Abele and Nicholas signed the acquisition deal, they agreed to stop marketing Surgex as of December 31.[13]

One of the company's chief weaknesses at the time was its limited sales coverage. In the United States, Medi-Tech was down to only three salespeople (located in Chicago, Atlanta, and New York) to call on radiologists, gastroenterologists, cardiologists, pulmonary surgeons, and general surgeons. International sales, which accounted for

These end-to-end goblets, designed to look like a balloon catheter, were presented to Abele and Nicholas by Medi-Tech's U.K. dealer when Boston Scientific went public. They represent the 50/50 partnership between the two founders.

A motion to change the name of the Society of Cardiovascular Radiology to the Society of Cardiovascular and Interventional Radiology is defeated.

Medi-Tech introduces the peripheral polyethylene dilatation balloon, which is stronger and less compliant than competitors' vinyl balloons.

Nicholas increases the forward spend in R&D as soon as he and John take control of Medi-Tech.

about 20 percent of total revenues, were conducted through 22 dealers, overseen by Medi-Tech's Western European salesperson, who was based near Amsterdam, Holland.[14] Nicholas beefed up the worldwide sales and marketing organization immediately.

Meanwhile, the company's research and development program was a unique hybrid of market-driven improvements and pure research. As R&D head Josh Tolkoff remarked, in the medical devices industry, much of the R&D was driven by the "D." Medi-Tech's products were often simple in theory, but there was no room for product failure, and they were very small with moving parts and had to meet very specific mechanical criteria.

Much of the conventional "research," or theory and ideas, came from the scores of doctors who approached the company with ideas and asked if they were feasible. For example, Dr. Wilfredo Casteneda, an interventional radiologist, worked with Medi-Tech on several products, including the Track Master (which removed stones from the kidney) and drainage catheters. "I used to visit the company [Medi-Tech] a couple of times a year to look at new designs they had and to give my critique," said Casteneda. "They listened."[15]

Likewise, Harold Coons, another interventional radiologist, worked with Medi-Tech. Coons was the first doctor in the world to implement a biliary soft stent. "It was just an endotracheal suction catheter that I cut off and stuffed in," he said. "It took me about two hours to get it in, and I thought, 'We've got to come up with something that will go in more easily.'" Bill Cook recommended that he talk with Medi-Tech about manufacturing such a device. "So I did," Coons said. "I sat down with John Abele and the R&D guys and explained what it was I wanted to make. They ended up making the Coons biliary soft stent, which was on the market for more than ten years."[16]

The Medi-Tech Balloon

While Medi-Tech was an early leader in noncoronary interventional products, the company had no stake in the cardiology balloon market. The leader was still USCI/Bard. When Medi-Tech decided to enter the balloon market, the company opted to develop its own balloon for peripheral vascular disease. The project was headed by Josh Tolkoff.

World Events

Visicalc introduces the first spreadsheet program for PCs.

Medical Milestones

Werner Forssmann dies.

Boston Scientific

Abele and Nicholas go on the road selling products, giving demonstrations, and attending conferences and trade fairs.

"Medi-Tech was much more involved in radiology and with radiologists than cardiologists," said Tolkoff. "So our discussions were, 'Well, why don't we cut our teeth on the radiology product, which is a little larger, and then once we have the technology in hand, we can move into the cardiology field.'"[17]

Although the manufacture of modern expanding balloons had been pioneered by Andreas Gruentzig, Medi-Tech bet it could build a better mousetrap. Tolkoff began his research by pulling all the old patents he could find on shrink tubing. Abele also traded ideas with John Simpson, the founder of the company that would later become Guidant, a leader in coronary artery balloons.

Making a balloon to expand in a human artery presented several unique challenges that required extensive knowledge of materials. For starters, the balloon had to be inelastic enough not to expand away from the hard plaque (Imagine a balloon squeezed in a fist; it assumes the shape of an hourglass) or get scratched by hard, calcified deposits. At the same time, the balloon could not overdistend because it risked bursting the artery, but it had to have enough force to flatten the lesion. Also, it had to be made of a substance that could be permanently attached to the end of the catheter—an especially difficult challenge since some plastics do not bond to other plastics with conventional adhesives or other techniques.

Medi-Tech's answer to these challenges was to pursue a new material. While John Simpson was using regular shrink tubing, and the existing Cook and Bard balloons were made out of vinyl, Medi-Tech began researching polyethylene balloons and applying shrink-tube technology to the polyethylene it had developed. Medi-Tech's processes produced the strongest polyethylene ever created at the time.

"The first technical breakthrough was learning about shrink tubing and how polyethylene materials could be cross-linked using electron beams to give them greater strength so you could do things

Above: The USCI display at the American Heart Association in 1981. This poster advertises the "[Gruentzig] Dilaca," the company's cardiology balloon. USCI was the leader in cardiology dilatation balloons.

Opposite: Pete Nicholas, center, works with Bob Brown, left, and Josh Tolkoff, right. Nicholas was well known for standing in front of white boards and large-format tablets and writing detailed and intricate plans as he talked and brainstormed in a public forum.

Iranian militants take over the U.S. embassy in Iran and take 62 Americans hostage.

Popular films include Manhattan *and* Apocalypse Now.

Josh Tolkoff and Bill Frait at the American College of Surgeons meeting.

without them tearing and breaking," Tolkoff said. "The second breakthrough—and we were really on our own—was the process work for how to actually make the balloons in the required shape."[18]

By 1978, Medi-Tech had developed a thirty-seven-step process to make a single angioplasty balloon. Later that year, the company received FDA approval to sell its peripheral angioplasty balloons.[19]

Within two years, Medi-Tech balloons were the industry standard for the treatment of peripheral vascular disease.

Dave Budreau quit Johnson & Johnson to join Boston Scientific in 1980 after meeting Bob Brown, vice president of sales, in a hotel room. "I walked in, and there was Bob sitting there, and he had a bunch of these catheters spread out on a table," Budreau remembered of his first interview.

> *I was used to selling titanium microneurosurgical instrumentation, you know, and what am I doing here? But Bob picked up a* Time *magazine, and on the front it said, 'New Treatments in Heart Disease,' and there was a cardiologist holding a balloon catheter. Bob said, "This is kind of what we're doing. We're not involved in the coronary artery at this time, but peripheral arteries. I'm not sure exactly what we've got, but we think it's going to be big in the future." He piqued my interest through the vision of the company, the mission of the company.*[20]

In fact, the company's mission, not its size or sales, was its strongest selling point when recruiting new employees. Medi-Tech had a strong appeal for idealists and pioneers, people who would be interested in helping Medi-Tech create a market for its peripheral angioplasty balloons. The bottom line at Medi-Tech was important—after all, it allowed for more growth—but equally important were the "soft issues" outlined by Abele and Nicholas. These ideas permeated the young company.

In the early 1980s book *Corporate Cultures: The Rites and Rituals of Corporate Life*, authors Terrence Deal and Allan Kennedy studied American corporations and assessed their cultural values. What they found was surprising at the time:

> *The health of the bottom line is not ultimately guaranteed by attention to the rational aspects of managing—financial planning, personnel policies, cost controls, and the like. What's more important to long term prosperity is the company's culture—the inner values, rites, rituals, and heroes—that strongly influence its success, from top management to the secretarial pool.*[21]

The authors concluded that, in the future, culture would become one of the defining characteristics of successful companies. A strongly cultured company would be able to respond to change and reach deeply into its shared belief system when challenges arose.

The book made a strong impression on Abele and Nicholas because, without having read it first, they had created a company where culture, mission, and values reigned supreme. Moreover, the company's business had the feel of a movement

World Events

John Lennon is murdered.

Mount St. Helens erupts.

Medical Milestones

Heliane Canepa joins Schneider as marketing assistant.

Boston Scientific

Peter Nicholas initiates a strategy of creating separate business units to better focus on the various markets being served by a single sales force.

The separate business units foreshadow the creation of Microvasive and Mansfield, in addition to Medi-Tech.

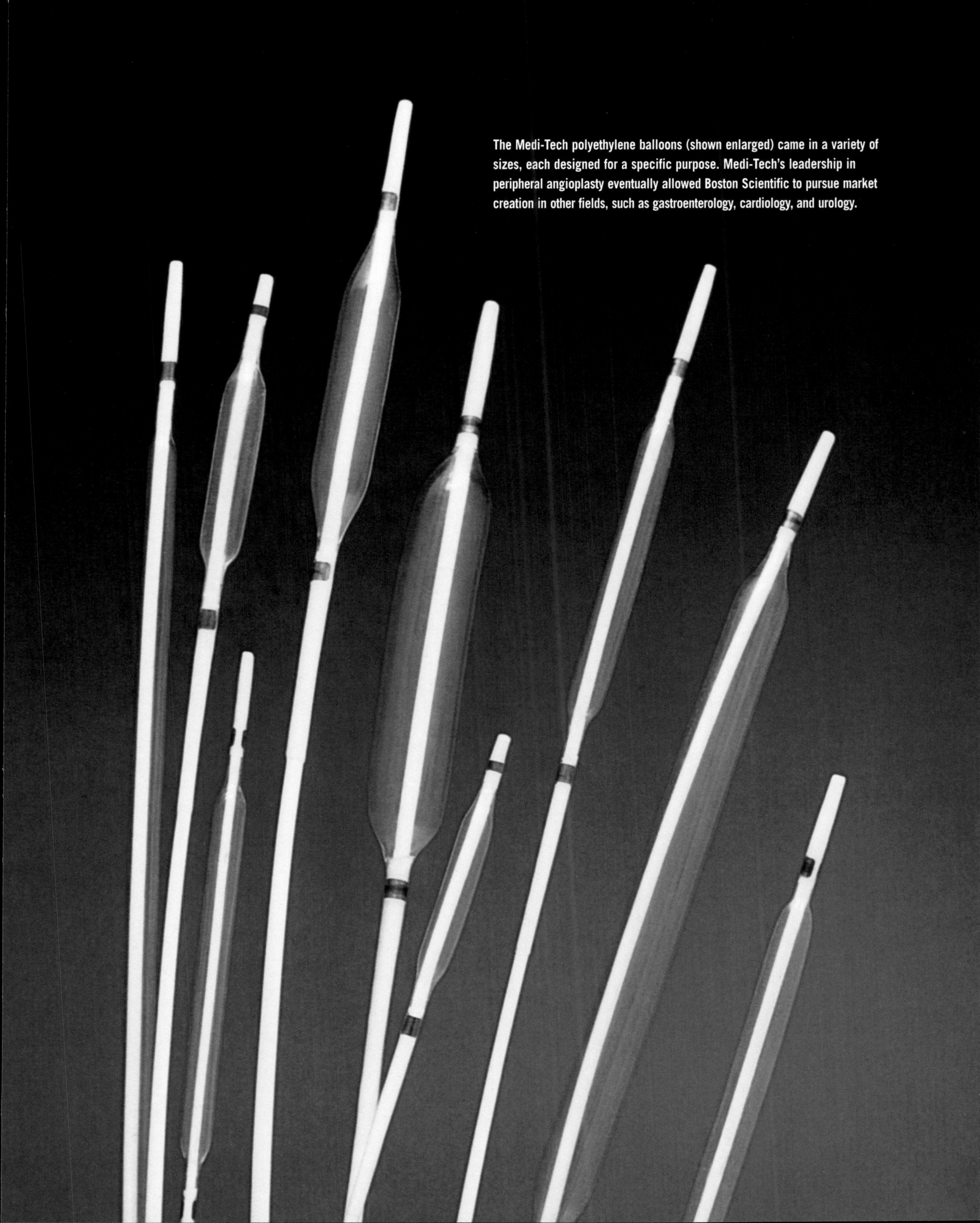

The Medi-Tech polyethylene balloons (shown enlarged) came in a variety of sizes, each designed for a specific purpose. Medi-Tech's leadership in peripheral angioplasty eventually allowed Boston Scientific to pursue market creation in other fields, such as gastroenterology, cardiology, and urology.

rather than a career path. A career in the very young discipline of interventional medicine wasn't for everybody, but those who did choose it believed deeply in what they were doing. They believed they were directly benefiting patients around the world. "We've got to have people who believe," Nicholas said.

> *Even if it's blind faith, they're willing to commit and believe, and we're willing to bring them in because of their demonstrated ability, their personal attributes that we think are in sync with ours and their willingness to be teammates. There was never a notion of hierarchy, there was never a notion of command decisions. On the other hand, there existed in a subliminal way ground rules, principles, values that we created and became the watchwords, the guidelines, and the guardrails that really defined and protected the company.*[22]

It was these values, and the fact that medical devices are not very capital intensive compared to pharmaceuticals, that originally brought Nicholas into Medi-Tech. Like Abele's attraction to the steerable catheter, Nicholas saw Medi-Tech as a platform on which to build an enterprise.

"In those days, most of the zealots in the business—and I was one of them—were more focused on trying to impact health care in a meaningful way, and if you did that, all this other stuff would happen," Nicholas said. "But the objective wasn't to make money. The objective was to do something that made a difference. You could imagine what would happen if that worked and one were to scale it up and develop a commercial game plan."[23]

A Maniacal Focus

The mission to positively impact health care meant Medi-Tech had a voracious appetite for expert salespeople, which presented an obstacle. As doctors explored more parts of the body with catheters, endoscopes, and other devices, Medi-Tech's line of products was multiplying exponentially. In many cases, an entirely new product was developed at a single doctor's request. "By 1979, the company had parts in cardiology, radiology, pulmonary, neurology, and gastroenterology," Brown said. "Medi-Tech salesmen were calling on all the different departments in a hospital."[24]

John Carnuccio, one of the early Medi-Tech salespeople, covered New Jersey, Pennsylvania, Delaware, Virginia, and West Virginia for Medi-Tech. "Much of what we were doing was pioneering selling," he said.

> *I remember talking to the physicians who I dealt with and showing them some of the technologies that our company was looking at. One of them was balloon catheters to dilate arteries. My best friend is a cardiologist, and he told me I was crazy for even considering this. It would never fly. But I was more than willing to take the risk.*[25]

Nicholas and Abele were unhappy that the Medi-Tech sales force was stretched so thin. Every new

1980...

World Events

The solidarity movement begins in Poland.

Medical Milestones

Barry Katzen presents his first in a long series of televised tutorials in percutaneous transluminal angioplasty.

Boston Scientific

Dale Spencer joins SCIMED from Baxter.

technique and every new specialty required a level of expertise and a vocabulary to communicate with the doctors who not only used the device, but often had a hand in developing it. This was markedly different from the accepted method of selling pharmaceuticals, in which a "detail man" would basically drop off brochures and samples. Medical devices demanded a much higher level of knowledge from the salesperson, and customer relationships were critical—something that John Abele understood from the beginning as he set out to become an educator/salesperson/communicator. Ideally, the Medi-Tech sales force should be patterned after his example.

But that wasn't possible if one salesperson had to communicate with six or seven medical specialists about procedures that often varied greatly in approach and efficacy. What Medi-Tech needed was a clear segmentation in its product lineup. "When I came to this company, every product was listed by general application," Nicholas remembered. "There was no effort to aggregate things for specific customers. We had to develop ways to think about segments because it was not just one customer."[26]

The best way to accomplish these two goals—having a force of expert salespeople/educators and dividing Medi-Tech's product lineup into its natural specialties—was to reorganize the company. The partners split the corporation into three autonomous operating units, each focusing on a medical specialty and having its own sales force and its own operating president. This move was guided by principles developed by Nicholas: that each company would have its own mission and values; that divisional opportunities would be fielded separately; and that leverage would be key, with all the companies committed to leadership in their markets.

Over the years, the company would constantly challenge itself on the dilemma of choosing between the customer focus of divisionalization and the leverage, economy, and branding benefit of centralization.

Mansfield Scientific

In February 1980, Boston Scientific bought Kimray Medical Associates (KMA), an Oklahoma company that sold thermal dilution catheters and manufactured and sold cardiac output computers.

A Medi-Tech sales training meeting in 1981. Throughout the late 1970s and into 1981, Boston Scientific reorganized into separate operating companies, leaving Medi-Tech to focus on peripheral vascular products. This sales force quickly became established as a leader and innovator in customer education and an advocate for interventional medicine.

These products were used together to measure the pumping effectiveness of the heart.[27] KMA also made the Greenfield vena cava filter system.[28]

This acquisition was important because of the company's focus on the heart. Without an approved PTCA balloon, Boston Scientific had no way to challenge USCI/Bard in coronary angioplasty, so the company was looking for other ways to establish itself in cardiology.

Soon after the acquisition, KMA moved to Mansfield, Massachusetts, and was renamed Mansfield Scientific. John Delph, a business unit manager with Abbott Laboratories' hospital division, whom Pete knew and brought in, was named general manager. Sales of the Greenfield vena cava filter, however, were transferred from KMA to the Medi-Tech sales force. Mansfield developed its own sales force for cardiologists. At the same time, the company began seeking FDA approval of a line of catheters for coronary angioplasty.[29]

Microvasive

Abele and Nicholas started a third division dedicated to gastrointestinal and pulmonary products. This, too, was accomplished partly through acquisition. In 1981, Boston Scientific acquired Endo-Tech, its largest competitor in the field of gastrointestinal and pulmonary endoscopic accessories from Katsume Oneida and Lew Pell.[30] Endo-Tech was part of a company that was initially called Machida and later became known as Pentax America.

With the acquisition complete, Endo-Tech was designated a separate division and given several existing Medi-Tech products, including retrieval baskets for retained stones, biopsy forceps, and cytology brushes. (Medi-Tech actually had more products in gastroenterology than Endo-Tech did at the time of the acquisition.) Robert DePasqua, initially hired to run Boston Scientific operations and who directed the rehabilitation of the mill in Watertown, was put in charge of Endo-Tech. Previously, DePasqua had held manufacturing, engineering, and production management positions at E. R. Squibb, Johnson & Johnson, and Millipore. "He was an incredible doer," Abele remembered. "He was a pied piper in terms of leadership, and funny, incisive, and decisive."[31]

In 1982, Endo-Tech's name was changed to Microvasive, and its operations were moved from Watertown to a new plant in Milford, Massachusetts. Nicholas said Bob was the individual who ultimately created the vision and strategic imperative that led to the creation of Microvasive.

"We felt that it was essential to be effectively autonomous," said Abele. "We would have financial control, and there would be overlap and so forth, but Microvasive needed a president. It needed the research and development, the manufacturing, and the sales and marketing in order to be responsive and effective in creating and

KMA also manufactured the Greenfield vena cava filter. After the acquisition, the division was moved to Mansfield and renamed.

1980...

World Events

The wreck of the Titanic *is found.*

Medical Milestones

Boston Scientific

BSC acquires KMA, maker of the Greenfield vena cava filter.

developing its marketplace."[32] And it needed a direct line to Nicholas so it could lobby effectively for investment dollars.

Spreading the Word

Political resistance to the acceptance of interventional medical tools was common, even though some of the devices had been around for a decade or more. It was fairly normal, remembered Abele, to have surgeons object that minimally invasive medicine was actually more difficult to practice than the open surgery they learned in medical school.

I remember showing a thoracic surgeon the steerable catheter and our cytology brush for taking cell samples of the lung to determine if the patient had cancer. And his response to me was "I can open up the patient's chest and remove that lung in the time that you would use that catheter." Unfortunately, surgeons seemed insensitive to the trauma of surgery to their patients and unaware that this new diagnostic technique could change treatment options.[33]

In 1982, the Medi-Tech salesforce held its first sales meeting in the new Watertown location. As an independent operating company, Medi-Tech contributed the largest portion of Boston Scientific's revenue through sales of peripheral angioplasty balloons. This group of salesmen considered themselves pioneers and traveled extensively.

U.S. speed skater Eric Heiden wins five gold medals at Winter Olympics in Lake Placid, New York.

Popular films include American Gigolo *and* Raging Bull.

Johnny Carson undergoes balloon angioplasty for a blocked leg artery. He later discusses his "balloon job" on The Tonight Show.

John Abele publishes an article on the physics of balloon dilatation in the American Journal of Roentgenology. *The article is cited hundreds of times in subsequent years.*

Dave Budreau quits J&J to join BSC.

Selling in this atmosphere had much more to do with the viability of the procedure than with selling Boston Scientific products against any competitive products; the best way to describe the competition was "relatively friendly." Manufacturers weren't so much competing for existing market share as trying to get their products accepted. Boston Scientific in particular worked toward expanding the market, spreading minimally invasive techniques into more branches of medicine, and developing more techniques.

This made new product introductions especially challenging. Rather than prove a Boston Scientific catheter was better than a Cook catheter, for instance, the company needed to demonstrate that its devices had a credible medical purpose, meaning that they reduced risk, trauma, cost, or time, or all four. Print ads were viewed suspiciously. It was much better to have a procedure published in respected journals, but that too posed hurdles.

The largest opportunity by far lay in converting the hundreds of thousands of traditional surgeries to Boston Scientific's catheter-based therapies. Also, because less-invasive procedures tended to be less risky and costly, they expanded the pool of candidates for any particular therapy to include

Charles Dotter took these catheters from a Medi-Tech exhibit and artfully arranged them in a vase. A year later, he took a picture and sent the image back to John Abele with an apology. Dotter kept the bouquet.

1981...

World Events

Ronald Reagan becomes U.S. president.

Prince Charles of England marries Lady Diana Spencer.

The IBM PC, using DOS, is introduced.

The U.S. Centers for Disease Control recognize AIDS.

U.S. hostages in Iran are freed.

Medical Milestones

Rohrer and Binnig invent the scanning, tunneling microscope.

Scientists at the New York Blood Center develop an experimental vaccine against hepatitis B.

Schneider and Gruentzig develop the first steerable guide wire; with twenty employees, Schneider moves to Zurich.

Boston Scientific

Drs. Wilfredo Casteneda, Barry Katzen, and Josh Tolkoff at the ESCVIR.

Interventional radiologists on Katzen's Caribbean cruise seminar.

Above: Endo-Tech, pictured in 1982 at a medical meeting. Just after this photo was taken, its name was changed to Microvasive and the subsidiary became a pioneer in the field of endoscopic accessories.

Right: This cartoon depicts the idea that radiology and other medical therapy might someday be served up like fast food. The cartoon proved to be prescient over the next decades as more medical procedures were performed on an outpatient basis, often because of less-invasive techniques.

both those who were too sick for surgery and those not sick enough.

"In these early days, there were few scientific clinical studies that would demonstrate the product's effectiveness," said Abele in 1997. "If you read the article, it would say, 'This is pretty neat and you ought to use it,' so it really wasn't scientific the way today's articles are because the studies were usually based on case studies with too few patients. Unlike today's multicenter studies with thousands of patients, we were persuading doctors to adopt techniques based on only limited information."[34]

Beyond journal articles, medical meetings were the most important way to connect with doctors. Companies trotted out their new products and showed how their physician customers could use them to their advantage. Young companies like Medi-Tech trained, demonstrated, recruited, and preached. Even before the era when big corporate money was poured into medical meetings, the gatherings were crucial to the spread of new procedures and technologies.

Films include An Officer and a Gentleman *and* On Golden Pond.

Sandra Day O'Connor becomes the U.S. Supreme Court's first female judge.

Pope John Paul II survives shooting.

Anwar Sadat is assassinated.

Muhammad Ali retires from boxing.

The number of positions in the Society of Cardiovascular Radiology expands from 75 to 100.

Two Rashkind umbrella occlusion devices begin FDA clinical trials for closure of ASDs and PDAs.

Van-Tec is founded by Jim Vance.

KMA moves to Mansfield and adopts name of the town.

Jimmy Dugan, left, shakes hands with John Abele after the mill sale is completed.

BSC buys Endo-Tech to help create markets for gastrointestinal and pulmonary products.

IN SEARCH OF HOME

WHEN JOHN ABELE FIRST MET ITZHAK Bentov in 1968, Bentov was running Medi-Tech out of the basement in his home. When the company introduced the steerable catheter, its operations moved to the basement at 372 Main Street in Watertown, Massachusetts, where they remained for eight years, gradually taking over the entire building.

By 1978, Medi-Tech had expanded sufficiently to require a second building, at 217 California Street in nearby Newton. Within a year of the buyout, Abele and Nicholas consolidated all company operations to the Barclay Chemical Building at 150 Coolidge Avenue in Watertown. They started on the bottom floor, which was approximately 20,000 feet, and slowly expanded upstairs.

Two years later, as Boston Scientific had once again outgrown its headquarters, Nicholas began searching for a new location that could accommodate the growing company for many years to come. At last, he stumbled upon what had been known as Aetna Mills, a historic landmark located along the Charles River that had served as a home for inventive Yankee entrepreneurs since the 1760s.

Interestingly, the mill housed its own small hospital, complete with crutches, a wheelchair, litters, and an assortment of medical supplies. "It was particularly poignant," said Abele, "because when we opened the medicine cabinet, some of the drugs were still there, including a bottle of pharmaceuticals from Lilly that dated back to 1920."[1] Also found during the renovation was an English-cast steel bell dated 1861. Weighing about seven hundred fifty pounds, the bell was once rung to summon employees to work at Aetna Mills.

When Abele and Nicholas acquired the mill, they created a small museum there to display some of this memorabilia—a museum which they occasionally used for meetings with physicians. And, rather than throwing out the remainder of the old mill equipment, they auctioned it to other mill owners, who moved it south.[2]

In addition to preserving artifacts, the partners left their own mark on the mill by adding some whimsical modern touches. In the lobby, they constructed a hologram display that depicts a three-dimensional image of a balloon catheter navigating its way around human organs. On top of the old chimney, they placed a weathervane displaying the company's logo, a ship in a balloon. After the windows fell out of the Hancock tower in Boston, they salvaged massive plates of the glass and turned them into transparent interior doors.[3] By October 1, 1982, the newly renovated building and manufacturing plant was operational.[4]

Two years later, an article in the local newspaper described the company's unique layout:

> *Medi-Tech has taken over the old woolen factory on Pleasant Street between the Sons of Italy and Bridge Street, and remodeled it into a sort of 'house-beautiful' showcase for a modern industrial plant. Visitors have to be reminded that all the brick walls have been sandblasted clean as they look around to see natural grain wood, soft carpets and modern, modular offices.*
>
> *General manager Joseph Ciffolillo is quick to explain his company's "less invasive surgery" products, but is just as enthusiastic to usher a visitor down to the "museum room"—where memorabilia found in the factory's massive remodeling has been assembled.*[5]

Boston Scientific purchased a small train of buildings that encompassed approximately 100,000 square feet of space.[6] The company initially rehabilitated only 40,000 square feet with plans for the rest over time.[7]

For the first five years, Boston Scientific was unable to purchase an additional set of buildings located on the other side of a road that ran through mill property. These buildings were owned by George Danas, who had become the arch enemy of the mill's former owner. The two owners battled over the use of the road, and Danas was notorious for causing traffic jams with his trucks.

"He was an obstinate guy," said Abele. "Many of the employees here disliked him and didn't want to deal with him. But Pete has this incredible ability to deal with people that nobody else wants to deal with. He saw George's best side, and finally they were able to work out a deal that was satisfactory to him and turned out to be great for us. We bought his buildings for a lot more per foot than our first building, but it allowed us to have the entire parcel."[8]

As Abele and Nicholas bought and refurbished the mill buildings, they increased the value of the neighborhood and became their own worst enemy from a real estate point of view because the renovations to the mill property made the land around them more valuable. To remedy this, Nicholas devised a checkerboard strategy in which Boston Scientific bought additional pieces of land, but not properties that were right next to each other. This later allowed the company to trade overvalued parcels.

Before Boston Scientific moved in, said Nicholas, the area looked like an "invasion of New York," with its rundown buildings and piles of discarded items. But when Abele and Nicholas first started to improve the area, they were met with resistance. "When you're working, particularly in an urban area like this, there are numerous agencies that you have to deal with," said Abele. "You have the town, you have MDC, you have state authorities, federal authorities, and the Charles River Watershed Association, which is a very powerful environmental group. Every time we trimmed a tree we had somebody on our back."[9]

As Boston Scientific continued to grow, Nicholas began eyeing additional properties in the neighborhood. In 1989 he created a color-coded poster, essentially a homemade Monopoly board, and used it to highlight targets, including a candy factory, a railroad, and a house that belonged to Mrs. Ryan and her team of trained pigeons. Then he rolled the dice.[10]

Pictured in 1928, the Watertown mill would later become home to Boston Scientific. A variety of interesting items were found during renovation of the more than 200-year-old building.

Medi-Tech salespeople attended as many as 10 medical meetings every year and set up booths showcasing appropriate products. Boston Scientific, for instance, was exhibiting at approximately 15 medical conventions yearly by the early 1980s. (This number would increase to 300 in five years.)[35] Some early Medi-Tech salespeople recalled flying to conventions on commercial airlines with their displays stashed in the overhead bin and being told to watch their expenses with an eagle eye.

"So we didn't do much advertising," said Abele. "We didn't think it was an effective use of dollars. But a good brochure was essential. We weren't just introducing products that were a variation of what people already had; we were creating new markets.... That's why we made the early hollow anatomical models, which allowed physicians to actually put catheters inside them. Not only did they learn, but we demonstrated how the product we made compared to what they were familiar with."[36]

But the live video demonstration course—a phenomenon pioneered by Drs. Peter Cotton and Joachim Burhenne in 1975—was perhaps the most effective marketing tool. Andreas Gruentzig relied heavily on the live demonstration course as he spread the word about coronary angioplasty; he is credited with establishing the standard format.

Gruentzig's demonstration style was adopted and championed by Barry Katzen, then a radiologist at the Alexandria Hospital in Virginia and a professor of radiology at George Washington University Medical Center in Washington, D.C. In 1980, Katzen presented his first televised tutorial in percutaneous transluminal angioplasty, using lectures, patient demonstrations, video, and audio. The demonstrations allowed for on-line communication among faculty, registrants, and angiographer. Registrants participated in decision making and were encouraged to discuss their own problem cases.[37]

Despite his lack of medical or engineering credentials, Abele was invited to talk about the physics of angioplasty at Katzen's first seminar and has been participating in his courses ever since. "It was really a revolution in education," he said. "Doctors would fight to get to these courses and watch these live cases. The video would zoom in and let them see things they couldn't see even if they were in the operating room. And it was no-holds-barred: The good and the bad were shown, and that has really changed the face of medicine."[38]

Abele participated in numerous seminars about transluminal angioplasty, including the 1982 Nuremberg symposium that brought together interventional pioneers such as Charles Dotter, Andreas Gruentzig, and Eberhart Zeitler. "I became sort of the guru in the technology of angioplasty," said Abele. "That was my slot."

Obviously, interventional medicine changed the role of the doctor. Medi-Tech's salespeople were often viewed as partners when it came to the use of the new techniques. Likewise, doctors were viewed as partners when it came to spreading the word of the techniques' effectiveness. For the first time, companies were hiring doctors to promote their products—a development that wasn't always wel-

1982...

World Events

Vietnam Veterans Memorial is dedicated in Washington, D.C.

Compact disc players are introduced.

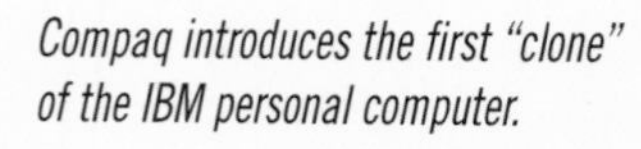

Compaq introduces the first "clone" of the IBM personal computer.

Medical Milestones

Zeitler and Gruentzig host a symposium on angioplasty in Nuremberg.

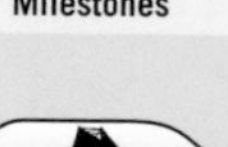

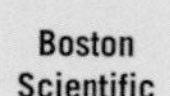

Boston Scientific

Moving day to 480 Pleasant Street, Watertown, site of the historic Aetna Mills.

The Radiology Society of North America meeting in 1982. At the time, this meeting was the largest scientific gathering in the world. It was also a critical venue for Medi-Tech to reach its market of angioplasters and interventional radiologists.

come in the more conservative halls of medicine. Yet this practice represented the future. Although Medi-Tech didn't create the movement, by its advocacy and involvement it helped lead the field and may have had a calming effect on profiteering and erroneous information.[39]

Fifteen Minutes of Fame

As Medi-Tech and companies like it worked to establish these techniques, the national media

Deal and Kennedy's book Corporate Cultures *is published.*

War erupts in the Falkland Islands in the South Atlantic.

Parade *magazine publishes article "Operations without Surgery."*

Endo-Tech changes its name to Microvasive and moves to Milford, Massachusetts.

played a significant role in swaying the general public's opinion. Interventional medicine had received some positive press already but had yet to really pierce the public's consciousness. That changed abruptly with a single event in 1980 that launched a national discussion and gave interventional medicine a powerful new kind of spokesperson: the celebrity patient.

At the time, few celebrities were bigger than Johnny Carson. Known as the "king maker" for his ability to spot talent and make people famous overnight, Carson hosted *The Tonight Show*, one of America's most beloved shows. Thus when the public learned that Carson had severe claudication due to arteriosclerosis in his leg and he chose a catheter-based treatment, it was a perfect opportunity for peripheral angioplasty to bask in Carson's fame.

Carson was scheduled for an operation at a Los Angeles hospital, but shortly before surgery, his doctor suggested he try balloon angioplasty to unclog his artery. If the angioplasty was successful, the doctor explained, there would be no surgery. If not, it would take place as planned. On the air, before the procedure, Carson told his perpetually chortling sidekick Ed McMahon that he was going to try a new therapy, calling it a "balloon job."

"They did the dilatation," recalled Bob Arcangeli, who was the Boston Scientific product manager for peripheral dilatation balloon catheters.

> *Carson came back to* The Tonight Show *two days later. In his opening monologue, he talked about this amazing new procedure where they took a balloon and inflated it in his artery, and before he couldn't walk upstairs, but now he could play tennis. He said it was the greatest thing. Instead of being out for two weeks recovering from surgery, the next day he was up and walking.*
>
> *People started referring to it as the Carson procedure, and sales of peripheral dilatation catheters just started taking off. We were a small company at the time, and one thing we couldn't afford was advertising and public relations. That publicity was worth millions.*[40]

Gradually, the mainstream media began to follow interventional medicine. On October 10, 1982, *Parade* magazine published an article called "Operations without Surgery," which detailed some of the ways in which catheters were revolutionizing medicine, including opening peripheral arteries, unclogging coronary arteries, treating high blood pressure, correcting scrotal varicoceles that can cause male infertility, and removing kidney stones.

In 1980, Johnny Carson was scheduled for surgery to correct severe claudication in his leg due to arteriosclerosis. Instead, he opted to try a peripheral angioplasty. The procedure worked, and Carson praised it on his famous television show, sparking a wave of interest in the novel technique.

1982...

World Events

Thomas Peters publishes In Search of Excellence.

Medical Milestones

Doctors implant the first Jarvik 7 artificial heart; patient Barney Clark lives for 112 days.

Boston Scientific

Abbott Labs acquires Sorenson Research; BSC becomes a supplier to Sorenson.

The article also described how a catheter had benefited a patient in unexpected ways.

> *Dr. J. Parker Mickle at the University of Florida in Gainesville used a balloon to plug a blood vessel abnormality in the brain of Ruby Lee Thompson, who had been shot in the head and the stomach by a holdup man. Following operations on her skull and in the large bowel, doctors also found an abnormal artery-vein connection behind and above her eyes. It threatened blindness, facial pain, agonizing head noises and stroke. Dr. Mickle moved a balloon-tipped catheter up from a leg artery to the site in the brain, inflated it, then detached the balloon, leaving it to plug the abnormal connection. After five weeks, the abnormality was gone; so was the tiny balloon—absorbed by the body. Mickle has done twelve similar operations, all successful.*[41]

Approximately a month after this article appeared, the *Wall Street Journal* published a story entitled "Long, Thin Tubes Take Place of Scalpel in Some Treatments." A medical products analyst said catheters had great appeal because "They promise the opportunity for doing procedures without the risk and often the cost of opening up the body." As the story noted, catheters were traditionally used to inject dyes deep into blood vessels or in conjunction with camera-like fiber-optic devices that could be attached to their tips. But, he said, doctors were no longer using catheters just to diagnose problems; they were using them to treat a variety of illnesses including heart disease and birth defects.

The article went on to quote catheter makers like Boston Scientific and said sales for therapeutic uses were rising much more rapidly than sales for diagnostic uses.[42] Minimally invasive medicine was finally making serious inroads.

Films include ET, The Extra Terrestrial *and* Gandhi.

AT&T agrees to sell 66 percent of its assets after losing a seven-year antitrust suit.

The FDA grants approval to the Eli Lilly Company to market insulin produced by bacteria, the first commercial product of genetic engineering.

Jamie Rubin is hired as vice president, human resources.

ANT'S
GRANT

CHAPTER FIVE

THE SEEDS OF STEALTH

1982–1991

The company always had just a voracious appetite for cash.

—Pete Nicholas, 1994

BY 1982, BOSTON SCIENTIFIC WAS EXPEriencing a fairly common problem among young, successful high-technology companies: it was starved for cash. With revenues of almost $13 million in 1982, Boston Scientific was going through money at an alarming rate.

Not only was it racing to fill orders and keep relatively high levels of inventory. The company was constantly having to retool production to keep up with the torrid pace of product innovation. Finally, the lead time between product development and its eventual market success was lengthening. Gone were the days when doctors and companies introduced products as soon as they were developed and gradually improved them after they were already in use. Instead, the FDA had steadily expanded its role in new product approvals, making it harder both to get products onto the market and to do the kind of iterative improvement that was standard in earlier years.

"We were certainly a significant cash user," said Pete Nicholas. "It wasn't like we were developing pharmaceuticals or building a plane. Devices traditionally took less time. And even though we complained a lot that the time length grew, the cycle time was not that onerous. We had the ability to develop on the fly, particularly in the early years. Still, the working capital required to finance our growth was outstripping our ability to produce cash."[1]

True to the earliest discussions of what Boston Scientific should be as a corporation, the founders plowed 100 percent of gross profit back into the company to support growth, which meant Boston Scientific essentially operated at a loss and had little cash on the balance sheet in case of a crisis. "But we were at a critical time period," said Abele. "If we didn't grow quickly, somebody else would close the gap, and they would lead the market."[2]

The FDA Roadblock

Indeed, the FDA had become something of a stumbling block for medical device companies. The Era of Cooperation, as Abele dubbed it, had seen the agency working to classify devices and procedures between 1976 and 1982. Later in the 1980s, however, the FDA entered a new period that Abele later nicknamed the "Era of Education." During this time, the FDA launched major educational programs for industry and users and began to develop guidelines for new classes of products.

While not entirely unwelcome, the FDA's approach to regulating medical devices had one major flaw. Much of the agency's experience was based on the approval of new drugs, which was a burdensome and long process. New medical devices were required to go through an abbreviated version of the drug approval process, something that Abele

Opposite: The Watertown Mill under reconstruction. The crane is removing the elevator through the roof. Throughout the 1980s, Boston Scientific continuously and rapidly expanded.

had written about in the 1960s as the Medical Device Act of 1976 began to take shape.

With the FDA basing its device approval process on the pharmaceutical approval process, product development slowed significantly. Boston Scientific had to carry out extensive bench testing, experimentation in animals, and sometimes lengthy clinical trials. While this process was justified in the case of a biological agent that altered the body's chemistry, medical devices didn't interact with the body on that level. Instead, their success was often dependent on the skill of the doctor who used them.

This FDA hurdle was common to all medical device companies, meaning Boston Scientific wasn't at a competitive disadvantage except in one glaring instance: Mansfield's lack of coronary angioplasty products. Whereas Medi-Tech's peripheral angioplasty balloon was the industry leader and accounted for about half of the company's revenue, coronary angioplasty was the crown jewel in the field of balloon angioplasty. And Boston Scientific was nowhere on the map.

"We should have had an approval of our coronary catheter in the very early 1980s," Abele said. "Our application had been filed and we were told we would get approval, but a well-publicized problem occurred in the field with another company's pacemaker catheter that caused the FDA to put everything on hold. So they basically went back to the drawing board. That set us back enormously. We really weren't prepared for that."[3]

Drug vs. Device Development

Regulating devices is very different from regulating drugs for a variety of reasons. The FDA has always been challenged to understand these differences.

FACTOR	DEVICE	DRUG
Influence of physician technique on result	*High*	*Low*
Rate of technical change	*High*	*Low*
Ability to evaluate performance attributes in vitro	*High*	*Low*
Effect of accessories and environment on performance	*High*	*Low*
Developer resources	*Limited*	*Many*
Technology	*Physical*	*Chemical, Biological*

1983...

World Events

Unemployment in the United States rises to more than 12 million, the highest since 1941.

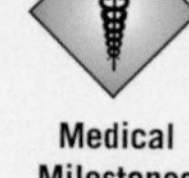

Medical Milestones

SCIMED begins angioplasty development.

Welch Allyn Inc. of New York introduces the first video endoscope.

Dr. Raimund Erbel develops the first PTCA perfusion balloon catheter for Schneider.

Boston Scientific

Boston Scientific posts sales of \$16 million. The company is severely drained of capital.

The Sorenson Deal

Boston Scientific needed money for a good reason: Nicholas was interested in rapid growth. Sales were climbing steadily, the company had participated in the early days of a medical revolution, and its products represented the intellectual horsepower of some of the world's great medical pioneers. In a significant way, this state of affairs tested the two founders and their lofty ideals. Boston Scientific was the market leader in certain areas—in some cases the only player—and it would have been a simple matter to pull back and wait for a lucrative acquisition offer. Abele and Nicholas would have been able to retire comfortably.

But the two men had founded their company with a different plan. Their strategy was based on building an enterprise that benefited public health and brought more accessible, lower-cost, lower-trauma medical options to patients. Their strategy aimed at industry leadership, not only in peripheral vascular or urology, but in all of less-invasive therapy. Cash and capital were the tools Nicholas would need to help Boston Scientific grow.

This left few options to raise needed money. The company could go public, which neither founder wanted to do, or it could put itself on the market to be acquired, which was even less appealing. Instead, Nicholas went back to his old contacts to look for an investor. In his days at Millipore, he had developed a close relationship with Abbott Laboratories' executive vice president, Chuck Aschauer. The timing was right for a conversation.

"I was tremendously excited with the opportunities in minimally invasive surgery and had tried to get Abbott to fund internal efforts in that area," Aschauer recalled. "But Abbott was putting heavy

This Swan Ganz–type thermal dilution catheter was manufactured by Mansfield for the Sorenson division of Abbott Labs. Although the product was not a huge success, the relationship resulted in an equity investment by Abbott in Boston Scientific.

Apple introduces the mouse and pull-down menus to personal computing.	*End of popular TV show* M*A*S*H.	*IBM introduces first personal computer with a hard disk drive built into it.*
James Gusella finds a gene marker for Huntington's disease.		*A motion to change the name of the Society of Cardiovascular Radiology to Society of Cardiovascular and Interventional Radiology (SCVIR) is approved.*
Joe Ciffolillo is hired from Johnson & Johnson. He recruits Dick Chenoweth.		*A 30,000-square-foot manufacturing plant in Milford, Massachusetts, is opened for Microvasive.*

money at that time into pharmaceuticals and diagnostics, and we had a price war going on in the hospital products area. They just didn't want to put the dough into that area. So it occurred to me and the planning guy at Abbott that maybe we could work something out with Peter."[4]

Yet the partners at Boston Scientific were paranoid about losing control of their business to another company. They were worried that another, more bureaucratic company might impose unhealthy controls on Boston Scientific and impede the company's rapid growth.

So in 1982, Boston Scientific and Abbott entered into a kind of "pre-engagement" agreement to feel out how a future equity deal might work between the two. Abbott had just acquired Sorenson Research, which made products for hospital intensive care units. Boston Scientific agreed to supply Swan Ganz–type thermal dilution catheters to Sorenson. This gave Abbott an opportunity to see how the company operated. "As one would expect in these situations, there were difficulties between Sorenson and us," said Nicholas.

> *They were a small player in a big market, and the major competitor—American Hospital Supply—was cleaning their clock. Sorenson was blaming their lack of success on our failure to make the right product. I think the quality of our product was O.K., but the thermal dilution catheter was a very touchy-feely sort of thing, and its softness changed according to temperature. The salesmen for our competitor said, "Their catheter is too soft," then went to another doctor and said, "Their catheter is too stiff." They planted that seed in doctors' minds, and they already had a great reputation. As a result, we were always chasing our tails.*[5]

Nicholas Makes a Deal

Despite the difficulties, however, Abbott was satisfied with Boston Scientific, prompting Nicholas to enter into negotiations with Abbott in early 1983 for

Medi-Tech was growing rapidly through superior relationships with physicians. Slides of bouquets of dilatation balloons were sent as gifts to physicians for them to use in slide talks.

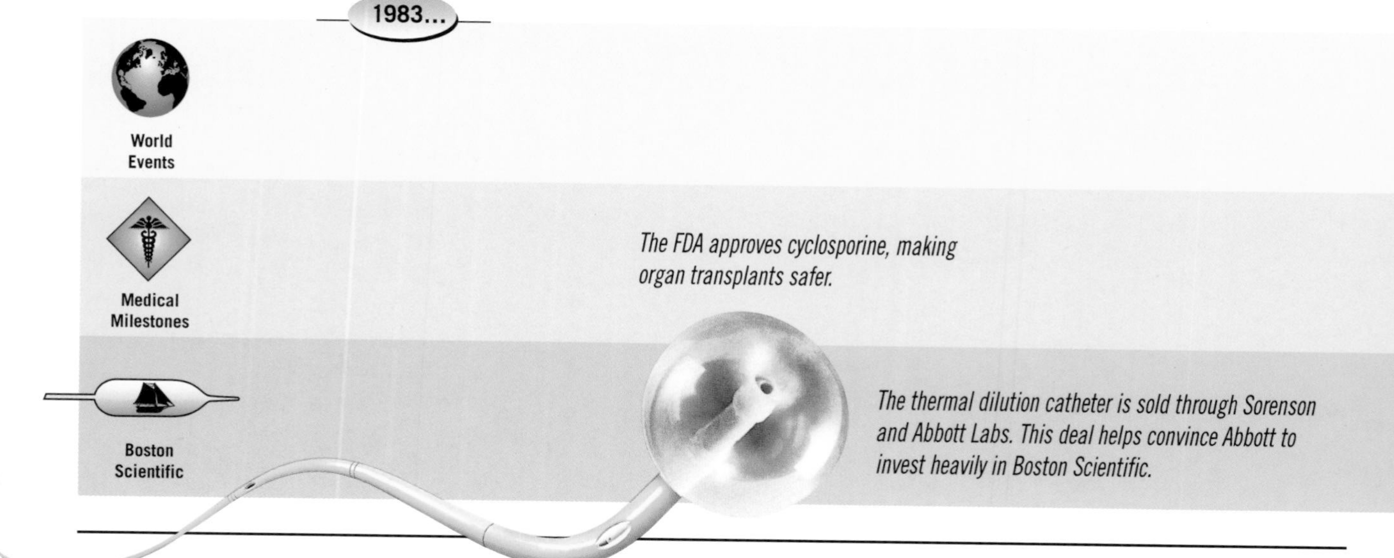

NICHOLAS AND THE BANKS

BOSTON SCIENTIFIC'S EARLY YEARS were fraught with challenges, not the least of which was the company's fitful relationship with the Boston banking community. During the company's first two years, Pete Nicholas worked hard convincing bankers to loan the company enough money to feed its growth.

At that time, the company had few concrete assets with which to protect a loan, and bankers were leery of Boston Scientific, partially because they didn't understand its products.

"We were viewed as a very risky start-up company," Nicholas said. "I jawboned them all into a banking relationship, and then we could never meet the conditions of our engagements. Our receivables were too high, or the European balance would be out of line or some customer's extension was too high."[1]

In the early years of growth, Nicholas churned through a number of different banks, continually searching for an institution that recognized Boston Scientific's unique business. "I suppose I wasn't the most generous person with the banks," Nicholas said. "My view always was, if you need to understand something, come in and talk about it. I'm not going to come down and sit on your doorstep and hold your hand every half hour with respect to every event that occurs in the world."[2]

What Nicholas experienced, however, was almost the complete opposite. When Boston Scientific banked with Merchants, the lending officer was so uncomfortable with how the company was conducting its finances that he sent a police officer, decked out in jodhpurs, polished boots, and gun, to Nicholas's home to deliver a registered letter from the bank—a letter demanding repayment of all loans and a termination of the banking relationship.

The Abbott deal was the work of Peter Nicholas, who was looking for a way to fund Boston Scientific's rapid growth without compromising its flexibility or putting it at the mercy of commercial banks.

The root of Boston Scientific's banking problems seemed to stem from clashing views of how to deal with such an entrepreneurial company. "It's a mindset the bank has," said Abele. "Whereas the banks may want to know what the 'feel' of the numbers they're financing are, just as important is the character of the people. We kept saying we wanted to meet the president of Harvard Trust. He kept putting it off, and it was literally two or three years before he allowed us to meet him, and then he made this kind of famous statement: 'I was afraid if I got to know you, it would color my interpretation of the figures.' Which, of course, we thought was the whole purpose of getting to know us."[3]

In 1986, Tom Piper, a professor at Harvard Business School (and a Concord neighbor of Abele and Nicholas), wrote a case study drawn from Boston Scientific. For his study, Piper substituted the names Peter Haskins for Peter Nicholas and Advanced Medical Technology Corporation for BSC. The following is a comment made by one of the loan officers approached by Haskins/Nicholas:

> *Peter Haskins is a very likable, magnetic person who puts you through challenging but enjoyable mental gymnastics during negotiations. He is also a grinder who comes back once a week with a new request. He never lets up when he wants something; just keeps coming at you and grinding away. Peter also tries to get to the highest possible authority, even on mundane issues.*[4]

At last, after years of trying to settle on a bank, Nicholas decided on another approach. "I concluded that we were asking the banks to be venture partners," Nicholas said. "But they were never really going to be venture partners. So we had to go out and find a relationship that was more accommodating to us, to eliminate the financing problem. Ultimately, that's what led to the Abbott relationship."[5]

a more direct investment. The deal that Boston Scientific and Abbott eventually worked out was a novelty in the business community. The partners agreed to sell 20 percent of their company to Abbott Laboratories in exchange for a $21 million investment over four years.[6] After nine years, Abbott reserved the right to buy Boston Scientific for a price that would be based upon a multiple of the average of two years' earnings. The multiple would be determined by the average earnings of an assortment of companies mutually selected by Abbott and Boston Scientific plus a "sweetener" if Boston Scientific's growth rate was higher than Abbott's.[7] The option window ran for six months starting on the anniversary date of the acquisition. If Abbott didn't exercise its right within that period, it forfeited the right to buy the company.[8] At the time of the deal, Boston Scientific had revenue of $16 million.

Besides creative terms, Nicholas insisted on a stipulation that was virtually unheard of for a company in Boston Scientific's position. There would be no contact between Abbott and Boston Scientific except for the very top executives. Jealous of its privacy and freedom, Boston Scientific was to be protected from outside influences.

"Because the arrangement contemplated a binary outcome, that is, they acquire us or they sell us back their investment," Nicholas said, "we were concerned that Abbott not be allowed to compete with us so as to dilute the value of our company, i.e., they not be allowed to trade on knowledge they gained through their association with us."[9]

In a metaphor often repeated at Boston Scientific at the time, the founders also didn't want aggressive underlings "pulling the roots out to see how the plant was growing." This was a critical element in the success of the deal.

"The arrangement was designed to be a win/win," Nicholas later said.

> *It was designed to enable Boston Scientific to garner the resources that we felt were necessary to make aggressive investments in growth opportunities with funds that were strategic in nature, and therefore came at a much greater premium than had we brought in a nonstrategic financial partner. Abbott was prepared to value the company on its initial investment. That value was somewhere around $100 million or $120 million, and a financial investor, a nonstrategic investor, would have valued the company in the $40 million or $50 million range. This meant that for the same amount of equity, through Abbott we were able to raise twice as much if not three times as much money.*[10]

Without realizing it, Abele and Nicholas had helped pioneer a model that future strategic partnerships in the industry would be based on. In those days, companies were valued on a multiple of earnings, unlike in later years, when this kind of math would seem like an incredible bargain. Shortly after signing the agreement, Aschauer attended a planning meeting at Boston Scientific and raised some concerns about Boston Scientific's redundant oper-

1983...

World Events

Films include The Big Chill *and* Flashdance.

Medical Milestones

Boston Scientific

The Microvasive sales awards. The unit was growing very quickly in the field of GI and endoscopic accessories.

ating units and its focus on many small markets. Abele responded with a letter in which he recapped the strategic goals of the deal:

> *I would like to re-emphasize that we have as much or more desire than you do to avoid being 5 percent shareholders in 20 markets.... I trust that it is becoming clearer, however, how our markets and technologies relate and are evolving and that one of our most fundamental objectives is to be market leaders. Yes, it would be possible to focus down on half a dozen projects ... PTCA, fiber-optic imaging, gallbladder ablation, urological stenting, etc., but it would not produce a market leadership strategy....*
>
> *We believe that to achieve success as a company, we must maintain the highest degree of focus on our markets and that the best way to do that is through the business unit approach. The "redundancy and inefficiency" you speak about we feel is more than offset by our ability to be close and responsive to our customers and markets.*[11]

At one point in their relationship, Aschauer even encouraged the company to dump its interest

Chuck Aschauer meets BSC staff. Pictured from left to right are Alan West, Bill Hawkins, Chuck Aschauer, Bob DePasqua, and Pete Nicholas. Abbott agreed to finance Boston Scientific.

The United States loses the America's Cup after 132 years of unbroken victory.

Tom Sos appears on the Today Show *to discuss renal PTA.*

John Abele and Peter Nicholas sell 20 percent of Boston Scientific to Abbott Labs for $21 million over four years.

in cardiology. "When they were struggling to put together a business, Medi-Tech was doing very well, and Microvasive was very promising, yet at the same time, they wanted a presence in cardiology," Aschauer remembered.

Mansfield just didn't have an attractive product line, and they were up against guys that were much bigger, and Mansfield's market shares were minimal. I kept telling Peter, "Look, you ought to dump that operation because there just isn't any way that you are going to mount an attack on that area." But Pete always had big dreams of being a force in cardiology.[12]

Although Boston Scientific considered the idea (Abele himself even supported it at one point), the partners ultimately refused to take this bit of advice. They figured the company could eventually leverage its strength in other areas into cardiology—a philosophy that became a hallmark of Boston Scientific's later success. Although the company dealt with so many specialties, everything was united by a common goal and, in many cases, by common products. Transferring the use of guide wires into cardiology from other specialties was a perfect example.

"The key to our success formula is the fact that we leveraged our efforts in each one of the specialties to the other specialties," Abele said. "What we learned in one, we applied to another. We took the concept of guide wires and catheters from radiology and applied it to cardiology, to urology, and to gastroenterology—as it turned out, very successfully."[13]

Joe Ciffolillo

With the financing in place, Nicholas focused on the internal environment at Boston Scientific. From the beginning, Abele and Nicholas had believed in an open flow of information. They had worked hard to imprint a flexible, nonbureaucratic structure on Boston Scientific—even to the point of excluding Abbott by contract and deliberately pushing the parent corporation into the background. Boston Scientific, through its operating units, was quietly orchestrating rapid growth and market leadership in all of interventional medicine, not just one or two areas.

"We were fiercely flat organizationally in research and development," said Al Couvillion, an engineer management consultant who was hired in 1984.

I'd be working along for a few months, and then one day Pete Nicholas would show up. He'd come in and he'd say, "How are you doing?" Then he'd spend two or three hours walking through the lab, talking to the technicians and assemblers, and it's a nonthreatening thing.[14]

Yet Boston Scientific was missing a critical element in its sales force. The company had traditionally hired technology experts and "put them in suits to go out and sell."[15] A true sales team had yet to form. While still negotiating the deal with Abbott in

World Events

Indira Gandhi, prime minister of India, is assassinated.

Standard Oil of California announces acquisition of Gulf for $13.2 billion, world's largest corporate merger.

A toxic gas leak in a Union Carbide plant in Bhopal, India, kills 2,500 people.

Medical Milestones

Boston Scientific

Bob Krajeski joins Microvasive as a sales rep.

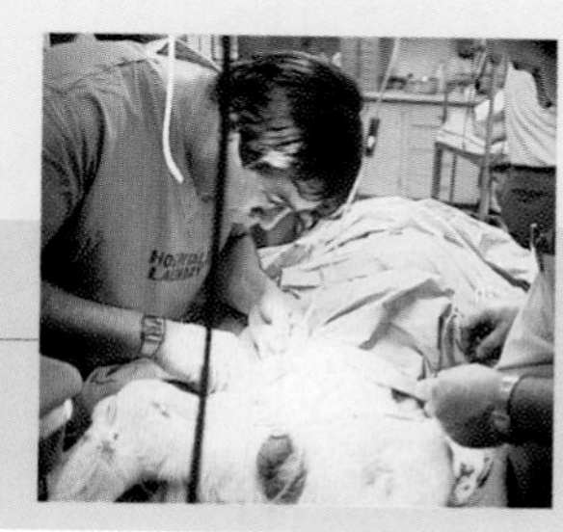

Paul Nardella evaluating a new catheter in a dog.

1982, Nicholas made a phone call to a man named Joe Ciffolillo, asking him to join Boston Scientific as the president of Medi-Tech. He wanted to put together the world's best medical devices sales team, and he believed Joe was the one to do it.

Ciffolillo was the perfect candidate to create a sales force at Boston Scientific's largest operating unit. A divisional president at Johnson & Johnson, Ciffolillo had been at the hospital supply giant for 20 years, having started as a trainee, and he was happy, secure, and comfortable in his position. Ciffolillo considered himself a "lifer" at Johnson & Johnson. "I thought Nicholas was out of his mind for asking me," Ciffolillo remembered.[16] After politely declining Nicholas's offer, Ciffolillo assumed that was the last he'd hear from Boston Scientific. To his surprise, Nicholas called back two or three months later, and now Ciffolillo found himself seriously considering leaving the upper executive ranks at one of the world's most powerful medical companies.

"Nicholas focused on creating something that would be unique," Ciffolillo said. "That's what intrigued me. We could integrate all the programs that were really strong at both Lilly and Johnson and exclude the programs that we thought were detrimental, bureaucratic, hazardous to your health, and politically motivated. Thus, we could create something new, something that was fast-tracked, dynamic, with rapid growth and deep penetration. And we would be able to really dominate a field that, at the time, we could barely define."[17]

After careful consideration, Ciffolillo decided to leave his "job for life." Pete later remembered having dinner with Joe and his wife, Joyce, at their house during the courtship and thinking that Joyce "thought Joe had gone around the bend." Ciffolillo's resignation at Johnson & Johnson was greeted with shock by his superiors. Two weeks after formally resigning, Ciffolillo got a call from Jim Burke, the chairman of the board at Johnson & Johnson. Burke didn't try to convince Ciffolillo to stay. Rather he wanted to know what had led Ciffolillo to make

Joe Ciffolillo, center, quit a senior position at Johnson & Johnson in 1983 to join Medi-Tech. He is flanked on the left by Bob Brown, vice president of international marketing, and on the right by Dick Chenoweth, Medi-Tech vice president of sales.

Ronald Reagan defeats Walter Mondale.

Popular films include Amadeus *and* Ghostbusters.

Optical disks for storage of computer data are introduced.

Apple introduces the Macintosh personal computer.

Pfizer Inc acquires Schneider Medintag AG, which has 32 employees.

In the United States, radiologists restructure the Society of Cardiovascular and Interventional Radiology.

Alec Jeffreys discovers technique of genetic fingerprinting.

Fifty Medi-Tech employees travel to RSNA in Washington, D.C., to man the expansive display.

Medi-Tech, with 24 sales representatives, is the largest operating company. Don Woods joins as a national sales manager.

Boston Scientific posts sales of $22 million.

such a decision and what Johnson & Johnson could do to instill some of the same entrepreneurial qualities that Ciffolillo sought at Boston Scientific.

Once at Boston Scientific, Ciffolillo, Abele, and Nicholas held many meetings to discuss "philosophy of management, philosophy of growth." Ciffolillo's aim was to change Boston Scientific's current practice of making salespeople out of those who understood the medical device technology. Instead, he wanted to hire winners with great communications skills, people with exemplary qualities, and teach them the technology. Ciffolillo embarked on a massive talent hunt to find the "kind of people who could maintain 40 percent annual growth year after year." To find the qualities he was after, he looked for collegiate athletes, class presidents, and cheerleading captains. In essence, he looked for people who were already leaders and who would surely carry that ethos into their jobs.

An offsite strategic planning meeting of the executive committee in Stowe, Vermont. The company's strategic planning was an intuitive process that moved in several directions at the same time as Boston Scientific sought to establish itself as a market leader and innovator in many highly specialized areas of interventional medicine.

"John initially didn't get a sense of what we were after," Ciffolillo remembered. "He understood globally, but not specifically. After we brought in a few people, we had a meeting at which he said, 'Do you know what you're doing?' I said, 'No, what are we doing?' He said, 'You are applying a cookie cutter formula. They all look the same. They all sound the same. They all act the same. You're getting rid of these people that know so much about the product.' I asked him to wait and see. Well, fortunately, John is the caliber guy that he is, and we were able to build the team we did."[18]

Six weeks after joining Boston Scientific, Ciffolillo hired fellow Johnson & Johnson employee Dick Chenoweth as vice president of sales for Medi-Tech. Bob Brown, who was vice president of marketing and sales, split his title and became vice president of international marketing.

"Getting Dick was a chip shot for me," Ciffolillo said. "He was an associate of mine for many, many years and probably the best sales manager in the entire medical device industry, so once I was able to get him, I didn't have to worry about the sales team. His assignment was to develop the highest quality, strongest sales and marketing organization in the United States for the medical device business."[19]

To his sales force, Chenoweth once said, "Total commitment is that special essence of a person that

1984...

World Events

More than 70 U.S. banks fail, the highest rate of bank failure since 1937.

Medical Milestones

Boston Scientific

Medi-Tech introduces 11 products at RSNA, including the Blue Max balloon for angioplasty cases, the Digiflex High-Flow catheter, drainage catheters, and uroradiology devices.

Medi-Tech's peripheral vascular angioplasty balloon is firmly established as the world standard.

takes them that extra mile—that brings out an extra effort of will when anything less than total success is completely unacceptable.... To be a star, you have to start each day with a commitment to yourself, your family, your company."[20]

Chenoweth tragically died of pancreatic cancer at age 45, about five years after joining the company. The team that he built, however, would form the core of Boston Scientific's executive leadership, and Boston Scientific would later name a space in corporate headquarters after him.

The salesforce that he and Ciffolillo created remained the standard bearer in the industry. Even if other companies had more revenue, salespeople from Boston Scientific were widely considered to be the most knowledgeable and customer oriented. The company had established itself as an educational powerhouse where physicians could go to obtain the latest information. At one point, acting in extremely enlightened self-interest, Medi-Tech salespeople were involved in setting up many local "angio clubs" across the country. These clubs helped newly minted interventional radiologists share experiences and continue the development of the field.

Just as Ciffolillo had hoped, competition was also a hallmark of Boston Scientific's various sales forces. During one sales meeting at the Scottsdale Conference Resort in Arizona, where the company's salespeople were competing against each other in team sports, Abele remembered one of the conference center's coordinators remarking that he had never seen such a competitive group of people. Yet the competition was based on a feeling of winning by doing better rather than making opponents lose.

Mining for Human Resources

As the new sales force coalesced, Boston Scientific leaders recognized it was time to do something else they had been resisting for cultural

Above: The Microvasive sales team engages in a friendly game of "football to the death" with the scenic Camelback Mountains behind them. The highly independent sales teams were known for their competitiveness. This group pioneered the sale of endoscopic accessories and penetrated deep into the operating room environment.

Below: The Medi-Tech sales force in 1987. Medi-Tech had the largest sales force in Boston Scientific and was the largest operating company, consistently accounting for about half of all revenue. It was the world leader in noncoronary angioplasty balloons.

This Medi-Tech exhibit appeared at the 1985 American Roentgen Ray Society. It is staffed by, left to right, Don Woods, Sue Sawyer, and Jeanette Miller.

reasons. With almost 200 employees, the company had no formal human resources organization. This was intentional. By pushing personnel duties onto managers, the company was requiring its managers to be accountable for their decisions, their business, and the people who worked for them.

"Pete felt very strongly there's a risk that managers might defer their personnel-related function to a department, and you didn't want that," Abele said. "That breeds an environment in which people don't do the most important part of their job, which is to lead and provide an environment where people can be productive."[21]

Yet the time had come to establish a formal personnel department. The company took out a classified ad seeking a vice president of human resources. Jamie Rubin answered the ad and was hired in 1982. Rubin had 10 years' experience running a human resources department, and although she wasn't looking for a job in any specific industry, she met with Ciffolillo and accepted the job soon after. "In those days, all you really had to do was show up and listen," she said. "You just couldn't help but be drawn into what was going on. It was also about Joe [Ciffolillo] and his passion and belief in this vision."[22]

As Rubin became acquainted with her new company, she recognized the value of the entrepreneurial culture that Boston Scientific had fostered yet also recognized that the company's rapid growth would have a significant impact on that culture. Boston Scientific was a very face-to-face company, she remembered, but technology and growth were forcing a change from within. This change wasn't always easy. Even voice mail posed a challenge because it was less personal.

These were critical years for Boston Scientific's growth and the formation of its culture. At one point during a meeting, Pete made the observation that in two years there would probably be more new people than the entire staff at the time. "Are they going to be more like us?" he wondered. "Or are we going to become like them?"

Even outside the company, Ciffolillo's arrival was watched as a watershed moment. Shortly after he arrived, he attended his first meeting of the Radiology Society of North America, which was the most important medical meeting for Medi-Tech. John Abele led him around the floor, introducing

World Events

An earthquake in Mexico kills 700.

Medical Milestones

With Professor Tassilo Bonzel, Schneider develops the first Monorail balloon catheter.

Lasers are used in the U.S. for the first time to clean out clogged arteries.

The FDA approves an implantable defibrillator.

Boston Scientific

Jerry Lacey joins BSC to develop international business.

Medi-Tech expands its line of nonvascular products and receives excellent market response, especially for Percuflex.

Arab terrorists hijack TWA airliner and hold 39 passengers, including Boston Scientific Vice President Bob Brown, hostage for 17 days.

him to colleagues and friends. In the course of their travels, they bumped into Bill Cook.

"John said, 'Bill, this is Joe Ciffolillo. He just joined us, and he's going to be running Medi-Tech. He comes to us from Johnson & Johnson,'" recalled Ciffolillo. "Bill, who is otherwise quite gregarious and friendly, looked at me eyeball to eyeball and said, 'Young man, I hope you're not going to screw up this great little company.'"[23]

The Seeds of Stealth

That remark was telling in many ways. Not only did it show the kind of friendly affection that existed in the medical device industry, but it revealed a crucial underestimation of Boston Scientific. This was also planned, for when Nicholas and Abele reorganized Boston Scientific into autonomous companies, they created an entity they came to call a "stealth enterprise."

When asked what Boston Scientific was, many of the company's own customers probably wouldn't have known. From the market standpoint, Medi-Tech, Mansfield, and Microvasive were three separate entities, each known for its strong interface

Each of Boston Scientific's three operating companies appeared independent. Mansfield, top, specialized in cardiology; Medi-Tech, middle, pictured at the 1986 RSNA meeting in Chicago, was a leader in PTA products; and Microvasive, left, pictured at the 1986 American College of Surgeons meeting, was active in nonvascular applications.

The U.S. becomes the largest debtor nation, with a balance-of-trade deficit of $130 billion.

On August 29, Mason Sones dies of lung cancer.

The U.K. begins screening blood donations for the AIDS virus.

John Abele writes an open letter to the SCVIR challenging them to expand their membership and fuel the growth of interventional procedures.

The Ultroid product shown at a Microvasive booth. The Ultroid was a well-intentioned failure.

with completely different groups of physicians. The larger corporation behind them was elusive and almost completely invisible, even in the medical device industry, and there were very few people openly drawing parallels between different medical specialties using the same devices to accomplish similar tasks.

Such independence among the divisions had its drawbacks, however. Each operating company had its own administrative function, its own research and development division, and its own sales team—which meant a significant overlapping of duties. Also, each operating company had to compete fiercely for the corporation's limited resources to better service its customers. But all of these disadvantages were outweighed by the major advantage that Abele had pointed out to Aschauer: intense focus on the customer.

The stealth angle was also a tremendous benefit. No one knew exactly how big or successful Boston Scientific was. No one knew it was growing around 40 percent every year. The partners recognized that the company's success could be dangerous because success in business always attracts competitors and, especially in the evolving fields of interventional radiology and therapeutic endoscopy, Boston Scientific was operating with relatively few competitors.

"There was no real incentive, from our point of view, for us to reveal the market share and size and shape of our data," said Nicholas. "Since we were the dominant player in almost every one of our businesses, revealing ourselves would just create a road map for others."[24]

This ad appeared in *Sports Illustrated* in 1987 promoting interventional medicine and specifically PTA. Although its operating companies were shrouded in secrecy, Boston Scientific worked hard to educate physicians and even the public about the benefits of interventional medicine. By the late 1980s, many procedures were credible and widely used.

A Wake-Up Call

The rationale behind the company's structure, its relationship with customers, and its competitive positioning in the marketplace could be summed up in a phrase: market creation. Boston Scientific's sales forces had been fanning out across the nation's hospitals and medical clinics, soliciting ideas from innovative doctors, and working with emerging interventional medical societies to find out what the marketplace needed and wanted. These ideas, with liberal input from the same people who would eventually buy them, were turned into reality, and it was up to the sales force to spread the technique beyond the original nucleus of early adopter physicians. It was more than informing doctors; it was being a responsible

World Events

Medical Milestones

Melvin Judkins dies in his sleep on January 28.

Boston Scientific

Boston Scientific posts sales of $31 million. Medi-Tech accounts for $17 million, Microvasive Endoscopy, $8 million, and Mansfield, $6 million.

Mansfield acquires Schiff Medical Electronics (cardiac-assist product line; intra-aortic balloon pump).

advocate; helping doctors establish practices that fostered new, less-invasive procedures; working with less-invasive medical societies to foster clinical trials; and keeping the media and public well informed.

"It was basically a road show," remembered Bob Krajeski, who joined Microvasive in 1984 as one of the division's 18 sales reps. "You just kept running from one hospital to the next, and people would ask, 'Boston Scientific who?' "[25]

So the "kimono stayed closed," in the words of Pete Nicholas, and Boston Scientific kept its three divisions, holding the public and even Abbott at arm's length. But behind the scenes there was a feverish effort to take advantage of Boston Scientific's relative obscurity while it lasted. When the managers gathered for monthly meetings to discuss growth and profit, the goal was maximum growth with a zero bottom line: no profit.

"That means if you lose money, you're in trouble because there's nothing to make it up," Ciffolillo said.

And if you've made money, you're also in trouble because you've lost the money to invest. I remember we'd have senior staff meetings about

An early clean room still under construction. This kind of facility and the large sales force were helping to create a cash crunch at Medi-Tech and the other operating companies.

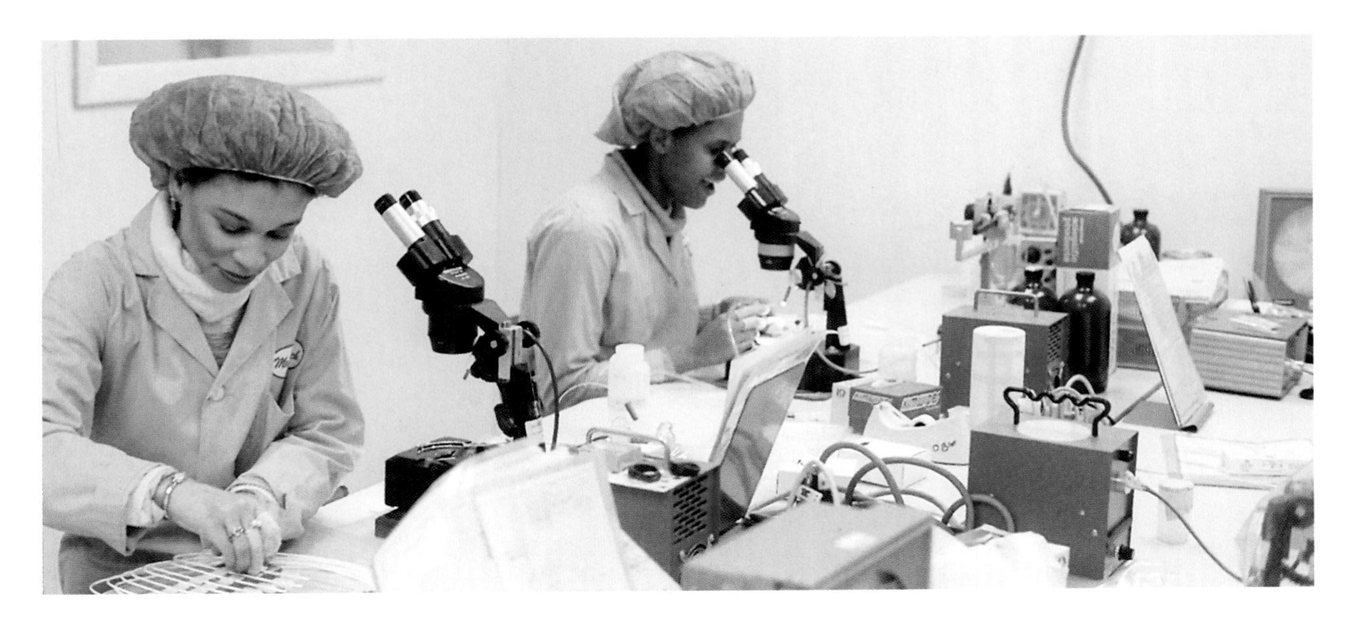

Films include Back to the Future *and* The Color Purple.

Andreas Gruentzig is killed when a private plane he is piloting crashes. In his obituary, Dr. J. Willis Hurst, chairman of Emory's Department of Medicine, calls Gruentzig "a national treasure."

On February 15, Charles Dotter succumbs to pulmonary insufficiency after surviving two coronary bypass operations and treatment for Hodgkin's disease.

The FDA approves Mansfield's PTCA catheters.

SEVEN STAGES IN THE EVOLUTION OF AN IDEA

IN THE MID-1960S, FAMED HEART surgeon C. Walton Lillehei came up with a humorous satire of how great ideas come to fruition. His list lampooned the conservatism of his time, when direct challenges to either doctors or conventional wisdom were rare. After Andreas Gruentzig, however, the situation changed, leading Abele to develop an updated spoof to reflect a time when people felt that anything was possible and probably worth investing in and promoting. He included his version in a keynote presentation on the history of angioplasty at the Society for Cardiac Angiography and Intervention.

1. Idea Stage:
(Lillehei, 1968) "Won't work. Been tried before."
(Abele, 1987) "What a fabulous idea. I want to try that on one of my patients."

2. After Successful Animal Experiments:
(Lillehei, 1968) "Won't work in man."
(Abele, 1987) "How do I become an investor? Is the stock public?"

3. After First Successful Clinical Patient:
(Lillehei, 1968) "Very lucky."
(Abele, 1987) To TV interviewer: "Yes, it is new, but in our hands, it has been quite successful."

4. After Four or Five Clinical Successes:
(Lillehei, 1968) "Highly experimental, too risky, immoral, unethical. I understand there have been several deaths they are not reporting."
(Abele, 1987) "In conclusion, Mr. Chairman, I believe that this advance is at least as important as Gruentzig's pioneering work years ago."

5. After 10 to 15 Clinical Successes:
(Lillehei, 1968) "May succeed occasionally in carefully selected cases, but most patients with the problem don't need the operation anyway."
(Abele, 1987) "We have arranged for training courses this year and coverage by NBC, CBS, ABC, CNN and *People* magazine."

World Events

Space shuttle Challenger *explodes, killing six astronauts and teacher Christa McAuliffe.*

Medical Milestones

Boston Scientific

John Abele presents Bob DePasqua with the Outstanding Performance Award for the year—a Suzuki Samurai.

6. After a Large Number of Successes:

(Lillehei, 1968) "So-and-So in Shangri-La has been unable to duplicate results. Not practical. Only experts can do it. I hear a number of patients are dying late and are unreported."

(Abele, 1987) Publicly: "Of course, the old procedure this replaced also had complications. In our recent work, we have focused on new indications and variations." Privately: "We better sell this company quickly, before the restenosis data get out."

7. Final Stage:

(Lillehei, 1968) "You know, this is a very fine contribution! A straightforward solution to a difficult problem. I predicted this. In fact, in 1929, I had the same idea. Of course, we didn't publish anything."

(Abele, 1987) "You know, I knew this technique wasn't going to work. I have been constantly demanding honest clinical trials. However, we have another breakthrough in technology, but my lawyer and advisors have told me not to talk about it."[1]

John Abele stayed deeply involved in the medical side of the business, networking between the various device companies and the professional medical societies that were slowly forming around various specialties.

Chernobyl nuclear reactor explodes.

Dick Rutan and Jeana Yeager pilot the airplane Voyager *around the world without refueling.*

Cardiologist Richard Myler appears on 20/20 refuting the possible overuse of PTCA.

Boston Scientific implements computerized MIS to decrease time between customer orders and delivery.

Boston Scientific posts sales of $47 million. Medi-Tech accounts for $22 million. Microvasive Endoscopy contributes $13 million and Mansfield $12 million.

growth, and we'd challenge each other. But we would invariably end up at the blackboard with a pro forma profit and loss—not for the year, not for the month—but for the week. As an operating guy, you were expected to fill in the blanks and know where we were going to be. These meetings were in the third week in the month, and we had to project out the last week to know if we had enough money, what was going on, and if there were any surprises.[26]

Management was committed to walking the tightrope of using all revenue to support their growth. Nicholas and Abele took low salaries and no dividends for the first thirteen years of the company's life.

But the team of executives didn't always get its projections right, and midway through 1983, Boston Scientific was forced to terminate about 35 employees, which represented a fairly significant downsizing in a company of only 200 people. This extremely painful task provided a wake-up call to the presidents running the three operating companies and to Boston Scientific itself. The company had to question if it was actually operating within the all-important philosophical framework of fast-growth, entrepreneurial, mission-oriented minimally invasive medicine, or if it had possibly overstepped its capabilities.

Blessed with the desire to look critically at itself, Medi-Tech hired a telemarketing company to survey its 250 largest hospital clients in the United States. The customers, without knowing they were being polled by Medi-Tech, were asked what they thought of Medi-Tech, its quality, its people, its products, and its service. By polling customers, Boston Scientific was trying to reach deep into its customer relationships to make sure the company was, in fact, everything its founders wanted it to be.

"We did not get the most wonderful news back that year," Ciffolillo said, "but we did that survey again for about the next six years."[27] Over these years, Medi-Tech representatives actively worked to address any negative comments, and gradually the surveys began to yield positive answers.

Building Markets

It was natural that Medi-Tech would be the focal point of this survey. In 1984, Medi-Tech was the largest operating company in Boston Scientific with 24 sales reps. Its peripheral vascular angioplasty balloons were firmly established as the world standard, and the treatment had gained acceptance in the public and within the medical community. Moreover, its sales force was the accepted leader in the field, having transformed Boston Scientific into a clearinghouse of information.

Medi-Tech might have been Boston Scientific's largest operating company, but Microvasive and Mansfield were both important to the company's overall strategy of market leadership. And although Mansfield was struggling in cardiology, Microvasive had become an early leader in gastroenterology and had basically pioneered the field of endoscopic

World Events

Whitney Houston and Madonna are pop divas.

General Motors overtakes Exxon as the biggest company in the U.S.

Medical Milestones

The first human coronary stent implantation occurs. A Schneider WALLSTENT endoprosthesis is used.

Pfizer Inc acquires Angiomedics.

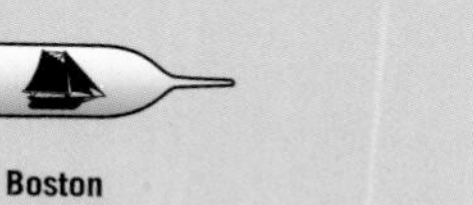

Boston Scientific

A demonstration of the Visicath at the 1986 American College of Chest Physicians. A novel product, the Visicath never succeeded.

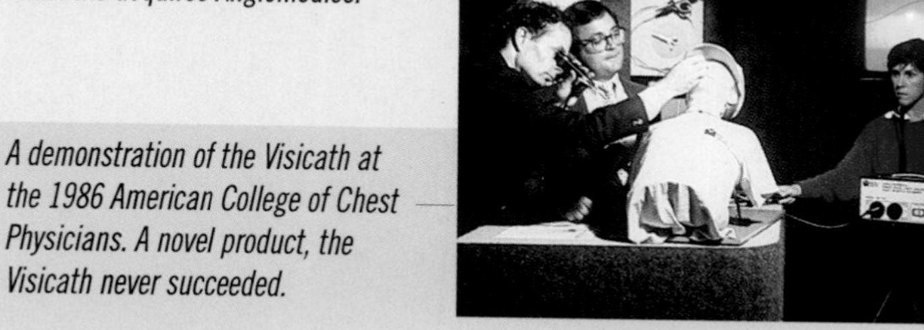

accessories (even while many outside companies were unaware that a "field" of endoscopic accessories existed).

As Microvasive grew, the company began to seek ways to expand both its market and the field of interventional urology, which was perhaps the oldest branch of less-invasive medicine.

In 1988, Boston Scientific bought Van-Tec, a Spencer, Indiana, company that, although it was only five years old, already had a history with Boston Scientific. When Van-Tec was acquired by Boston Scientific, it was a $10 million business with 200 different product codes. The company had a new 40,000-square-foot manufacturing facility and 66 employees. Van-Tec had pioneered the use of pigtail ureteral stents, which were used to hold open obstructed ureters. The product line also included dilatation catheters and stone removal equipment for the kidneys.

The Van-Tec purchase was no surprise to either Boston Scientific insiders or Jim Vance, the founder of Van-Tec. Boston Scientific had helped fund the company during its early years and had always planned on buying it. Vance, a former employee of Bill Cook's and a key figure in the development of the pigtail ureteral stent, founded Van-Tec in 1981. Vance had known John Abele since the early 1970s, when both were working to breathe life into minimally invasive medicine. Vance approached Boston Scientific in 1984 seeking funding and the opportunity to distribute Boston Scientific products. Nicholas, sensing an opportunity, agreed.

In 1988, Boston Scientific bought Van-Tec, thus giving a major boost to its urology-based business. Van-Tec's first big product was a pigtail urinary stent developed by Hal Mardis, left, a Johns Hopkins–trained urologist.

"He told me Boston Scientific could fund our start-up," Vance remembered. "He told me, 'If your business really takes off, we'd like to have an opportunity to buy you in the future.'"[28]

Nicholas and Vance agreed to an amount Vance would need for his company. Vance took only half of the proposed amount, started his company in the garage, and ran tight.

The company's first big product, the pigtail urinary stent, was jointly developed by Vance and Dr. Hal Mardis, a Johns Hopkins–trained urologist. "The ureteral stent was actually fairly revolutionary because it used a guide wire," Mardis said.

> *The pigtail held the catheter in place, and it allowed you to put it up over a guide wire because other catheters were not designed to be put over a guide. They just put a stiffener inside the catheter, but that was a clinical problem because if the ureter was obstructed, you risked perforating the urethra and not getting the catheter up. My recommendation was to put a guide wire that bypasses any obstruction up first, then put the stent over the wire. It was a very safe and effective way to get a stent up.*[29]

Reagan admits secret arms deal with Iran in breach of U.S. arms embargo.

Films include Blue Velvet *and* Crocodile Dundee.

Ivan Boesky pleads guilty to insider trading.

Bert Vallee and coworkers find the tumor angiogenesis factor, which was first predicted by Folkman in 1961; it stimulates growth of new blood vessels.

Doctors record 25,000 AIDS cases in the U.S.

British surgeons perform the world's first triple transplant (heart, lung, and liver).

Construction gets under way to expand two Watertown Medi-Tech facilities—Medi-Tech West, formerly the Boston Gas Company, and Medi-Tech South, previously the Damco building.

After the acquisition, Boston Scientific brought in Dale Jackson to run the Van-Tec plant. Jackson had worked at Baxter for 14 years, earning a reputation as "The Preacher" for his inspirational talks to employees. This trait was welcome at Boston Scientific, which Jackson remembered as a refreshing change.

"I could only describe it as walking from a dungeon into the daylight," Jackson said. "The people were running around. They had more to do than they were going to get done that day. There were looks of frustration on their faces, but at the same time, I knew that those were the people who were going to be here bright and early the next morning and that their frustration was from their inability to get everything done that they wanted to do."[30]

Jackson began working to modernize and grow the Spencer, Indiana, plant. Within only a couple of years, both the size of the building and the number of product codes had doubled.[31]

Boston Scientific's culture changed how Van-Tec related to both its market and the medical community. Prior to the acquisition, the company had been working with Dr. Joe Dowd to refine an existing balloon for dilating the prostatic urethra. This procedure was used as an alternative to prostatectomy, or removal of the prostate gland. Dowd, an important leader in the development of less-invasive medicine, was chairman of the Urology Department at the University of Oregon and treasurer of the American Urological Association.

There he had met Jim Vance and had begun working on a new urology balloon. After the acquisition, Dowd found himself working with Randy Tuomisto, a Boston Scientific employee.[32] He next met John Carnuccio, a Boston Scientific employee "who seemed to be the spokesperson for getting things done."[33] Before long, the team had developed a minimally invasive alternative to a prostatectomy.

Boston Scientific wanted to call the product the "Dowd balloon." The doctor, however, balked. He had heard of legal troubles experienced by doctors who put their names on products, so he hired a team of lawyers to represent his best interests.

> *On the scene came a guy named Joe Ciffolillo. He wasn't a lawyer, but he turned out to be my advocate. He was advising me personally as to how I could get the best deal with Boston Scientific, and yet he worked for them. Then in the other ear, I have my partner saying, "Don't deal with that. Have your own lawyer. You're going to get nailed." So I went that route, and I hired a private attorney who was $600 an hour. What a mistake! Although this was not Boston Scientific's business, they were on my side.*[34]

The Dowd balloon, as it was eventually named, was introduced as an alternative to prostatectomy, but its long-term effectiveness was not as good as trials suggested, and it was eventually dropped from the product line.

Joe Lacman, a nonvascular development engineer, transferred to Spencer in 1988 as head of urology research. "Van-Tec had a very good technology platform in ureteral stents, catheters, and

1987...

World Events

Black Monday: world stockmarket prices crash.

Reagan announces the nation's first trillion dollar budget.

In the U.S.S.R., Mikhail Gorbachev campaigns for glasnost and perestroika.

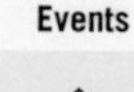

Medical Milestones

Laparoscopic cholecystectomy becomes a hot topic at the American College of Surgeons meeting and remains so for the next five years.

Emory University receives NIH approval for angioplasty-versus-surgery trial, the first to test multivessel PTCA versus coronary artery bypass graft surgery.

Boston Scientific

Boston Scientific gets a record bond to refinance Watertown Mill.

Mike Mabrey joins Boston Scientific as Medi-Tech's vice president of operations. He reports to Pete Nicholas directly.

A Face Company

As a small company, Boston Scientific thrived on open communication. It was a face-to-face kind of company where people regularly gathered to exchange ideas, develop new strategies and devices, argue and defend positions, and knit together a cohesive team with a remarkably consistent approach to its mission of rapid growth across many medical specialties.

Yet that same growth began to pose a major challenge in the early and mid-1980s. As the three separate divisions became more entrenched and the number of employees mushroomed, it was becoming harder and harder for ideas to flow across the whole corporation and harder for the leaders of Boston Scientific, the parent corporation, to distribute their message deep into the company.

Technology, which was undergoing its own revolution, offered both a promise and a peril. In the early 1980s, voice mail was introduced as a new way for people to leave messages for each another. Originally, many people at Boston Scientific saw voice mail as a replacement for the answering machine and were unabashedly opposed to it—after all, the company of personal communication had created a culture that didn't like talking to machines.

Yet voice mail had one potent advantage that answering machines didn't. Once a message was received, it could be forwarded directly to different mailboxes, spreading the original voice message intact and quickly. Nevertheless, Boston Scientific's three operating companies remained reluctant to adopt voice mail. Finally, however, the sales force of Mansfield, the smallest company within Boston Scientific, agreed to try it out.

The results of this enhanced communication within Mansfield were almost instantaneous and positive. The productivity of the entire team measurably increased as the salespeople exchanged messages with ease, handled complaints more quickly, and swapped ideas through voice mail. And, salespeople being salespeople, the barriers to further acceptance were quickly broken. The next company to sign on with voice mail was Microvasive, then Medi-Tech, the largest group, and finally the corporate offices. After company-wide acceptance, voice mail became a powerful internal tool for Boston Scientific.

Richard Myler's 10th anniversary PTCA course in San Francisco.

The Executive Committee in 1987. John Abele and Pete Nicholas are seated in front.

During a 6 A.M. aortic valvuloplasty registry meeting in 1988, cardiologists share data on the new procedure. Mansfield Scientific organized and hosted this informational meeting, which was held at the American College of Cardiology.

wire forming, which is the base technology for retrieval baskets and kidney stone retrieval baskets," Lacman said. "Basically what we did after we acquired Van-Tec was iterate and expand the living daylights out of those product lines."[35]

The Mansfield Story

While Van-Tec added a new push to Boston Scientific's urology business, the cardiology business in Mansfield wasn't faring so well. The Mansfield coronary angioplasty balloons didn't receive their first FDA approvals until 1985, well after USCI/Bard and Advanced Catheter Systems were established as the industry leaders in coronary angioplasty. That same year, Mansfield received approval to market dilatation balloons for pediatric pulmonary valvuloplasty, or opening damaged pulmonary valves within the heart. Five years later, Mansfield received approval for a balloon for adult aortic valvuloplasty.

"The aortic valvuloplasty approval, all told, took over three years because in addition to developing the product, we were also developing the technique and the patient selection criteria," remembered Janet Bologna (later Sullivan), who started in 1986 as a manager of clinical research.[36]

The 1990 approval of the adult aortic valvuloplasty balloon represented a major victory for Mansfield because it was the company's first big product in treating heart disease. Nicholas had spent

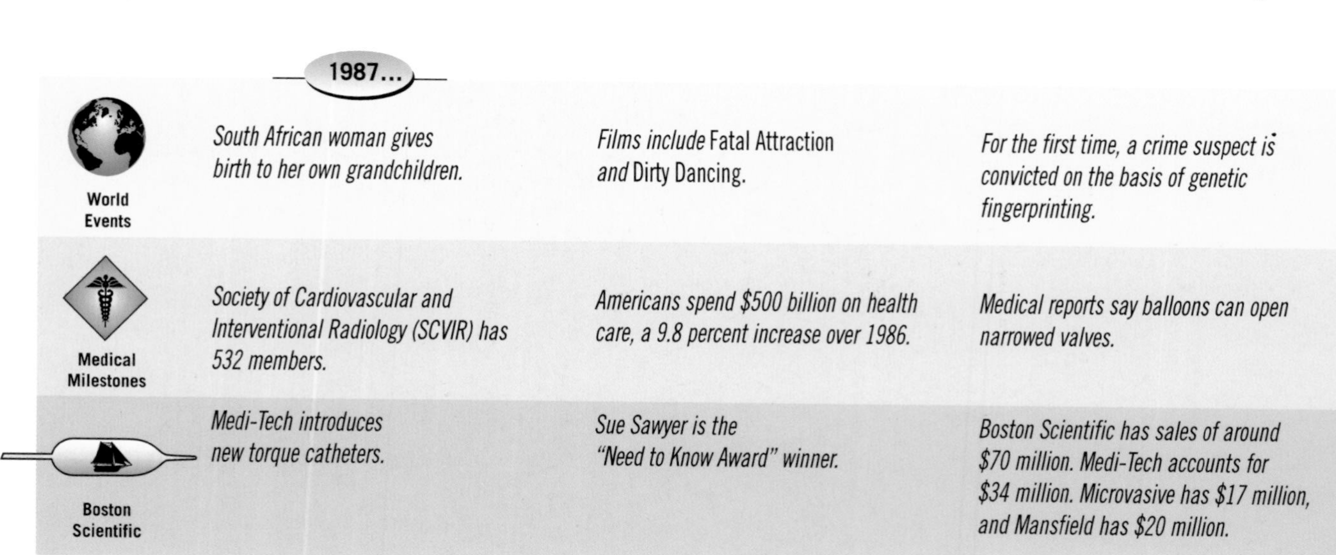

almost 10 years trying to establish the company in cardiology—sometimes considering outrageous plans along the way. In the mid-1980s, he considered selling the Greenfield vena cava filter to fund a stronger effort in cardiology. At various times he talked to the CEOs of Bard and Cordis, trying to buy all or part of their cardiology businesses. These efforts didn't bear fruit.

Although Mansfield wasn't destined to dominate the coronary angioplasty market, it did gain a following for its valvuloplasty products. Like the other divisions, Mansfield sponsored educational seminars that received high marks from the attending physicians. "In this era of criticism and distrust of the scientific-industrial collaboration," wrote Dr. William O'Neill in his introductory remarks to one seminar, "the conduct of Mansfield Scientific serves as a refreshing model for future industrial-scientific collaboration."[37]

Mansfield also got several favorable press reports regarding its techniques. One of the more interesting media accounts was called "A Reason to Dance," which appeared on a Philadelphia TV program called *Prime Time* in 1986. The television news magazine told the story of Kim Stedman, a 17-year-old ballerina in New Jersey who was one of the first people in the world to undergo balloon dilatation of a narrowed valve. Her doctor used a Boston Scientific device to perform the procedure.

Pulmonary valvuloplasty went on to be widely used in patients with congenital pulmonary valve disease. Pediatric cardiologists accepted the procedure relatively quickly.[38]

These same results could be claimed by many Boston Scientific products, and the company was rapidly creating new markets. By this time, Boston Scientific had hundreds of product codes across multiple manufacturing facilities and its three operating companies.

At Medi-Tech, this rapid growth had created a manufacturing problem, and the operating company was churning through manufacturing executives, none of whom lasted more than a year. Much of the challenge for a medical device company is in manufacturing because each of the hundreds of tiny products has to meet medical manufacturing excellence criteria. In the mid-1980s, Ciffolillo began to look for a new manufacturing expert, but Pete Nicholas took it one step further. Instead of a new manufacturing executive for Medi-Tech, in 1987 he recruited Mike Mabrey as the new head of manufacturing for all of Boston Scientific.

Mabrey had 20 years' experience at Baxter in various manufacturing, engineering, and corporate jobs. Once at Boston Scientific, he joined the executive committee, which was the first time operations was represented at that level. Pete Nicholas viewed Mabrey's introduction to the company and his role within the company as so important that Mabrey reported directly to him instead of to Joe Ciffolillo.

Building International Sales

Throughout most of the 1980s, Boston Scientific realized the majority of its growth and sales from the United States, although it could count on overseas

Boston Scientific opens a manufacturing facility in Denmark, its first outside the United States.

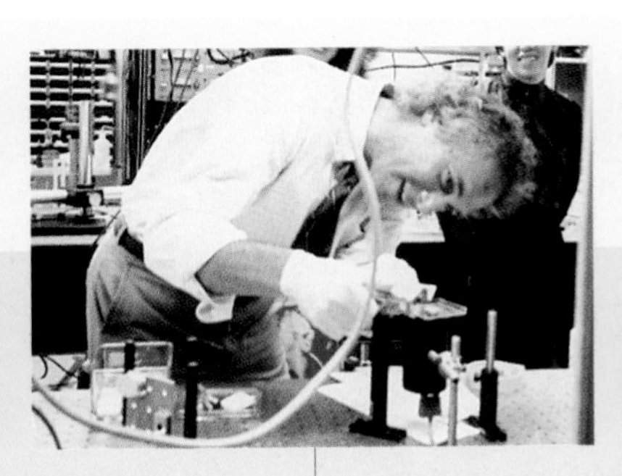

Dr. Jeff Isner demonstrates laser angioplasty.

John Abele, John Carnuccio, and Kurt Amplatz on a beach in Sardinia during a medical conference.

markets for about 20 percent of overall sales. Medi-Tech especially did well overseas. Nicholas remembered, "We handled international sales through distributors in Europe and through our own organization in Japan."[39]

Medi-Tech's international sales were managed by Bob Brown, who had set up the network of European distributors in the 1970s and early 1980s. Yet sales seemed low to Pete Nicholas, who saw others in the medical device industry reaping half of their total revenues from overseas. At around the same time Nicholas was coming to the conclusion that Boston Scientific needed to strengthen international sales, he received a phone call from Jerry Lacey.

"It was very difficult to find someone who could effectively run the company overseas, but Jerry Lacey had direct international operating experience," Nicholas said. "He was very comfortable with Japan and very comfortable with Europe."[40]

Lacey had been president of Millipore's international division until 1981, when he left to become president of a company called Dyonics, which developed arthroscopy products. Dyonics was a subsidiary of the Roehr group, and in 1985 Roehr announced it was merging Dyonics with another unit. Lacey was offered a job in Philadelphia, which he didn't want, so he called Nicholas looking for options. That's when Nicholas offered him the opportunity to "really develop" the international business at Boston Scientific. Lacey accepted the challenge and began working for Boston Scientific in 1985.

Jerry Lacey, left, was hired by Nicholas in 1985 to help build international business. John Carnuccio, right, who had joined as a Medi-Tech sales rep in 1980, moved into international sales.

His first move was to create Boston Scientific International Corporation (BSIC). Over the next six months, Lacey and Brown worked together to impose a basic structure on the jumbled distributor business. But it wasn't destined to be an easy year.

1988...

World Events

Gorbachev consolidates power in the U.S.S.R.

George Bush defeats Michael Dukakis for the U.S. presidency.

U.S. dollar has roller-coaster year.

Medical Milestones

The FDA adopts a new policy to speed drug approval.

Schneider Medintag AG's name changes to Schneider (Europe) AG.

SCVIR membership rises to 747.

Boston Scientific

Jerry Lacey talks to doctors in Rouen, France.

John Abele writes an article for Seminars in Interventional Radiology *about the profession's future.*

THE LONG FLIGHT HOME

BOSTON SCIENTIFIC TRIED ITS BEST to stay out of the media. But avoiding public attention wasn't always easy—especially when one of its key employees was taken hostage by Lebanese terrorists.

The nightmare ordeal began on June 14, 1985, on board TWA flight 847. Bob Brown, then Boston Scientific's director of international marketing, thought he was returning home from a meeting in Athens of the European Society of Cardiovascular Radiology (which later changed its name to CIRSE, the Cardiovascular and Interventional Radiology Society of Europe).

As it turned out, however, Brown was beginning a zig-zag flight over the Mediterranean—a flight that would ultimately land him in Beirut, where he would be imprisoned for 17 grueling days.

Not 20 minutes after the Boeing 727 left Athens, two well-dressed Muslim men hijacked the plane, recklessly brandishing a 9 mm pistol and two grenades. The hijackers, fanatic members of Islamic Jihad, first ordered Captain John Testrake to fly the plane to Beirut.

Initially they were denied permission to land—until one of the hijackers pulled the pin from a grenade. "He is desperate," the pilot calmly told the control tower. "We must land at Beirut. There is no alternative."[1]

Airport officials at first refused to refuel the plane, but the terrorists began beating the passengers, threatening to kill them. "I ended up on the floor back by the galley," Brown remembered, "and when they landed the plane the first time in Beirut, they wanted me to move into another spot on the floor. I didn't move fast enough, so one of the men kicked me in the face."[2]

At last the plane was refueled in exchange for the release of 19 women and children. While on the ground, the hijackers made a number of demands, including the release of hundreds of imprisoned Shiite Muslims.

The hijackers next ordered the pilot to fly to Algiers, where they released more women and children in exchange for fuel, food, and water.

Once this exchange was completed, the plane looped back to Beirut, where the pilot was able to land it just seconds before running out of fuel. The hijackers demanded to talk with representatives of the Shiite Amal militia to demand freedom for imprisoned Shiites. When their request was not met, they shot and killed U.S. Navy diver Robert Stethem, dumping his body on the tarmac.

"The State Department actually called my wife and told her I was the one who was killed," Brown said. "One of the women who was released—she spoke German—told the press that a mariner had been killed. A mariner in German is a navy person, but they interpreted it as Marine. I was the only former Marine on the plane, and therefore they thought I was the one who was killed. It wasn't until they sent a limo out to pick up my wife that they showed her a distant video of the navy man on the tarmac. He was wearing jeans, and I never wore jeans when I traveled on business. My wife knew that, and she said, 'That's not him. He doesn't wear jeans.' "[3]

After one more stop in Algiers, where more passengers were released, the 40 remaining passengers, Bob Brown among them, were locked up in safe houses in southern Beirut while the terrorists made their demands to foreign governments.

"They didn't treat us very well," Brown said. "I lost 17 pounds, and I lived on the floor. No windows, no furniture, just a concrete floor."[4]

Seventeen days later, after intense international negotiations, the last of the passengers were freed.

"I'd never seen so many cameras in all my life," said Brown of his homecoming.[5] Following the ordeal, he conducted a number of interviews with the national media to talk about the traumatic ordeal.

"I don't think Boston Scientific liked that too much," he said. "They're kind of low-key people, John especially."[6]

Brown resented someone being hired over his head; a rift was opening between Brown and the company he had joined in 1971 as the first sales manager. Then shortly afterward, he was kidnapped and held hostage by Iranian terrorists. Just after he returned, he and Lacey sat down to discuss Brown's role in the company. The two men couldn't reconcile themselves in the end, and Brown left the company.

"It was an amazing ride, and to some degree I regret not staying at Boston Scientific," Brown said in 1998. "It was a lot of fun. It really was."[41] He later helped found his own materials company, which eventually supplied nitinol, a nickel and titanium alloy, to Boston Scientific.

After Brown's departure, Lacey enlisted the help of John Carnuccio, then the product manager for the Blue Max angioplasty balloon at Medi-Tech, and again retooled the company's approach to overseas markets. Lacey and Carnuccio identified six countries that were key to Boston Scientific: Germany, France, Great Britain, Italy, Spain, and Japan.

A meeting of Boston Scientific International Corporation executives in Watertown. The original BSIC operated very independently of its U.S. cousins.

World Events

A tidal wave kills 3,000 in Bangladesh.

Films include Beetlejuice *and* Die Hard.

Medical Milestones

U.S. survey shows that daily aspirin halves the risk of heart attack.

U.S. surgeons implant the world's first plutonium-powered pacemaker.

Boston Scientific

Boston Scientific International forms international subsidiaries in Germany, France, and Japan, eliminating the dealerships.

The BSIC display in Nuremberg, Germany, during the 1988 Zeitler Meeting. It is led by Hans Peter Strohband. Germany was a focus market for BSIC.

"We took on the relationships of all the dealers," Lacey said. "We wrote the contracts. We qualified them, meaning that we went around and made sure that somebody was qualified to be our dealer. We trained their sales forces."[42]

Lacey next met with Nicholas and outlined two basic ways to approach overseas business: by medical specialty (radiology, cardiology, etc.) and by geography. He requested a specialist for each of the product lines. Nicholas agreed but told Lacey to "pay as you go." With this understanding, Boston Scientific International split the world into two regions—Europe and everywhere else—and contacted Erik Anderson, who had recently left Surgimed, a Danish catheter company. Boston Scientific waited twelve months for his noncompete clause with Meadox, which had purchased Surgimed two years earlier, to run out, then brought him to the United States to introduce him to Boston Scientific people, products, and technology.

That year, Boston Scientific International opened up a manufacturing facility, run by Anderson, in Denmark. Called Boston Scientific A/S Denmark, this first facility located overseas opened in 1987 in Jyllinge, Denmark.[43]

"Denmark was not a country you'd think of going to at first, but it turns out there were a number of catheter companies in Denmark for historical reasons," Abele said. "So it was a fertile ground for people who knew that technology. Anderson, in fact, had been running a catheter company. When we brought him on board, he had built that company from scratch, and it expanded substantially. It was a key move in growing the European business and providing a

McDonald's opens 20 restaurants in Moscow.

A panel of physicians and medical school faculty urges revision of training, stating that schools are not training physicians to be socially conscious or skilled in doctor-patient relationships.

Medicare hospital payments altered; new doctor fee structure proposed in which family doctors receive more money and specialists receive less.

Surgeons in the U.K. perform the first brain cell transplants.

Boston Scientific acquires Van-Tec in Spencer, Indiana, which has a large business in interventional urology.

Boston Scientific has sales of $99 million. Medi-Tech has $43 million, Microvasive Endoscopy $16 million, Microvasive Urology (Van-Tec) $12 million, Mansfield $27 million.

Boston Scientific International accounted for about 20 percent of sales. Pictured, left to right, are Hans Peter Strohband, head of BS GmbH Germany; Pierre Marchesin, head of BS SA France; Peter Nicholas; and Jerry Lacey, president of BSCI.

base for product development outside of the U.S. FDA purview."[44]

In 1988, Boston Scientific took the next step overseas, founding direct international subsidiaries in Germany, France, and Japan for marketing and sales operations.[45] This was an enormous development and eliminated the distributor structure that had been in place, thus signaling a major commitment overseas.

Despite this level of effort, however, the company's international operation still generated only around 20 percent of total sales and sometimes even less. This was an indication not that international sales had become static but that the international unit couldn't keep pace with the domestic units. By the late 1980s, Boston Scientific's domestic operation was growing by approximately 40 percent annually—a very difficult act to follow. Also, said Lacey, the international market was full of medical and pricing idiosyncrasies that made it difficult to establish a solid business.

"In the United States, the nonvascular businesses were growing very well because they were able to sell disposable biopsy forceps," Lacey said. "Overseas, we couldn't give them away. We had a very good business with the radiologists, but we didn't have any business with cardiologists because we didn't have a competitive product. Our sales forces were more or less specialized in peripheral vascular."[46]

The Growth Challenge

With 40 percent growth every year, there could be no doubt: Boston Scientific was a growth enterprise, and the founders' formula for success was working. In its core businesses—Medi-Tech and the nonvascular companies—Boston Scientific continued to do well throughout the late 1980s.

1989...

World Events

In the ocean off Alaska, the Exxon Valdez *causes the world's largest oil spill.*

East Germany opens its borders, including the Berlin Wall.

Oliver North is found guilty of crimes in the Iran-contra scandal.

Medical Milestones

David Auth creates Heart Technology.

SCVIR membership is 1,200.

Symbiosis is founded by four Cordis engineers.

Boston Scientific

"The key growth areas at that time were not only peripheral angioplasty but the Greenfield vena cava filter and the whole area of percutaneous drainage—whether it be biliary drains, nephrostomy, or abscess drainage, which was fairly new at the time," remembered Dave Budreau, one of five regional sales managers for Medi-Tech.

Moreover, the company was busily keeping up with changing market conditions. "For example, Medi-Tech saw a big opportunity in guide wires," remembered Tom Keenan, product manager for guide wires. "They were a fundamental tool for an enormous variety of procedures, and new technologies and applications were expanding their variety and use. Medi-Tech wanted to be a full-line company to service all of the specialties."[47]

One of the reasons Alan Milinazzo left Baxter to join Mansfield as a salesman in 1987 was this ability to focus narrowly on customers. "At Baxter, my background was very broad," Milinazzo said. "Boston Scientific really drilled into specific franchises and, maybe more importantly, into disciplines at the physician level."[48]

It would be impossible to overstate how important this connectedness was to the company's success or how profound an influence it allowed Boston Scientific to have on interventional medicine. Boston Scientific was entrenched in a web of doctors, developers, community leaders, inventors, and pioneers—some of whom worked for the company and many who did not. The company took an active role in promoting interventional medicine, helped develop new techniques, and then helped

As the operating companies grew, they each fought to establish a full range of products. This prototype guide wire machine was part of Medi-Tech's push into guide wires. Yet by the late 1980s, the organization was suffering from overlap between its operating companies and expensive triplication of many functions.

A major earthquake rocks the San Francisco Bay area.

Banks post heavy 3rd quarter losses.

Study shows that, due to skyrocketing malpractice insurance, an increasing number of obstetricians are no longer delivering babies.

At the AHA meeting in New Orleans, many inquire about the PTCA Glider, biopsy forceps, and the intraluminal ultrasound machine.

train more doctors to use its devices and therapies. In any of Boston Scientific's businesses, perhaps only 200 opinion leaders determined the tone and substance of discussions of minimally invasive medicine, so it was critical for the company to remain close to these individuals.

This reason, in addition to the desire for a stealth enterprise, had been a powerful incentive to create the separate entities behind which Boston Scientific remained shrouded in secrecy. But by the late 1980s, the structure that had once been so necessary and powerful was beginning to create serious problems. When Pete Nicholas and John Abele formed their partnership in 1979, the company had sales of less than $2 million. By the end of the 1980s, sales teetered on the brink of $100 million.

Throughout all this growth, the company held profit to a minimum and walked a very fine line between explosive growth and disaster. In 1988, the inevitable finally happened. For the first time in its existence, Boston Scientific lost money. According to the *Boston Globe*, it lost $900,000 on sales of almost $100 million.[49] Pete Nicholas disagreed with the numbers, but the basic truth was incontrovertible: Boston Scientific took a loss.

A Cultural Reorganization

The problem was fairly obvious and common to companies with multiple operating units. Boston Scientific was paying a premium for triplication of almost every function, including marketing and sales, manufacturing, and administration. This had been justifiable when the company was originally split into operating units, but the inefficiencies had grown with the company. Worse yet, internal rivalry was becoming more and more destructive as the units were forced to compete ever harder for resources from the parent corporation.

On December 31, 1988, after pinpointing the strengths and weaknesses of each operation, Nicholas announced a reorganization plan that consolidated all Boston Scientific companies into a single operating company, eliminating the existing three presidencies.[50] The new organization, with corporate headquarters in Watertown, brought together managers for research and development, sales and marketing, manufacturing, finance, and human relations. As part of this move, there was significant discussion about which department managers belonged near each other and would benefit the most from proximity.

The former independent companies became divisions that retained the brand names of Mansfield Scientific, Medi-Tech, and Microvasive.[51] At the same time, Van-Tec, which was acquired almost simultaneously with the reorganization, was folded into Microvasive and ceased to exist as a separate entity, although separate revenue figures were kept for sales in urology and gastroenterology. (Later it would become apparent that urology deserved its own platform for growth and intense customer focus. True to the established pattern, Microvasive would be split into two operating com-

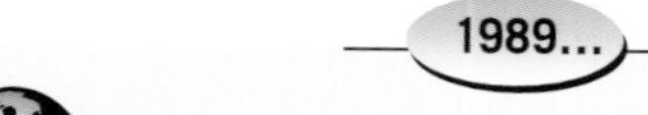

World Events

Medical Milestones

Bristol-Myers and Squibb announce a merger.

Boston Scientific

New Medi-Tech catalog is promoted at RSNA meeting; demonstration emphasizes breadth of its product line.

Dr. Josef Rabkin from Moscow poses with John Abele during Rabkin's visit to the United States.

panies, Microvasive Endoscopy and Microvasive Urology. John Carnuccio would become head of Microvasive Urology, while Stephen Moreci would take over Microvasive Endoscopy. Moreci, an old Johnson & Johnson colleague of Ciffolillo, had been working at Mansfield since joining Boston Scientific in 1984.)

Although it was a major milestone in the company's strategic approach to its business, the reorganization was not significant from a customer's point of view. The companies still maintained independent sales and marketing teams. The greatest benefits were internal, and many had to do with Mike Mabrey. Manufacturing leadership was consolidated under Mabrey, who assumed responsibility for the sites in Mansfield, Milford, Spencer, Watertown, and Denmark.

In a 1989 company newsletter, Nicholas detailed the reasons behind the reorganization:

> *This new organization enables BSC to optimize the use of its resources by creating a single corporate management, which permits a truly corporate overview of opportunities and a real perspective on what is best for BSC. For the first time, it enables us to develop, communicate, and embrace common goals and shared values throughout the corporation,*

Pete Nicholas, left, and John Abele, right, fooling around. The partnership between the two had deepened over the years as they learned to rely on each other's strengths.

Films include Batman *and* Driving Miss Daisy.

The stock market climbs to new high.

The S&L bailout crisis eases.

AZT is found to help early AIDS cases.

The FDA retests generic drugs; drug companies admit fraud.

Boston Scientific has sales of $116 million. Medi-Tech posts $63 million, Microvasive Endoscopy $18 million, Microvasive Urology (Van-Tec) $14 million, and Mansfield $21 million.

All companies are consolidated into one, which markets under the names Mansfield (cardiology), Medi-Tech (vascular), Microvasive (urology and endoscopy), and BSIC (international).

which will then become and remain the driving force behind BSC's response to our converging markets. It permits greater coordination of our selling and product management groups without diluting our existing commitments to the markets we serve. It permits us to more effectively pool and utilize our operations and development resources.[52]

The reorganization also streamlined the upper executive ranks. Joe Ciffolillo, former president of Medi-Tech, was tapped to run all three Boston Scientific companies. At Mansfield, John Delph, former president of the company, had already left Boston Scientific and been replaced by an old J&J colleague of Ciffolillo's named John Pavlic. Microvasive was headed by Bob DePasqua.

There were some internal difficulties, however, as Ciffolillo came in over Pavlic and DePasqua, giving the appearance that Medi-Tech was the most important company.[53] But the reorganization had asked employees to shed those kinds of old loyalties. In fact, Pavlic and DePasqua were part of the executive committee and voted on the new structure that would ultimately claim their jobs. Shortly after the move, both DePasqua and Pavlic left the company.

Issues like this were by far the most difficult part of the reorganization, not the administrative task of combining three companies. In fact, John Abele would later refer to the move as a "cultural reorganization."

"From an employee perspective, it passed the common sense test," said Jamie Rubin, vice president of human resources.

Employees had already identified many of the things that were driving and motivating the change. They knew there was redundancy in some of the R&D. The R&D folks knew they were working on the same projects, but they weren't leveraging well. The administrative folks knew that there was duplication of effort to do some of the financial procedures. The operations folks knew that the needs of the business and the customer weren't being served because you had one plant that wasn't to full capacity and another one that was on back order. The kind of people we selected had a broad enough base in terms of business knowledge and acumen, so we didn't have to convince the organization that this was right. They already knew it.[54]

The reorganization reduced the internal rivalry among the operating companies and allowed the opportunity to trade technologies between the divisions. This fit in with the company's goal of market leadership, which meant more than having successful products in one or two medical specialties. It meant leadership in all of interventional medicine, which translated into moving techniques and equipment from one specialty to the other. Internally, the term for this was "leveraging technology," which included brainpower and assets. With all the companies pulled under one corporate umbrella, this became intuitive.

Larry Jasinski, Medi-Tech product manager, moved into "product development coordination" in 1989 before there was any formal name for it. "I

The Boston Scientific senior staff holds a meeting in Brewster, Cape Cod.

was doing coordination among divisions because we would make a balloon that would work in a blood vessel," Jasinski said, "but it would also work in the ureter, in the bile duct, and then everywhere else. At Medi-Tech, I was having trouble getting financial support for one of the things I was trying to do. I started reaching out to other divisions, and soon we were saying, 'Well, we should have somebody doing that for the company.'"[55]

By almost any measure, the reorganization was a success, but no measure was as germane as profitability. Within a year of the reorganization, Boston Scientific was back in the black, earning $23.5 million on sales of $159 million. In 1991, it earned $42 million on sales of $243 million.

This profit was significant. Throughout the deal with Abbott and during the years of rapid growth, Boston Scientific had consciously avoided making too much money and reinvested everything. But now, nearing the ninth anniversary of the Abbott investment, it was time for Boston Scientific to face its past, and Nicholas wanted to make sure that the company was fully valued for a very good reason: the period that would determine Abbott's purchase option price had begun.

In the late 1980s, with the purchase option for Abbott about to begin, Boston Scientific undertook a reorganization that was designed to maximize the company's profitability. For their part, Abbott managers began to study Boston Scientific.

Poland elects Lech Walesa president.

South Africa frees Nelson Mandela. Germany reunites.

Films include Goodfellas *and* Dick Tracy.

Congress passes a deficit-reduction bill that would raise taxes $164.4 billion over five years.

Stephen Covey's book, The 7 Habits of Highly Effective People, *appears.*

Iraq invades Kuwait.

The Oregon Health Sciences University establishes the Dotter Interventional Institute.

A Philadelphia TV station airs a segment about a young dancer who wants valvuloplasty so she won't have a scar on her chest.

A four-year-old is the first human to receive gene therapy.

FDA cites Mansfield's pioneering efforts in development and evaluation of valvuloplasty as one of the nine most significant regulatory approvals of the year.

Microvasive splits into Microvasive Urology and Microvasive Endoscopy.

Boston Scientific has sales of $159 million. Medi-Tech has $82 million, Microvasive Endoscopy has $25 million, Microvasive Urology has sales of $21 million, and Mansfield has $31 million.

Nicholas and Abele, however, were also careful not to fishbone the company just to avoid an acquisition by Abbott. As Nicholas pointed out to Chuck Aschauer at Abbott, making Boston Scientific profitable at the expense of its product development, employees, and manufacturing could easily backfire if Abbott chose not to acquire it.

The Long Debate

By the mid- to late 1980s, interventional medicine had essentially won over the public, but mainstream doctors remained somewhat resistant. "Many of our physician customers viewed the procedures we were working on as experimental research and with limited application to whatever they did," said Abele. "So we were always very interested in getting publicity for the procedure as opposed to just the product."[56]

For the most part, patients supported Boston Scientific's work, but the media coverage of minimally invasive medicine in the 1980s began to reflect some of the subtle issues that shaded the entire field. Increasingly, it wasn't only a question of "Would it work?" but a multitude of concerns, including "Who should do it? Is it overused? Is it cost-effective? Just because we can do it, should we?"

On November 13, 1986, the network television news program *20/20* featured a doctor performing coronary angioplasty and discussed some of the issues that had sprung up regarding the high-profile treatment. Medical reporter Dr. Timothy Johnson noted the following:

> *When angioplasty was first tried on a human patient nine years ago, its future role in the treatment of heart disease was obviously uncertain. However, since that time, the number of cardiologists doing it and the number of procedures done each year have grown dramatically—over 100,000 projected this year alone. But as the numbers have grown, so too has the criticism by some surgeons and other concerned physicians.*

Despite the growing popularity of angioplasty, Johnson explained, cardiologists had been unable to solve one major problem—restenosis. This occurs when arteries that have been unblocked by angioplasty close again and have to be redone. According to cardiologist Richard Myler, who also appeared

A scientific poster for valvuloplasty at the 1987 American Heart Association meeting. The issues surrounding the spread of interventional medicine grew increasingly complex heading into the 1990s.

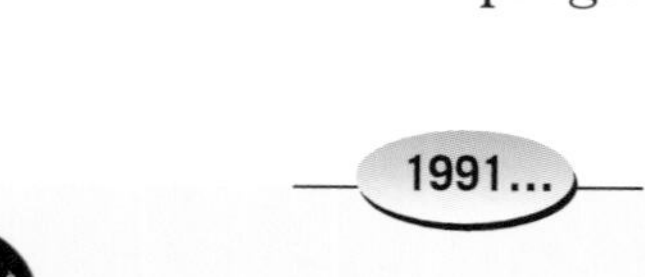

World Events

The Soviet Union dissolves.

In Lebanon, hostages are freed.

Medical Milestones

Boston Scientific

BSC earns $42 million on sales of $243 million.

on the segment, the incidence of clinical restenosis was about one in five, or possibly as high as one in four.

Johnson also noted that the increasing use of angioplasty for multiple blockages in more than one artery had put some cardiologists in competition with surgeons. Lawrence Cohn, a heart surgeon at Brigham and Women's Hospital in Boston, said, "I think we would make a serious mistake if multiple vessel coronary angioplasty were widely done by every angioplaster, even the novice."

Also featured on the show was Dr. Nicholas Kouchoukos of the Jewish Hospital in St. Louis, who wrote an editorial in a leading medical journal that criticized how coronary angioplasty was being used. Kouchoukos said angioplasters were encroaching on surgeons' territory: "Surgeons are perhaps upset by that. I am more upset by the fact that we do not have objective evidence in a very organized and prospective way to tell us that the procedure is better or worse than coronary bypass surgery."

Johnson commented: "This criticism by surgeons irritates Dr. Myler, who suspects the surgeons fear that multivessel angioplasty could take away business. Obviously, the patient doesn't care about this potential territorial and financial struggle between surgeons and angioplasters.... Angioplasty has truly revolutionized the treatment of some serious heart cases. And while it will continue to have its excesses and limitations, it is a revolution that is far from over."[57]

A year later, in an entirely different field, Abele wrote an editorial in which he questioned whether interventional radiology was living up to its original promise:

> *Formerly the province of the adventurous and the intrepid, interventional procedures are now performed by radiologists with a broad range of experience and academic standing.... From the less controversial needle biopsy to the controversial laser angioplasty with stenting, drainage, and numerous other procedures in between, the role of the interventional radiologist is growing in importance and prestige. It has the potential of becoming the 'General*

Dr. Richard Myler, left, with John Abele, right. The two shared correspondence throughout the 1970s development of PTCA and both knew Andreas Gruentzig. In the 1980s, as PTCA became more widespread, Myler commented on it for the network news show *20/20.*

Persian Gulf War; Iraqi forces are driven from Kuwait by a United Nations coalition.

A new plant to support the rapidly growing urology business takes shape in Indiana.

John Abele writes editorial, "Objective Assessment of New Technology." The editorial was a critical view of the process for developing new procedures.

Medical technology meetings became increasingly sophisticated. The 1989 RSNA meeting, inset, and the 1989 American College of Surgeons meeting both boasted large, interactive displays.

Surgery' of the future. The development of the field has been compromised, however, by a lack of organizational leadership. Factional disagreements, controversy over the role and definition of the interventionalist and a focus on research and academic activities have prevented the societies from developing a strong lobby in medical, economic and political power structures. The enormous potential for interventional procedures to contribute to lowering risk, trauma, recovery time, and the cost of health care is still vastly misunderstood and underappreciated.

1991...

World Events

Films include Terminator 2 *and* Judgement Day.

Bush and Gorbachev sign Strategic Arms Reduction Treaty (START).

State and local governments have worst fiscal year in decades.

Medical Milestones

Boston Scientific

Abbott Labs sends group of executives to scope out Boston Scientific as the purchase option date nears.

Abele made a plea to the Cardiovascular and Interventional Radiology Society of Europe and the Society of Cardiovascular and Interventional Radiology of the United States to devote more effort to promoting the value of interventional radiology "to the public, to the government, to the primary care physician, to the insurance companies, hospital administrators and all those people who may influence the acceptance of this specialty."

He ended by saying:

> *As a friend, but an "outsider," I am sensitive to offering gratuitous criticism and suggestions, but so many good things are happening technically and medically that to see less than the full promise of Interventional Radiology achieved is frustrating and disappointing. We owe it to Charles Dotter and the other pioneers, as well as to prospective patients, to help their dreams come true.*[58]

Also in 1987, Emory University, an institution world renowned for its heart research because of Gruentzig's work, received National Institutes of Health approval for an angioplasty-versus-surgery trial. This was the first randomized trial in which PTCA was pitted against coronary artery bypass graft (CABG) surgery.[59] In 1989, additional trials of PTCA versus CABG in multivessel disease got under way in the United States and Europe.[60]

The debate promised to extend into the indefinite future.

The inaugural meeting, in London in 1989, of the Society of Minimally Invasive Therapy. The society was one of the first to recognize interventional therapy in all its forms as belonging to the same school of thought.

The Bank of New England files for bankruptcy protection in the third largest bank failure in U.S. history.

Federal Deposit Insurance Corporation asks Congress for $70 billion in additional borrowing authority for its Bank Insurance Fund.

Boston Scientific posts sales of $243 million: Medi-Tech has $115 million, Microvasive Endoscopy has $45 million, Microvasive Urology has $29 million, and Mansfield has $54 million.

CHAPTER SIX

AN ADVOCATE FOR CHANGE

1992–1994

Three powerful forces—technology, global health care reform, and the new paradigm for business—are reshaping the world of medicine. Others may feel threatened by change. We welcome it. We hope to lead it.

—Joseph Ciffolillo, John Abele, and Pete Nicholas, 1992

IN THE EARLY 1990S, MEDICINE UNDERwent the most sweeping societal changes since the rise of modern surgical, interventional, and therapeutic techniques. This widespread instability was provoked by the skyrocketing cost of health care. Since the 1980s, health care costs had been increasing by almost 15 percent a year, driving up the cost of insurance. By the early 1990s, this burgeoning expense had put so much pressure on the system that something had to give way. Millions of Americans opted to forego expensive health insurance.

As a candidate in the 1992 presidential race, Bill Clinton proposed universal health coverage for Americans, coupled with cost controls to keep the expense of health care in line. After he won the election, Clinton sought to make his health care reform a reality and appointed the Clinton health care task force, led by his wife, Hillary, to study the subject and develop recommendations. The debate was loud and acrimonious.

Before long, almost every player in the health care arena was drawn into the fray as the task force assessed hospital fees, pharmaceuticals, surgical equipment, diagnostic fees, and preventative medicine.

Opposite: The brochure for the Microvasive Ultraflex esophageal prosthesis. Throughout the early 1990s, Boston Scientific's nonvascular businesses were the fastest growing in the company.

No successful bill to reform health care ever came out of the debate, but the effort ushered in a fundamental change in health care delivery in the United States. Health maintenance organizations (HMOs) began to multiply. These new mass insurers cut costs by signing up large numbers of people and used bargaining power with hospitals and doctors to keep prices down. Concurrently, the HMOs imposed guidelines on their members, such as dictating which doctors could be visited, which diagnostics were covered, and how long people could stay in the hospital.

The immediate effect of managed care on Boston Scientific was mildly negative. In 1993, the most raucous year of the debate, the company's growth rate dropped to 16 percent. Its stock also suffered, along with that of most medical companies.

But this was more of a reflexive whiplash across the entire medical industry than anything targeted at Boston Scientific. In truth, the company occupied one of the stronger positions in the entire health care debate and remained optimistic.

"We view this time of change and confusion as an opportunity to contribute further to the discussion," stated Boston Scientific's 1993 annual report, "to offer patients information and clear choices; and to develop and advocate innovative alternatives (treatments) that reduce risk, cost, trauma, and recovery time."[1]

This issue was so important to the company that almost the entire 1993 annual report was devoted to a discussion of the debate. On its cover, the company asked:

What is health care reform? It is not simply universal access, affordability and security for all—as important as these goals are. It is also "value." But what is "value?" Who decides? Who pays? How is it measured? Over what period of time? The central question we must answer together is: "What is appropriate?" not "What is possible?"

Advances in medicine, however, are continuing to make the impossible possible. This is creating a demand that costs more than society can or is willing to pay. Reform requires increased participation by patients as well as doctors in making tough choices. It requires increased measurability and visibility to understand the impact of these decisions, and constant improvement by providers of care and suppliers of technology to make better use of limited resources.

To innovate.
To do more, better, for less.[2]

All of the precepts that Boston Scientific had been preaching for decades suddenly became national priorities. Medicine had to become less expensive, yet effective, and not require such a major investment on the part of hospitals, doctors, and patients. Boston Scientific had predicted this long ago and positioned itself as the only deeply rooted company that was active in many of the young disciplines and devoted solely to interventional medicine.

But managed care wasn't without challenges for Boston Scientific. The company had traditionally sold directly to doctors and hospitals. In the era of managed care, Boston Scientific suddenly had a new customer: the economic buyer. This kind of customer included hospital chains, outpatient clinics, the federal government, and even

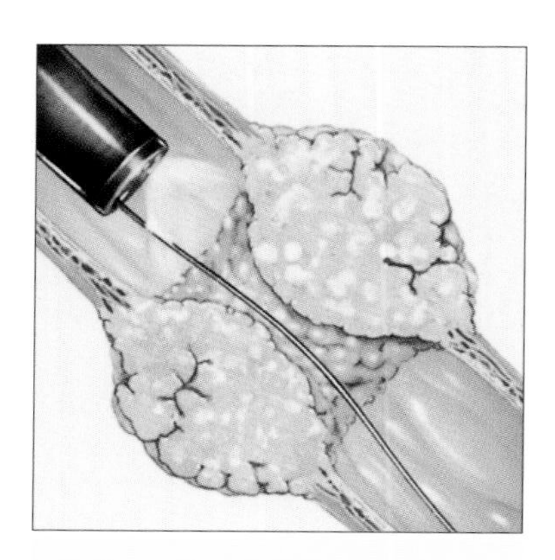
Pass guide wire beyond lesion.

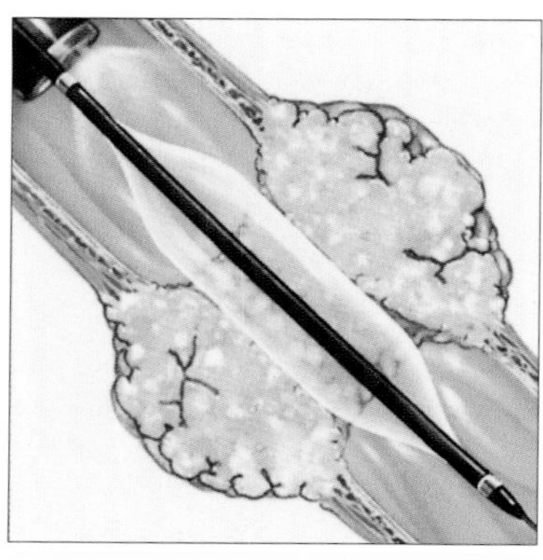
Pass balloon over guide wire and dilate lesion.

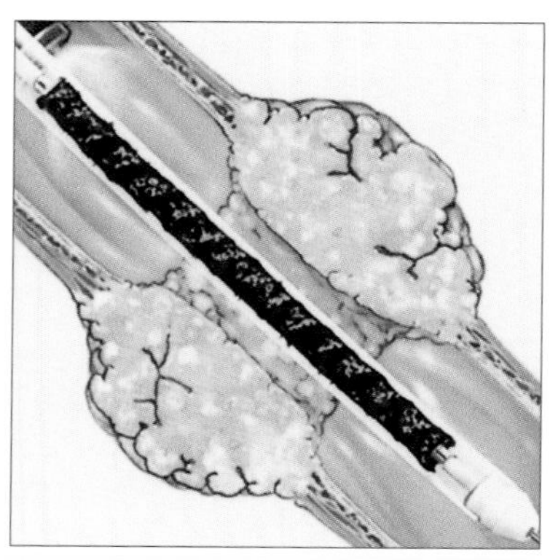
Introduce wax-covered collapsed esophageal stent.

1992...

World Events

The Yugoslav civil war spreads to Bosnia.

The U.S. intervenes in Somali famine.

Medical Milestones

The development and use of intravascular ultrasound languishes due to the nation's struggle to control health care costs.

Boston Scientific

Larry Best joins the company as chief financial officer.

large insurers, and these new customers were more interested in bottom-line results than the physician/decision-maker Boston Scientific had been serving.

Under this new model, Boston Scientific was expected to provide economic analysis for every product and procedure as well as efficacy and safety studies. This focus on cost raised further questions, such as whose perspective was important when it came to measuring cost? the patient's? the payer's? the hospital's? society's? insurance companies'? Or others'? These questions would not be easily answered.

This series of drawings shows an esophageal stent being put into place. Even into the 1990s, after interventional medicine had become more widespread and accepted, Boston Scientific was a commanding market leader in the GI market.

The Piper Calls

To Pete Nicholas the era was fraught with risk. In his view, the rise of economic buyers put the company in peril. "Nobody could understand it," Nicholas remembered.

> *We had come off three or four good years with strong growth. We had a very intact team. We had strong relationships with our customers. What was all this business about risk? It was enterprise risk that I was talking about. I was talking about the risk of sustained leadership and the risk of maintaining what I viewed as sustainable long-term competitive advantage. The political system is basically unfriendly to the notion of profit in health care. And here was the idea that some of the larger companies, which had much greater currency and much deeper pockets, could develop predatory pricing*

Wax dissolves.

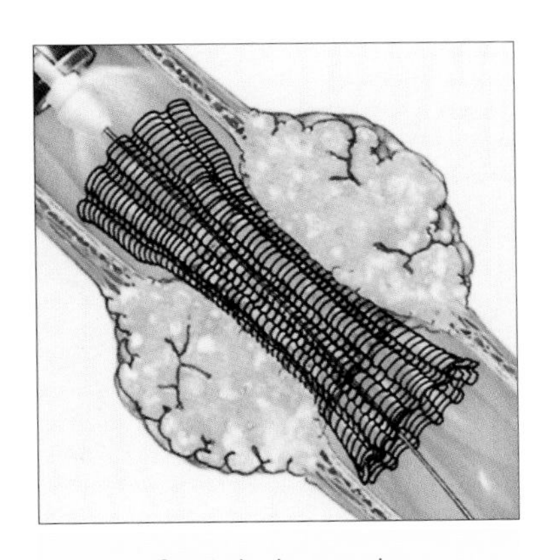

Stent slowly expands.

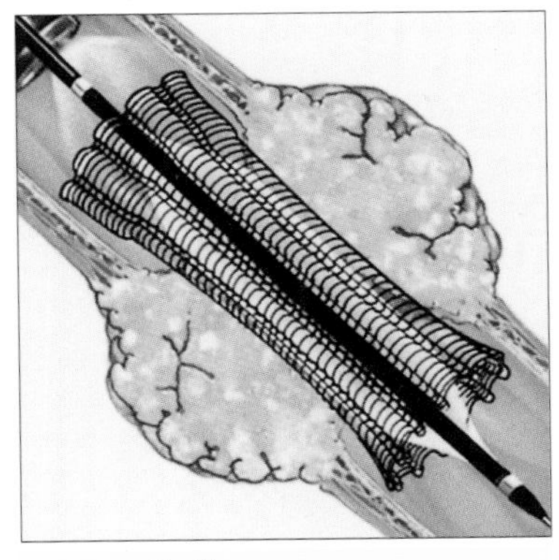

Continuous expansion pressure presses against lesion.

Rio de Janeiro hosts the Earth Summit.

Riots break out in Los Angeles after four police officers are acquitted of all but one charge in the beating of Rodney King.

A study suggests that angioplasty is being overused.

Boston Scientific goes public. John Abele and Pete Nicholas sell 25 percent for $450 million; at time of the IPO, BSC sales were $230 million, but because of BSC's quiet nature and confusing structure, many people thought they were only $50 million.

behavior aimed at taking us out in a number of ways. It was my view that in order for us to be able to compete in that world—which did not exist yet but was coming—we had to substantially bulk up, with size and technology.[3]

Yet before Boston Scientific could "bulk up," it had to deal with its past. Nine years before, Nicholas had set up a deal with Abbott Laboratories to help finance the company's early growth with a "buy option" at the end of that period. Throughout the relationship, Boston Scientific management had held Abbott at arm's length. As a result, the two companies had no interlocking board members, no intercompany projects, and no working relationship beyond the financial obligation, although Chuck Aschauer kept very involved in Boston Scientific's business.

"We created a situation with Chuck Aschauer of complete openness and transparency so that he, as an individual member of Abbott's executive committee and eventually board, was in a position of being able to say to Abbott's executive committee and board that he was up to speed with respect to all BSC issues," Nicholas said.[4]

In 1992, as Abbott's option to buy Boston Scientific matured, there was the very real possibility that Pete Nicholas and John Abele and the entire team of Boston Scientific management would become employees of Abbott Laboratories. Their strategy of the previous nine years had been to reinvest everything and make Boston Scientific grow quickly, yet show a profit near the end to make Boston Scientific's valuation a better reflection of the company's actual worth in the marketplace, or in Nicholas's words, "fully max out our financial profile."[5] The 1989 reorganization had turned Boston Scientific into a profitable company.

"Whether we wanted Abbott to buy us was of no importance," Nicholas said. "We had made this bargain and given them that option. We probably orchestrated the process a little bit to make us less attractive because I don't think we wanted to sell. It had nothing to do with any self-enrichment objective. It had to do with John's and my view that to allow Abbott to take this

By 1992, Boston Scientific offered thousands of products, each designed for a particular purpose. Pictured are an assortment of Boston Scientific products, including (from left to right across both pages) a ureteral stent, an abscess drainage catheter, an endoscopic biliary stent, an endomyocardial biopsy forceps, an endoscopic biopsy forceps, a urological biopsy forceps, a peripheral balloon dilatation catheter, a gastrointestinal balloon dilatation catheter, a coronary balloon dilatation catheter, three guiding catheters, and three urological stone removal instruments.

World Events

Hurricane Andrew ravages South Florida and Louisiana.

Medical Milestones

The Wall Street Journal *reports that angioplasty slows the increase in bypass surgeries.*

Boston Scientific

Boston Scientific announces an exclusive agreement with Hewlett-Packard to market and sell catheter-based intraluminal ultrasound imaging systems.

company over would have been the beginning of the end to this company as an agent for change."[6]

As Abbott began its investigation into an acquisition, it became fairly obvious that any move would be replete with difficulties. There was a significant cultural gap between Boston Scientific, a fast-growing device company that thrived on flexibility, and Abbott, described by Nicholas as "a product of the fairly massive, slow-moving, supertanker kind of drug industry mentality."[7]

Abbott itself had changed considerably since it had loaned Boston Scientific the original $21 million. By 1992, Abbott's pharmaceutical and diagnostic businesses were both booming. A medical device firm like Boston Scientific would have diluted the company's focus—especially at the going price. To buy Boston Scientific, based on the formula the two companies had agreed upon, would cost Abbott about $900 million.

Nevertheless, the deal deserved serious consideration on both sides. In August 1991, Abbott issued a confidential preliminary report estimating that the market for less-invasive hospital products was more than $1 billion annually and would continue to grow by double-digit leaps—especially considering that HMOs favored less-expensive interventional therapies and were willing to reimburse for them.

The comprehensive report also provided a rare glimpse into the Boston Scientific of the early 1990s. The company maintained three domestic plants and one international plant with about 1,500 employees worldwide. Each of the four operating divisions (Medi-Tech, Mansfield, Microvasive Endoscopy, and Microvasive Urology) "has a different position in and approach to their respective markets."[8] The international division, meanwhile, operated through three subsidiaries, which accounted for about 45 percent of international sales. The rest was sold through distributors.

Within its individual markets, Abbott noted that only two divisions had sales of more than $100 million, while the company "has not been able to achieve significant share in the PTCA market because of its limited product line and comparatively small sales force."[9] The report went on to note, however, that small markets were part of the company's success:

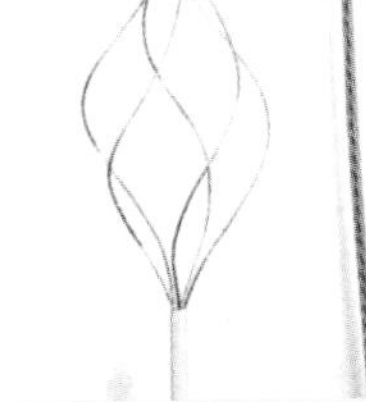

BSC has driven its sales by entering, and sometimes creating, relatively small

Unemployment in the U.S. reaches an eight-year high.

David Auth, creator of the Rotablator, takes Heart Technology public.

The Mansfield EP division is formed.

Gastrointestinal endoscopy is the fastest growth area for Boston Scientific.

markets with a wide variety of products. They place a high premium on being first-to-market, and attempt to offer complete lines to lock up customers. This philosophy has resulted in a product catalog with more than 1,700 catalog numbers. In addition, over 1,500 custom products are sold.[10]

Lastly, the report listed Boston Scientific's relative strengths and weaknesses. The company had developed a network of medical thought leaders and had an organization that allowed for quick decision making. It approached every market with a full line of products and had divided its sales organizations by specialty, which allowed "greater product pull, and an enhanced image." The report went on to predict that BSC sales would top $500 million by 1995.

On the downside, Abbott noted that the company suffered dearly for lack of a competitive PTCA balloon and that "BSC is weakest in cardiology, the largest segment of the less-invasive market." Also, Abbott observed that planning at Boston Scientific tended to be done on a short-term basis, even going so far as to say that "LRP-type planning is apparently non-existent." (Of course, this wasn't entirely accurate because Boston Scientific had a long-range planning function, but the efforts weren't formally documented.)

Finally, the most negative attribute from Abbott's point of view was management's uncertain position in relation to an acquisition: "In addition to Nicholas and Abele, the two principal shareholders, at least 40 other key employees will profit handsomely if BSC is acquired, obtaining approximately 10 percent of the purchase price. Their willingness to continue with BSC if acquired is not known."[11]

This was a critical point, prompting Abbott in late 1991 to sound out the company's senior management. "I had to sit there and smile for three days and explain our businesses in such a way that they didn't sound so great," remembered Joe Ciffolillo. "But down deep, I was as enthusiastic as hell about our business. I had to answer the questions honestly, but whenever they questioned something, that gave me the license to tell them all the bad things, and I took that license. When I came back after the third day, Pete said, 'How did you do?' I said, 'I don't think they're going to buy it.'"[12]

Ciffolillo's intuition was soon confirmed. Abbott issued another report that suggested the risks of acquisition were too high. The main deterrent, according to the report, was the alienation of Boston Scientific's senior management, many of whom would leave if Abbott took over the company. In January 1992, Abbott formally announced it would not buy Boston Scientific.

The Kimono Opens

Abbott's decision raised an entirely new dilemma. As a 20 percent owner of the company, Abbott was now in the market to unload its shares of Boston Scientific, meaning Boston Scientific was still vulnerable to a major outside influence. Nicholas and Abele hoped to find a more strategic buyer for 20 percent of their company.

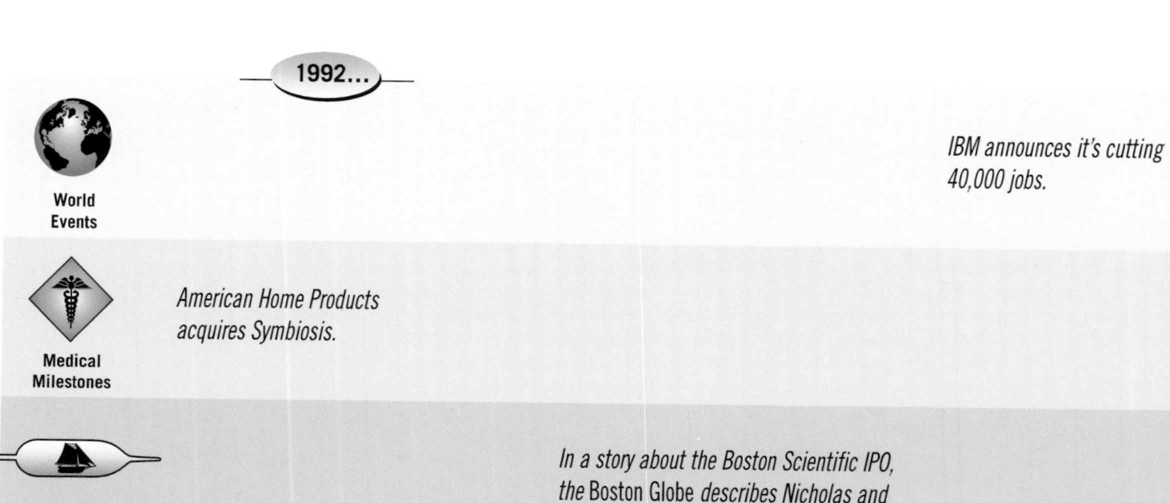

In 1992, Boston Scientific announced its plans for an initial public offering. As the IPO approached, Peter Nicholas, left, John Abele, center, and Joe Ciffolillo, right, traveled around the country giving presentations and promoting Boston Scientific to the investment and financial communities.

On February 19, 1992, Nicholas and Abele mailed a letter to Boston Scientific's employees discussing their plan:

Looking back over the past 12 years since our founding, we can all take great pride in our accomplishments. We are today a widely respected supplier of cost-effective medical devices. We are a thought leader in our chosen markets worldwide. Our relationships with physicians are stronger than ever, as is also our capacity to develop, manufacture and supply a wide variety of innovative "alternatives to surgery" that reduce risk, cost, trauma, and recovery time for the patient. We are financially sound as we plan for the post-Abbott plan....

The purpose of this letter is to tell you we have concluded the best way to accomplish [our plan] would be through an Initial Public Offering of BSC stock. Accordingly, we have initiated the rather involved process that should enable us to sell stock to the public.[13]

This decision had enormous implications for Boston Scientific. According to the *Boston Globe*, the partners were very reluctant about an initial public offering, or IPO:

It was the day they fervently hoped would never come.... To be fair, it wasn't so much the money that bothered the co-chairmen of Boston Scientific Corp. It was the fact that the two had to pose there smiling on the floor of the New York Stock Exchange, and formally cash in something they deeply cherished: their privacy.[14]

As Boston Scientific began the IPO, most people—including employees, competitors, and the general public—learned that they had made the same mistake Bill Cook had made when he met Joe Ciffolillo in 1983: They had grossly underestimated Boston Scientific's size and reach and had made the mistake of assuming Boston Scientific was a one- or two-technology company instead of one of the world's largest enterprises devoted to interventional medicine.

The Federal Reserve Board lowers two significant short-term interest rates to 3 percent, their lowest in 29 years.

Batman Returns *is the year's top-grossing film.*

Cost containment pressure and delays in new product approvals continue to affect the entire medical industry.

The company announces plans to acquire the 350-acre former site of Prime Computer's Natick headquarters, called Carling Park. Plans are canceled two weeks before closing date.

"Unlike most rapidly growing medical device companies," reported PaineWebber in 1992, "[Boston Scientific] is broadly diversified, not dependent upon a single product or even a single market.... [It] holds a leadership position in most markets in which it competes."[15]

While many competitors assumed the company had sales of about $50 million, in reality Boston Scientific reported sales of $230 million.[16] As the *Boston Globe* noted, Boston Scientific raised the art of being low-profile to a new low.[17]

Going public also had internal ramifications. Boston Scientific had existed so far without much of a corporate presence. There weren't established communication programs or much of a proven method for the parent corporation to effectively communicate with the four highly independent operating divisions.

To help employees understand their motives, Pete Nicholas and John Abele gave talks around the company in which they listed the possible negatives of going public, including the short-term focus of the stock market and a spotlight on the company's strategies, and then talked about the upsides. "At the same time, it enabled us to develop a currency for growth through acquisition using stock value," they said.[18]

The partners, who both stood to make a tremendous amount of money from an IPO, also quieted any suspicions that they were simply cashing out. Both Nicholas and Abele had publicly and loudly proclaimed for years that Boston Scientific was never founded for personal enrichment. During coverage of the IPO, the *Boston Globe* even dubbed

John Abele, posing in 1992 with a group of cardiologists. From left to right are Abele, Richard Myler, M.D.; J. Margolis, M.D., from Miami Heart; Nobayoshi from Japan; and Spencer King from Emory University. By now, Mansfield had an established valvuloplasty balloon but was still lacking a blue-chip coronary dilatation balloon.

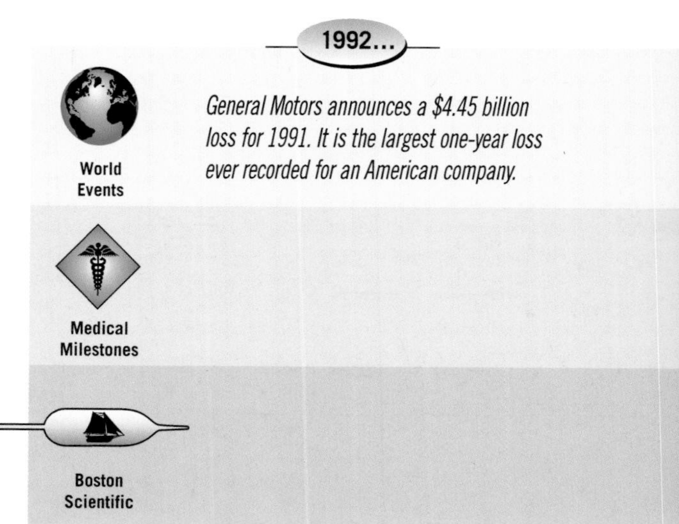

them the "reluctant millionaires."[19] Moreover, Abele and Nicholas used the IPO to reward employees with ownership in Boston Scientific.

Boston Scientific's introduction to the public marketplace was a carefully orchestrated maneuver. The company had no intention of being mistaken for a high-tech start-up, so it chose PaineWebber and Goldman Sachs, both very large financial institutions with high credentials, to underwrite the offering—instead of a firm that specialized in medical technology companies. And, instead of offering stock on the younger, more high-tech NASDAQ exchange, Boston Scientific chose to offer its initial shares of stock through the more conservative New York Stock Exchange.

Finally, in the month prior to the IPO, Abele, Nicholas, and Ciffolillo traveled extensively to promote Boston Scientific, which they had always tried

During the IPO road show, Abele, Ciffolillo, and Nicholas had to talk to many potential investors in a very short time. They traveled by limousine and occasionally by private jet.

to avoid doing in the past. During their presentations, they didn't talk about future products—a common practice during IPO roadshows—and instead focused on their record and the mission and goals that drove Boston Scientific forward.

"None of us had done this before," Ciffolillo remembered. "You work with your investment bankers to develop slides and tabletop presentations and then use them to tell people where you are and where you're going. Well, we had three pretty headstrong people, and all three of us started getting bored with this flip-job thing. So we started being more casual and talking, which made it flow better. Then as we got more casual, we just said what came to mind. We were three people who loved the subject we were talking about, who could get up and talk for hours about it."[20]

The trio seemed to experience more than their fair share of complications while they traveled the country promoting Boston Scientific. They arrived in Los Angeles just after the high-profile Rodney King case ended with the acquittal of L.A. police officers. As the plane landed, the passengers looked out and saw plumes of smoke and realized the city was in the middle of major rioting. The group, which had never been comfortable with the limousine service

1992...

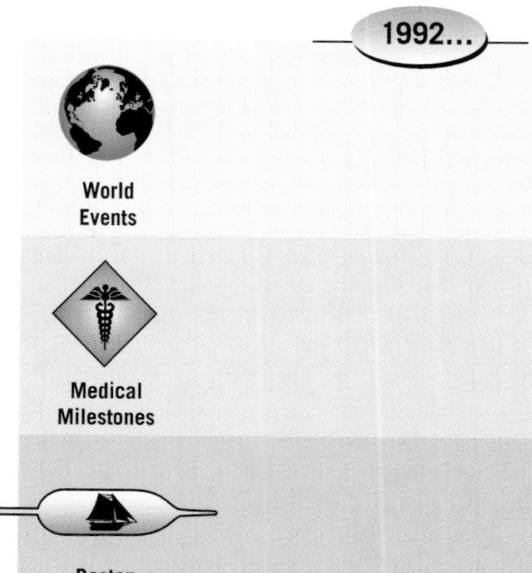

Laparoscopic cholecystectomy found safe.

Sales are $315 million, with Medi-Tech at $141 million. Mansfield has $58 million, Microvasive Endoscopy has $78 million, and Microvasive Urology has $38 million.

supplied by the banks, instead rented a van to travel through the city.

Back on the East Coast two weeks later, the team had a presentation scheduled at the Waldorf-Astoria Hotel in New York City. In the confusion before the event, John Abele got separated from his colleagues and somehow ended up at a Mary Kay convention while the other two sweated out his absence. He arrived just in time to give his third of the presentation.

The presentations themselves, however, went extraordinarily well, and word began to leak out that Boston Scientific would have one of the largest medical IPOs in history. Goldman Sachs's representatives often introduced the company as the "Microsoft of the medical device industry." Throughout, Abele, Nicholas, and Ciffolillo were more concerned with communicating the purpose of Boston Scientific. It was a company that wanted to empower patients and offer treatment alternatives that were less costly, less traumatic, and less risky.

The stock was scheduled to go out at $21, but the market hiccuped just before the offering. Nicholas pulled the price back to $17 a share, even though they could probably have gotten more. For outsiders, his move was a sign that Boston Scientific would wear its public mantle responsibly.

Reaping Rewards

On May 19, 1992, Abele, Nicholas, and Ciffolillo watched from the floor of the New York Stock Exchange as Boston Scientific rode the Big Board ticker for the first time. In all, the company offered 23.5 million shares of common stock at $17 per share. Of those shares, 18.8 million were offered in the United States and 4.7 million were offered outside the country. Boston Scientific granted the underwriters an option to buy an additional 3.525 million shares to cover over-allotments.[21] This sale represented about 25 percent of the company and netted $450 million, most of which was used to liquidate the Abbott Laboratories investment. For its initial investment of $21 million, Abbott received about $400 million in cash only nine years later.

Abele, Nicholas, and their respective family trusts retained a controlling interest in the company. Based on Boston Scientific's market valuation, their stakes in 1992 were valued at more than $500 million each.

The stock sank to $14 in June of that year, but it spent most of the summer valued at around $20. "The stock stinks," declared analyst Kurt Kruger a few days after Boston Scientific stock closed at around $15. However, he added, "We like it. We want to like it. We're recommending it, and now we're sitting here with egg on our faces." Kruger said the threat of President Bill Clinton's health care reform hurt medical stocks, but he estimated that Boston Scientific could grow to $500 million in sales by 1995.[22]

This kind of tortured but loving relationship with analysts turned out to be typical of Boston Scientific as a public company. "We were a model that was not immediately apparent to the marketplace," Nicholas said.

An HPN market report predicts that endoscopy will represent half of all surgeries in 1995.

When we went public, we ended up being a company whose sales in certain segments were larger than maybe the market thought the total segment sales were. It caused an awful lot of people to go back and redo the market math, and we didn't help them a lot because we didn't really tell people how much of our $300 million in revenue was international or Medi-Tech or cardiology.

We became a darling of Wall Street within that small intelligentsia of people who are very focused on this business, but we were also an enigma and somewhat of an anathema because we were viewed as kind of a stealth enterprise. That is something analysts really don't understand or think about. We're not focused on value in the stock market. We've been focused on value to our customers, and our view is that if we do that well, the value of the market will reflect it.[23]

At the end of the year, Boston Scientific put together its very first annual report, a document the company designed more for its employees than for the public. Five pages of the document were devoted to printing the name of every Boston Scientific employee. The cover was simple, emblazoned with the company's trademark image of a ship in a balloon, along with the company's philosophy:

To BSC, less-invasive medicine is improved outcomes: patients returning to work sooner; patients of all ages benefiting from improved quality of life. It is physicians across diverse medical specialties doing more for less; intervening in new ways that reduce trauma, risk and cost. To BSC, less-invasive medicine is procedures, not just products. Knowledge, not just technology. To BSC, less-invasive medicine is a wide open playing field, with no boundaries but those defined by doing the right thing. Matching a need with a procedural solution. Being driven by a set of values and principles to make a difference.[24]

Similarly, the letter to shareholders was devoted to describing Boston Scientific's mission, explaining some of its recent moves, and talking about how the company was responding to the powerful changes rocking the world of medicine, including global health care reform and high technology:

Abbott Laboratories deserves a special note of recognition and gratitude.... Our ten-year association was a critical block in BSC's success. Without it, we could not have become the company we are today. In addition to Abbott's wise counsel, its investment allowed us to keep most of the ownership of BSC in the hands of our people. Today, even after our public offering, the men and women of this company own 75 percent of its equity.[25]

In 1992, the first time it publicly announced sales, Boston Scientific reported revenue of $315.2 million, a 37 percent increase from 1991.[26] The company had 2,051 employees, including 1,272 in operations, 156 in administration, 176 in research and development, and 447 in sales, marketing, distribution, and administrative support. Of the

1993...

World Events

The GATT trade agreement is signed; NAFTA is approved.

The Maastricht Treaty takes effect, forming the European Union.

Medical Milestones

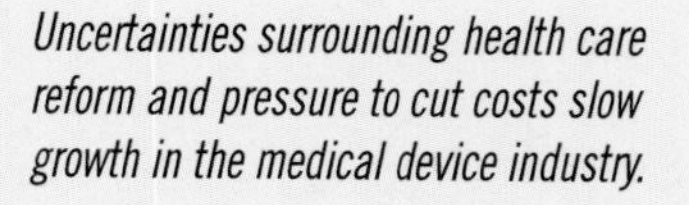

Uncertainties surrounding health care reform and pressure to cut costs slow growth in the medical device industry.

Boston Scientific

The FDA approves Synergy, the first in a family of new-generation convertible PTCA catheter systems under development at BSC.

Shares plunge to $10 as the medical industry is rocked by the health care reform debate.

total number of employees, 178 worked outside the United States.[27]

A week after the IPO, Boston Scientific elected Charles Aschauer to the board of directors.[28] Later that year, Joel L. Fleishman, first senior vice president at Duke University, joined the board.

The executive committee included Nicholas, Abele, Ciffolillo, Michael Mabrey as vice president of operations, and Robert Anderson as general counsel. Later that year, Larry Best joined Boston Scientific as the chief financial officer. Formerly, Best was a partner in the Boston office of the accounting firm Ernst & Young.[29]

Elbow Room

Although going public had its drawbacks, it was a critical element in Nicholas's strategy for the future. The IPO gave Boston Scientific a degree of freedom and capital it had never had before. At this point in its history, considering the rapidly changing face of medicine, Boston Scientific had desperate need for both. The company was at a critical juncture: it needed to grow even faster and cover more specialties or it risked becoming a small part of an industry that had grown beyond it, an interesting footnote in the early days of interventional medicine. This was the time when Nicholas's talk of "enterprise creation" would really be put to the test. The company wasn't looking to become the world expert in just one field or a small player in many, as Aschauer had criticized it for doing years before. Rather, it sought market leadership in all of interventional medicine. It wanted to lead the revolution, not be swept away by it.

The first order of business, however, was securing more space. Early in 1992, Abele and Nicholas announced that Boston Scientific was looking for new headquarters and might even consider moving out of Watertown because the site was developed to its limits.

Local officials, who had grown accustomed to the homegrown company, were dismayed. In the *Middlesex News*, Chamber of Commerce director Hope Tsacoyeanes said, "We were very, very disturbed at the thought of losing them. The thing about Boston Scientific is that they give back to the community. They keep a very large presence in town."[30]

Boston Scientific had been active with the Watertown Boys and Girls Clubs and often opened its facilities to outside groups. In addition, the company granted a scholarship to a Watertown student each year, and it kept its property in immaculate shape. In a July letter to Nicholas, town manager Joseph Painter implored the company to stay:

> *I would like to take this opportunity to offer our assistance in encouraging your remaining and expanding in Watertown. We would like to ensure [that] the benefits of retaining your Watertown location be significant and feasible. Our cooperation could include attractive financing through the Watertown Industrial Development Finance Authority, other lower cost financing available through joint State-Town programs, assistance on negotiations with Guilford Industries regarding the railroad right-of-way access, and an efficient process for new construction or rehabilitation.*[31]

Despite this apparent cooperation from town officials, some residents believed Boston Scientific's intention to move was due in part to unfriendly treatment from the local zoning board. Boston Scientific and the town government had a history of disputes involving parking and a number of other issues. One of the main disputes concerned the company's efforts to connect two of its buildings along Pleasant Street. Boston Scientific won approval from the planning board, but its request was later denied by the zoning board of appeals. The company challenged the ruling in land court, and the court decided that the matter should be reviewed again by the board.[32]

Boston Scientific declined to pursue the matter, however, and on July 20, 1992, the company announced plans to acquire the former site of Prime Computer's headquarters in Natick, Massachusetts, for $26 million. Nicholas announced he would shift headquarters and at least some manufacturing from Watertown to the sprawling Natick campus. Located on Route 9, just a mile from the Massachusetts Turnpike and overlooking Lake Cochituate, the facility featured a 4,600-square-foot fitness center, a 45-seat auditorium, and extensively landscaped grounds.[33] Nicholas said he was particularly drawn to the 300,000 square feet of manufacturing space and the large conference rooms.[34]

Vacated by Prime in 1991, the Natick campus "had become yet another symbol of the deterioration of the state's minicomputer makers, which included Wang Laboratories Inc., Data General Corp., and Digital

Equipment Corp.," according to the *Boston Globe*. Before Prime took over in 1979, the buildings were home to the Carling Brewery.

"Those buildings have many living lessons in them," Abele told the *Boston Globe*. "We just wonder whether those ghosts will be positive or negative."[35]

On October 6, 1992, roughly two weeks before the scheduled closing date, Boston Scientific abruptly canceled its plans to buy the Natick campus. The company did not elaborate but simply said that "certain contingencies had not been satisfied." The announcement stunned and baffled many people who were not on the inside and touched off widespread speculation about Boston Scientific's motivation.

The *Tab*, a local paper, reported that Natick business officials were excited when Boston Scientific agreed to buy the biggest vacant commercial office space in town. "But the dream turned sour in October when Boston Scientific officials announced the deal was off," the paper reported. "Although a full explanation was not given, it appeared that the company wanted guarantees that local and state taxes would be fixed for five years, which the town is prohibited from doing by state law."[36]

In reality, the company's refusal to consummate the deal had more to do with environmental and

Both pages: In 1993, Boston Scientific announced plans to purchase Carling Park in nearby Natick. The attractive waterfront property was large, but Boston Scientific still planned on expanding.

World Events

Floods ravage the Midwest.

Britain and Ireland work toward the Ulster Peace.

Medical Milestones

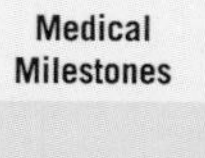

Boston Scientific

The sales force is expanded to 330.

Boston Scientific begins expanding in Spencer, Indiana, and Denmark.

Jean Baptiste Honore of France, at 89 years old, receives the first Boston Scientific percutaneous aneurysm graft and returns to his normal routine in three days.

labor issues than tax privileges. Nevertheless, Boston Scientific reopened its search and by early 1993 was eyeing a 53-acre parcel on the South Boston waterfront known as the Subaru Terminal. At the time, the property was being used to store equipment and dirt used in the construction of the Third Harbor Tunnel to Logan Airport and to park automobiles unloaded at a nearby ship terminal.

As Boston Scientific considered its alternatives, even discussing moving out of Massachusetts,

1993...

World Events

The FBI raids the Branch Davidian religious cult compound near Waco, Texas.

Inflation remains low.

Boeing announces thousands of job cuts.

Medical Milestones

C. R. Bard pleads guilty to 391 counts of manufacturing unapproved heart catheters, which caused one death and 20 emergency heart surgeries.

Heart Technology's Rotablator receives FDA approval for use in coronaries.

Boston Scientific

At the 1993 RSNA meeting, among the new products Medi-Tech introduces are an abdominal aortic aneurysm graft and drug delivery systems.

Opposite: The Natick site eventually became headquarters for Boston Scientific, and soon the corporate and administrative offices began moving over from Watertown, which was converted entirely into a manufacturing facility.

the trustees of Carling Park Trust, along with state and local officials, tried to woo the company back to Natick. They dropped their price by $4 million, resolved the zoning issues, arrived at an assessment agreement based on purchase price, and offered to help with environmental permits.[37] Their efforts paid off.

On May 20, 1993, Boston Scientific announced it would buy Carling Park. The company planned to use the Natick complex as its new corporate headquarters and house its manufacturing in Watertown.[38]

After signing the deal, Nicholas said, "This remains a very expensive state to do business in. Massachusetts, long term, is not an attractive place to be for manufacturing." But Boston Scientific was reluctant to set up headquarters in another state. "We have a team here, and we don't want to put that at risk," he said.[39]

As Boston Scientific moved to Natick, it was a large enough company that Abele and Nicholas found themselves in a strange position. Their company had always thrived on closeness, openness, and the ability to move quickly. Even while it was growing so quickly through the 1980s, it retained the flavor of a small company since, in fact, it actually was three small companies united under one corporate umbrella. After the reorganization and the public offering, however, Boston Scientific began to confront an issue that would become more relevant as time passed: how to maintain its culture while becoming a multinational, public corporation.

Also, the company didn't have an organized approach. Boston Scientific still didn't have a sophisticated internal communication apparatus in place. "We've always considered ourselves great communicators," said Jamie Rubin. "But as you grow larger, it's about the tools and methods that you use to communicate. One of John's favorite sayings is, 'You don't know what you don't know.' Unfortunately, it can be difficult to find out what you don't know. There was no formal method of communication."[40]

While the company was growing quickly and moving into friendly markets without provoking strong controversy, the issue of internal communication was mostly cerebral. In the coming years, however, when the company's culture, integrity, and framework would be tested severely, the ability to quickly move messages through the organization and make decisions would become critical.

Expanding Ireland

As the domestic side of Boston Scientific continued to outgrow its administrative and manufacturing facilities, the overseas division was getting smaller by comparison. Though the company's

Bill Clinton is inaugurated as U.S. president; he introduces legislation containing managed competition proposals as part of his health care reform.

The top-grossing film is Jurassic Park.

Sales are $380 million; earnings are $70 million. Medi-Tech has sales of $160 million; Mansfield, $62 million; Microvasive Endoscopy, $111 million; and Microvasive Urology, $46 million.

The Carling Park deal is revived. Boston Scientific pays $22 million for the facility, which will house corporate administration, marketing, sales, R&D, and a pilot plant.

Danish manufacturing facility had more than tripled in size through recent construction projects, the international division accounted for only 13 percent of sales in 1992—not a very impressive number in the medical devices field.

There were myriad reasons for this, including the unique and challenging obstacles that Boston Scientific subsidiaries encountered in each of their respective countries. Similar to taste in food and clothing, the medical communities' preferences and needs were different in each Boston Scientific country.[41] In Japan, for example, a Boston Scientific newsletter noted:

> *Due to the relatively heavy consumption of salt and dried foods in the Japanese diet, the incidence of gastrointestinal disease is higher in the Japanese market than in other major markets in which international operates. Accordingly, relative sales in this product area are higher in Japan than in Germany, France, or Denmark.*
>
> *Because the Japanese consume only small amounts of meats and fat in their diet, the incidence of vascular and coronary artery disease is correspondingly lower in Japan than in other countries. Nonetheless, Japan is a good market for dilatation products, and Boston Scientific enjoys an important place in the radiology dilatation market.*[42]

After taking into account the differences from country to country, Boston Scientific management believed there were still fertile markets to be tapped overseas. Intent on increasing its presence in Europe, on February 2, 1994, Boston Scientific announced plans to construct a manufacturing facility in Galway, Ireland. Mike Mabrey headed up the project to establish the company's second international plant. Unlike in Denmark, where the focus had been solely to supply Europe and develop outside the FDA's reach, the facility in Ireland would focus on manufacturing efficiency and take advantage of Ireland's business-friendly atmosphere.

"We needed a major location that could supply products for the international division," Mabrey said. "A lot of the major device companies operate in Ireland. So we went over and tested the

1994...

World Events

After a raucous debate, Congress abandons health care reform.

Medical Milestones

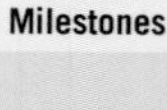

Boston Scientific

water and decided it was the right time for Boston Scientific. We found this very small building, roughly 20,000 square feet, that used to belong to Wilson's Sporting Goods. We did a renovation there, and at the same time, we were trying to build a new manufacturing facility so we could get started very quickly."[43]

The plant, which was to be constructed in three phases, would ultimately encompass 400,000 square feet and employ more than 2,000 people. "The Ireland facility will be strategic to our growing international business and will at the same time serve to reduce the Company's overall effective income tax rate," Nicholas said.[44] The Galway plant began shipping product in September 1994.[45]

That same year, Paul LaViolette, formerly president of the USCI division of C. R. Bard, became president of Boston Scientific International. He replaced retiring Jerry Lacey.[46]

"Basically, international had always been an afterthought," LaViolette said. "When I came on, international was growing at about 13 percent a year. The first thing we did was to say, 'How do we strengthen the current companies that we have?' We began by making management changes in Japan and in France."[47]

In the mid-1990s, Boston Scientific expanded its overseas capacities in France (above) and Denmark (right). The Denmark facility would be eventually be closed in favor of production in Ireland.

Opposite: The Boston Scientific offices in Tokyo were located on several floors in this complex. Japan remained an important market for Boston Scientific, especially its radiology products.

Republicans gain control of the House and Senate for the first time since 1954.

Civil war erupts in Rwanda.

Paula Corbin Jones files a sexual harassment suit against Clinton.

Managed care sparks the trend to merge and consolidate health care services; BSC's customers want fewer suppliers who can provide a broader range of products.

Boston Scientific buys Datascope's angioplasty business for $3 million, acquiring Integra PTCA catheters.

The combined effects of new manufacturing and new management finally began to raise international's growth rate. In 1994, the international division grew by 18 percent.

At the Frontier of Medicine

At home, Boston Scientific continued to delve into its various specialties. As technology proliferated, Boston Scientific became involved in some very exciting research projects, each offering the potential to change the course of treatment for thousands of patients. This ability to help people was one of the major psychological benefits working at Boston Scientific and something oft repeated by its employees.

To gain access into new markets, or create markets that hadn't existed only a couple years before, Boston Scientific continued to rely on its proven methods. When a specialty or technology became important enough to warrant it, a new division or sales force was created to fiercely specialize in that area. One of these was formed on June 1, 1992. Called Mansfield EP, the new division was designed to focus solely on electrophysiology, a specialty within cardiology that dealt with the heart's highly complex electrical conduction system.[48]

Market leadership in cardiology remained an important—and still missing—piece of Boston Scientific's plan. In January 1993, years after the original target date, Mansfield received FDA approval to market Synergy, the first in a family of new-generation PTCA catheter systems. Although there had been four or five other PTCA catheters from Mansfield, none had been successful, and Boston Scientific had been forced to watch companies like USCI/Bard, ACS, and Schneider grow rapidly in the exploding cardiology market.

A Breakthrough in Ultrasound

Fortunately, Boston Scientific's fortunes were not tied to cardiology. Its Medi-Tech division main-

1994...

World Events

The Russian army invades Chechnya.

Medical Milestones

Senator Edward Kennedy submits a bill to speed federal decisions on new medical devices.

Boston Scientific

The company holds 90 U.S. and 85 foreign patents and has 102 U.S. and 131 foreign patent applications pending.

The new manufacturing plant in Galway, Ireland, begins shipping product.

The plant in Galway, Ireland, was announced in 1994. Within a few years, Galway would grow into Boston Scientific's largest overseas manufacturing facility.

tained market leadership in peripheral vascular therapy, while Microvasive Endoscopy and Microvasive Urology continued to dominate their smaller, but no less demanding, fields. At any given time, Boston Scientific had hundreds of projects going, many of them partnerships with other companies or doctors. One of these—the company's intravascular ultrasound project—came to fruition in the early and mid-1990s.

Boston Scientific had long sought a way to provide inside visibility of a catheter at work, including the novel but ultimately unsuccessful Visicath project of years before. Similarly, a project to develop an intravascular ultrasound device had been con-

The IRA announces a cease-fire in Northern Ireland.

Boston Scientific introduces a new marketing division, Insurg, to provide gynecological diagnostic and therapeutic devices. The division is disbanded that same year.

ceived in the mid-1980s, when it became possible to shrink ultrasound devices to catheter size. At the time, however, even the larger external vascular ultrasound probes were handmade and cost as much as $5,000 each, far too much for a disposable device.

Boston Scientific took the approach that any device needed to be cost effective, and to that end the company formed a team to develop and commercialize a low-cost minuscule ultrasound device that fit inside a human vessel, or was "intravascular."

By 1988, Boston Scientific, working with Diasonics, a California ultrasound console manufacturer, was ready to announce its first intravascular ultrasound device at the RSNA meeting. Used to view the inside of vessels, it was approved for a wide variety of noncoronary indications.

Although this technology had the potential to be a breakthrough medical development, the partnership with Diasonics had soured, leaving Boston Scientific looking for a new partner. At last Boston Scientific settled on Hewlett-Packard, which had a medical division based in Andover, Massachusetts. The partnership agreement was announced in mid-1992, and shortly after, the two companies introduced the HP Sonos intravascular imaging system, which used Boston Scientific's catheter-tip ultrasound transducers to provide high-resolution, 360-degree internal images of the blood vessels and heart chambers.

This device turned out to have many unforeseen benefits. Prior to its development, the medical establishment assumed that arteriosclerosis was an isolated phenomenon, meaning that only one area of an artery would occlude while the rest remained relatively free from obstruction.

"When we look at a coronary angiogram with an x ray, we see an open area and a narrow area," said Bob Arcangeli, who worked on the development team. "Once we got in with ultrasound, we saw a completely different picture. We saw that the open areas were just those areas that had not closed down yet, but were on their way to closing down. Arteriosclerosis can be a very diffuse disease that is present throughout the entire coronary artery system."[49]

While intravascular ultrasound would remain a limited but important technique in the years to come, the arrangement between Hewlett-Packard and Boston Scientific would not last, eventually ending in a lawsuit.

The Gauntlet Is Thrown—To No Effect

Although the government-directed efforts at health care reform fizzled, they had set in motion profound changes. Cost had suddenly moved to the forefront as a major issue, and larger companies were naturally at an advantage through economies

Opposite: A Microvasive booth at a trade show in the mid-1990s. Microvasive Endoscopy was the fastest growth segment in Boston Scientific. Like Medi-Tech, all the divisions relied heavily on trade shows to reach potential clients and opinion leaders.

1994...

World Events

A major earthquake hits Los Angeles.

Medical Milestones

Many raw materials suppliers halt sales to Massachusetts medical device companies for fear of liability lawsuits.

Boston Scientific

Boston Scientific is number eight on the Boston Globe*'s Top 100 list.*

Boston Scientific Europe has great success with Ultraflex stent family of products.

Mexico devalues its currency and shocks international investors.

Key executives join Boston Scientific, including Art Rosenthal in research, Paul LaViolette in international, and Bob Hargraves in information services.

N. J. Nicholas, Peter Nicholas's brother, joins BSC board.

of scale. Also, as interventional medicine gained more publicity and became even more widespread, patients began to demand it in place of traumatic and time-consuming surgery whenever possible and doctors began to rely on the tests with increasing frequency. Paradoxically, the very qualities that made it so desirable also made it the subject of controversy.

On November 11, 1992, an article appeared in the *New England Journal of Medicine* suggesting that coronary angiography was being overused. This article was covered widely in the mainstream press, including the *Boston Globe*:

> *Half of the more than one million high-technology tests done in this country every year to diagnose clogged arteries are unnecessary or could be postponed, Boston-area researchers estimate based on a small study of patients being released today.*
>
> *The study suggests that overuse of coronary angiography, as the test is called, could partly account for the dramatic increase over the last decade in heart bypass surgery and balloon angioplasty to clear blocked blood vessels, despite the drop in heart disease in the United States.*
>
> *Because the test allows physicians and patients to see blood vessel blockage, the urge to "fix the plumbing" takes over and surgery or angioplasty is done, even though clearing out the blockage has not been proven to reduce heart attack risk, said Dr. Thomas B. Graboys, one of the authors of the study published today. He says that in many cases medication would be the preferred treatment.*[50]

On November 25, 1992, the *Wall Street Journal* picked up the thread but extended the cry of "overusage" to PTCA itself: "The rise in the number of coronary bypasses—long criticized as too expensive and sometimes unnecessary—is slowing, according to a report by HCIA, a health-care information company in Baltimore. In contrast, according to HCIA, the number of balloon angioplasties grew steadily to more than 300,000 last year from about 200,000 in 1988."

Ultimately, while sides were drawn in the sand and research was debated, coronary angioplasty continued to be a heavily used procedure.

Later, the *New York Times* covered the implications of managed care in an article entitled "When Doctors Say Yes and Insurers No." Writer Gina Kolata described how intravascular ultrasound was languishing due to the nation's struggle to control medical costs. Cardiologist Jeffrey Isner of St. Elizabeth's Hospital in Boston told Kolata that the high-tech test "could be the most important change in the way we evaluate patients with coronary disease in the last 30 years." According to Kolata, the test "shows the inside of a patient's blood vessels with detail so fine, and images so pure, that the only thing comparable is to split open the blood vessels at autopsy and look at them."

But each intravascular ultrasound procedure cost several thousand dollars, and insurance

World Events

The top-grossing film is Forrest Gump.

Medical Milestones

Boston Scientific

Forbes *magazine publishes an article about Abele and Nicholas, calling them "An Odd Couple."*

Microvasive Endoscopy receives FDA approval in September 1994 to market the Ultraflex esophageal stent system for treatment of advanced esophageal cancer.

companies were beginning to refuse to pay for such expensive tests.[51]

This debate, which was conducted in the nation's hospitals, newspapers, and living rooms, certainly did not end when national attention finally shifted away from health care sometime in 1994. Instead, it simply went underground, to continue indefinitely as more complicated procedures become possible and an aging population needs ever more medical support. Boston Scientific, however, remained willing to confront the questions raised by managed care. In its 1994 annual report, the letter to shareholders contained an eloquent statement of the company's future in health care:

As the health care system continues its transformation, so does our market. The trend to merge and consolidate health care services gathered steam in 1994 and is likely to continue.... BSC entered 1994 ready to respond to these rapidly changing market demands. During the year, we invested strategically in a number of initiatives that will enable us to maintain our powerful competitive advantage. We leave 1994 positioned to offer one of the broadest product lines in the world for minimally invasive therapies and prepared to take advantage of the opportunities that exist globally in less-invasive medicine.[52]

The U.S. economy remains strong.

Boston Scientific has sales of $450 million. Medi-Tech has $181 million; Mansfield, $68 million; Microvasive Endoscopy, $141 million; Microvasive Urology, $55 million; others, $5 million.

TITAN

CHAPTER SEVEN

BUYING POWER

1995–1997

The acquisitions have helped the company to reach a certain strategic mass which should enable it to compete more effectively in, and better absorb the pressures of, the current health care environment of cost containment, managed-care, large buying groups, and hospital consolidations.

—Boston Scientific's 10-K Report, 1996

THROUGHOUT THE FRACTIOUS HEALTH care debate of 1992 and 1993, many people had pointed to the growing strength of managed care as the savior of the system. It could, they said, control health care costs better than a federally managed national health care program such as the Clintons were proposing. By stressing preventative medicine and cost control through sheer size, managed care represented free market forces.

This cheerful optimism would be sorely tested. However, after the Clinton health care debate fizzled out because of the political impossibility of restructuring the U.S. health care system, managed care had proliferated.

Logically, companies like Boston Scientific would seem likely to welcome managed care—and it's true that the system presented great opportunity for a company that was focused on reducing time, trauma, and cost to patients. But managed care was not without tremendous challenges. Instead of fundamentally changing the delivery of health care, insurance companies and providers began to look for easier ways to save money. The most logical was cost reduction.

Soon, managed care plans, with their thousands of patients and lists of approved doctors and procedures, began to put even more pressure on the system to reduce or shift costs. As a result, hospitals and health care providers struggled to form voluntary buying groups, which could bring enormous price pressure to bear on supplier companies like Boston Scientific. Columbia, which owned its own network of hospitals, was a successful early model for these buying groups. (It was later involved in a billing fraud scandal that derailed its efforts.)

Most of the buying groups didn't fare well. Because of their voluntary membership, early participation was fairly low. And confusion often resulted because national buying groups weren't capable of making allowances for regional and local differences. At Boston Scientific, which at first had only two or three people dealing with the economic buying groups, there was a sense of watchfulness in upper management. In the early 1990s, the company formed an advisory group that was composed of leaders from many different segments of the health care system, including the president of Columbia and the chairman of the Mayo Clinic Foundation.

"The people who attended these meetings were people who ran medical schools and health care systems," said John Abele, himself a participant. "We were trying to understand what the critical issues were and therefore what we should be doing as a supplier of technology."[1]

At the same time, Boston Scientific was slow to partner with any of the buying groups because it was apparent they were based on flawed economics. Ostensibly, the groups offered volume discounts to

Opposite: Vascular graft manufacture in Meadox. These Jacquard looms were used to knit fabric for endovascular stent grafts. Boston Scientific bought Meadox during a buying binge in 1995 and 1996.

their members and relied on voluntary participation from suppliers. However, since buying participation was voluntary, companies like Boston Scientific were put in the position of offering deep discounts with no guarantee of greater sales volume.

With this kind of diffuse pressure, it wasn't long before something shifted. The industry of medicine began a rapid and profound consolidation. Hospitals began buying one another, and larger, regional health care systems spread across the landscape. This consolidation had the same effect as the theorized buying groups: downward pressure on prices by purchasing in greater volume. Soon Boston Scientific formed a Corporate Marketing Group, which was devoted to selling to the new larger entities.

In the early 1990s, Peter Nicholas had warned Boston Scientific of the risk inherent in managed care, and both founders spent a lot of time talking about Boston Scientific's place in the future. At the time, before the Clinton health care debate and after several strong financial years, this red flag seemed like "a bit of an extraordinary statement." As it turned out, the statement wasn't extraordinary but prescient. By 1995, the risk had become apparent; Boston Scientific found itself under increasing pressure to cave to buying consortiums and in danger of being outflanked by much larger rivals. Fortunately, Boston Scientific had a plan.

Nicholas called it "strategic mass." This concept was different from critical mass, or the idea that once a company reaches a certain size, it can achieve economies of scale and grow very rapidly. Under the Nicholas vision of strategic mass, Boston Scientific wouldn't seek size for the sake of growth. Instead, it sought targeted leadership in its specialties, and it sought size for the sake of influence in the emerging world of dollars-and-cents health care. Acquisition would be the tool Nicholas would use to accomplish his vision.

Nicholas's first experience with this idea, and the difficulties it entailed, had come in the early 1980s. A habitual deal maker, Nicholas was continually exploring alliances and acquisitions with many companies. At one point in the late 1980s, Johnson & Johnson had even expressed an interest in buying Boston Scientific—something that Boston Scientific management seriously considered but ultimately didn't pursue.

Around the same time, Nicholas made overtures to the board of directors at C. R. Bard, hoping to orchestrate a merger. But nothing ever materialized. "We were never really able to make sense of that company or have conversations with its management that were responsive to our view and vision of the world," Nicholas said. "I made a very determined effort to merge with Bard and spent the better part of a year in periodic discussions with its CEO and chairman of the board. It was largely that experience that was in the back of my mind all the way up into the nineties."[2]

When Nicholas again approached the idea of rapid growth through acquisition, however, Boston Scientific was in a much better position. The IPO had given the company a vast amount of currency. In the early 1990s, Nicholas held a meeting in New

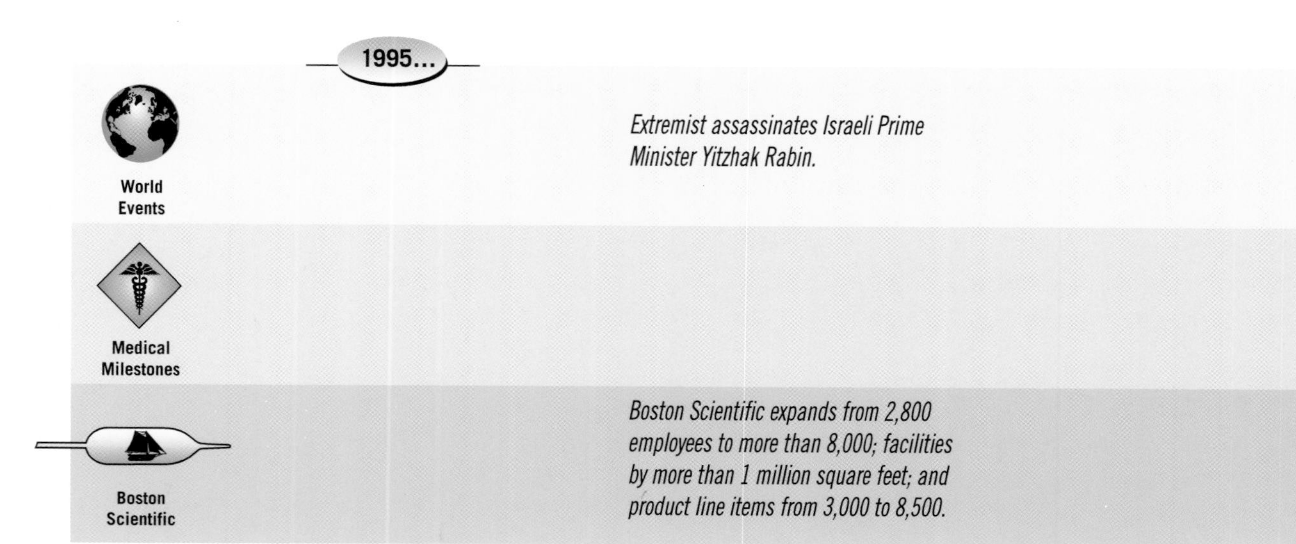

York and outlined an ambitious plan to acquire multiple medical device and technology companies that would complement Boston Scientific.

"Pete has always loved big marker boards so he could outline his planning in extreme detail," remembered Abele of this meeting. "And he did that. You could look at the board as he wrote and see the outline emerging. It had a diagrammatic structure and lists that were carefully tabulated and indented to show how each of these activities related to one another. I see this kind of planning sometimes with consultants, but what's different about the way Pete does it is that it's not prepared. It comes out of his head and flows, and he's constantly writing and erasing, and you can see a structure emerge before your eyes."[3]

The structure that emerged that day addressed Boston Scientific's two major weaknesses. At the time, its international sales remained only 20 percent of total sales, and it had never gained a significant share of the important PTCA (percutaneous transluminal coronary angioplasty) market. Nicholas's acquisitions, if they were successful, would address each of these weaknesses while strengthening Boston Scientific's hold in its traditional specialties.

Of the companies that Nicholas outlined that day, all but one would join the Boston Scientific family over the next three years as he orchestrated an incredible string of acquisitions, each with its own character. Some of the acquisitions were strategic in nature, while some were designed to add products and reinforce technologies. Boston Scientific would acquire Cardiovascular Imaging Systems, SCIMED, Vesica, Heart Technology, EPT, Meadox, Symbiosis, MinTec, and Target Therapeutics.

SCIMED

Announced near the end of 1994, SCIMED's acquisition was the biggest and most important in Boston Scientific's history. Looking back two years later, a Merrill Lynch report remarked that Boston Scientific "has been the most aggressive of medical device companies in relation to its size, and for the most part, it has been a smart acquirer and integrator. Its first and best was SCIMED."[4]

At the time, however, the SCIMED acquisition appeared a good deal riskier. Outsiders wondered

At the end of 1994, Boston Scientific announced the upcoming acquisition of SCIMED, a Minneapolis-based interventional cardiology company with a leading position in PTCA catheters. The $870 million transaction gave Boston Scientific a developed cardiology business and a thriving overseas division. This building was added in 1997.

CARDIOVASCULAR IMAGING SYSTEMS

ALTHOUGH SCIMED WAS UNDOUBTEDLY the largest and most strategic of Boston Scientific's acquisitions, it wasn't the first the company targeted. A few months before announcing SCIMED, Boston Scientific had unveiled its intention to buy Cardiovascular Imaging Systems (CVIS) for approximately $100 million.

Based in Sunnyvale, California, CVIS developed intravascular ultrasound imaging catheters. Its technology complemented Boston Scientific's existing project in intravascular ultrasound, which was relocated to Sunnyvale.[1] The acquisition was anticipated to help intravascular ultrasound grow and aid in the development of interventional procedures.

"Catheter-based intraluminal ultrasound is in its infancy today," Pete Nicholas said in 1994. "The merger will provide Boston Scientific with the scientific and commercial resources needed to quickly realize both the vascular and the nonvascular potential of this technology. By our working together and leveraging the technology from both companies, the development of new devices focused on reducing the cost and improving the accuracy of diagnosing and treating lesions deep within the body will be greatly accelerated."[2]

The deal, however, was complicated even before it was finished. On January 19, 1995, the Federal Trade Commission (FTC) voted unanimously to block Boston Scientific's acquisition of CVIS. According to the FTC, the acquisition would enable Boston Scientific to monopolize the tiny market for intravascular ultrasound imaging catheters.[3]

Richard Ferrari, president and CEO of CVIS, said, "BSC and CVIS are disappointed that the FTC has chosen to intervene in this case. The combination of our two companies is needed to move this important technology forward.... I fear that the FTC's actions will harm, not promote, patient health."[4]

The FTC's ruling did not come entirely as a surprise. Prior to the CVIS acquisition, Boston Scientific had been working with Hewlett-Packard to develop an intravascular ultrasound device. That relationship soured, however, when Boston Scientific announced it wanted to buy CVIS and SCIMED and asked Hewlett-Packard to be a partner in the new group. Hewlett-Packard declined.

"They said, 'Okay, we'll step aside,'" Joe Ciffolillo said. "We took it at face value. Mistake. Little did we know that Hewlett-Packard had

World Events

An earthquake in Kobe, Japan, kills 5,000.

Medical Milestones

Boston Scientific

Boston Scientific acquires SCIMED (cardiovascular), CVIS (intravascular ultrasound), Vesica (urology), Meadox (textile vascular prostheses), Heart (Rotablator), and EPT.

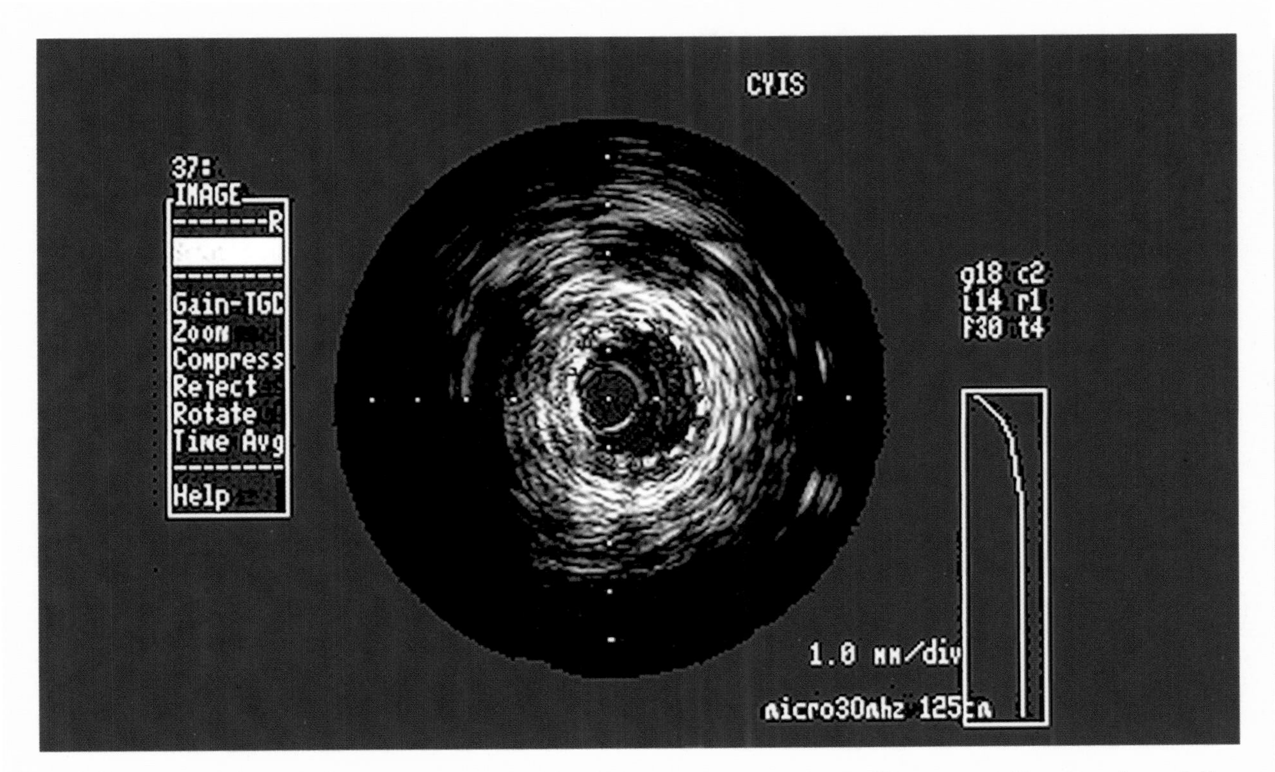

such phenomenal clout in D.C. They were behind the scenes, really leveraging."

Boston Scientific agreed to negotiate a deal with Hewlett-Packard. On February 23, the FTC and Boston Scientific entered into an agreement requiring Boston Scientific to license certain intravascular ultrasound technology and supply-related devices to Hewlett-Packard.

Court proceedings were dismissed, and the merger was completed on March 9.[5] Later, however, Hewlett-Packard initiated a lawsuit against Boston Scientific regarding the project.

In the meantime, Boston Scientific and CVIS continued to develop the technology. It was important, said Abele, because it gave physicians the ability to "look from inside out in the body."[6]

The leaders of Bosnia and Herzegovina, Serbia, and Croatia sign a peace treaty.

The company forms an alliance with B&K Medical to develop and market catheter-based intraluminal ultrasound imaging systems for nonvascular applications.

Mike Berman is named COO of SCIMED.

if Boston Scientific was completing the necessary due diligence for such a major acquisition. According to Pete Nicholas, however, there was no lack of due diligence. He took the position that Boston Scientific had already done a lot of due diligence on critical issues and that many of the other questions had been addressed by Boston Scientific's knowledge of SCIMED management and its performance in the marketplace. His interactions with the company officers had only reinforced his positive impressions, and he felt that an extensive due diligence could waste precious time and sour the management and personnel, making a smooth integration unlikely.

"The due diligence period could be relatively short," agreed Larry Best, Boston Scientific's CFO. "That's because we were really not buying bricks and mortar. How you value a building that is owned by a company is pretty irrelevant. What's relevant is the technology we were acquiring and what we thought of the success of that technology as a part of Boston Scientific."[5]

Boston Scientific announced on November 8, 1994, that it was buying SCIMED in a stock swap valued at about $870 million. The *New York Times* covered the acquisition, saying, "The two medical

Dale Spencer, president of SCIMED, was responsible for pushing the company into cardiology in 1982. With Peter Nicholas, he negotiated the deal to sell SCIMED to Boston Scientific.

Vesica Medical

DEEPENING ITS HOLD IN INTERVENTIONAL urology, Boston Scientific completed the acquisition of Vesica Medical Inc. on March 23, 1995.[1]

Based in San Clemente, California, Vesica focused on the treatment of hypermobility, the most common form of stress urinary incontinence, afflicting approximately 2.7 million women in the United States alone. Hypermobility of the bladder neck occurs when the muscles of the pelvic floor weaken, often as a result of childbirth. An innovator, Vesica developed a less-invasive therapy to stabilize the bladder neck using pelvic bone anchors and support sutures that are deployed through small incisions. At the time of the acquisition, Vesica's system had been used in more than 700 procedures by more than 75 physicians.[2]

As with other acquisitions, this one boosted both parties: Boston Scientific expanded the focus of its urology division beyond stone management into incontinence, and Vesica gained the opportunity to expand rapidly through access to Boston Scientific's strong sales force and substantial resources.

1995

World Events

France elects Jacques Chirac as president.

Medical Milestones

Boston Scientific

Dale Spencer joins BSC as director and executive vice president but announces his operating role retirement shortly after the SCIMED's acquisition.

device companies would continue the growing trend toward one-stop shopping demanded by hospitals and large managed health care buyers."[6]

SCIMED fitted perfectly in Boston Scientific's product lineup. The company had a major share of the coronary angioplasty market and had one of the industry's most developed overseas divisions. When the acquisition was finalized on February 24, 1995, Boston Scientific gained a leadership position in interventional cardiology and became a truly global company.[7]

At the time of the acquisition, SCIMED was run by Dale Spencer, who had joined the company from Baxter in 1980. In 1982, Spencer recommended that the company concentrate on developing a leading position in interventional cardiology. The board of directors accepted his recommendation and gave him the responsibility to "develop a compelling, financeable, credible plan on how we were going to do that."[8]

As SCIMED moved into interventional cardiology, Spencer fought hard to keep the company independent, but like Boston Scientific, he found his company in need of cash. In 1983, he even approached Abele and asked if Boston Scientific would consider manufacturing a peripheral vascular line for SCIMED, an effort that would save money and allow SCIMED to pay "on the come" (or not pay up front). Boston Scientific declined, leaving SCIMED to support its early growth through a research partnership.

The company that Spencer eventually put together was not the first to introduce a coronary angioplasty balloon. (SCIMED's was even introduced after Boston Scientific's.) But SCIMED was aggressive and well managed. By the late 1980s, SCIMED had captured almost 30 percent of the market for coronary angioplasty balloons.

"It was just execution," Spencer said. "People put too much emphasis on planning and not enough on execution. It was clearly a simple plan. Have the best product. Have the highest quality product. Have the highest quality organization that moves faster than anybody. Speed, innovation, and quality was our slogan."[9]

Right: Mike Berman was named chief operating officer of SCIMED the year after the acquisition. He had come to Boston Scientific as marketing manager with SCIMED.

Below: Boston Scientific elected to keep the SCIMED brand and dissolve Mansfield.

The Supreme Court rules that SCIMED must pay $68 million to two subsidiaries of Pfizer, one of the largest patent-infringement awards in U.S. history.

It was exactly the kind of company Nicholas was interested in. He had first approached Spencer about a strategic merger during an industry meeting in Boca Raton, Florida. After listening to Spencer's presentation, Nicholas "maneuvered myself around in order to make contact with him."

> *I'll remember this to my dying day. We were on the second floor of essentially a connector between two buildings. He walked by in one direction and I was going by with Larry Best in the other direction. I congratulated him on his presentation, and then I took him off to the side and said, "Dale, I think it would make sense for you and I to get to know one another better, and I would very much enjoy meeting with you to not only do that but also engage in a discussion about our businesses." He said, "I would very much enjoy that as well."*
>
> *We arranged a private dinner in Minneapolis. We had a three- or four-hour dinner, and it was at dinner that I became so comfortable with him that I revealed to him my strategy of strategic mass, how it made sense. He was very excited by it.*[10]

These first discussions entailed a strategic merger between Boston Scientific and SCIMED. The two companies had complementary strengths: Boston Scientific's peripheral vascular, urology, and endoscopy divisions meshed perfectly with SCIMED's cardiology and international units.

But a series of patent infringement lawsuits soon changed the course of the conversations. The most important lawsuit came from Pfizer Inc and involved a patent owned by a German inventor, Dr. Tassilo Bonzel, for a coronary angioplasty catheter. At the same time, Advanced Catheter Systems (ACS) filed a patent infringement suit against SCIMED.

According to the *Boston Globe*, "Schneider AG, a Swiss unit of Pfizer, bought exclusive worldwide rights to the [Bonzel] device in 1988. A year later, Schneider granted a U.S. license to its American affiliate, Minneapolis-based Schneider Inc. The Swiss and U.S. Schneider companies jointly sued SCIMED, claiming that it had violated Bonzel's patent."

SCIMED lost the 1993 trial, then challenged the decision in the U.S. Court of Appeals. When the Appeals Court voted against SCIMED, the company took its case to the Supreme Court. In November 1995, the Supreme Court rejected SCIMED's appeal and ordered the company to pay $68 million to the two subsidiaries of Pfizer. It was one of the largest patent-infringement awards in American history, weakening SCIMED significantly and teaching a hard lesson about the value of patents.[11]

When Boston Scientific acquired it, SCIMED had sales of about $260 million and a talented team of executives. Dale Spencer, however, would not remain with the company; he announced his retirement as chairman and CEO in conjunction with the sale.[12]

"Dale will be remembered as that person who most fundamentally shaped the vision of SCIMED and provided the essential leadership as President and then Chairman upon which SCIMED's undisputed industry leadership was built," announced Boston Scientific in its annual report.[13]

The Federal Reserve Board lowers interest rates twice.

The Million Man March is staged in Washington, D.C.

Jim Corbett becomes new president of Boston Scientific International.

Pete Nicholas, left, David Auth, center, and John Abele, right, celebrate the acquisition of Heart Technology. That year, Nicholas was on a roll and successfully negotiated six strategic acquisitions.

Boston Scientific retained the name SCIMED because of the respect it commanded in the market, and Mansfield was dissolved and folded into the new division.[14] At the time, Dan Cole was president and COO of SCIMED. Cole was to be groomed to take over Boston Scientific, and after the acquisition he took responsibility for Boston Scientific's cardiology and vascular divisions. After Cole moved to Natick, Mike Berman, a SCIMED employee since 1986, was given local responsibility for SCIMED.

Under Cole's and Berman's leadership, SCIMED grew more than 30 percent in 1995, accounting for about 50 percent of Boston Scientific's 1996 revenues of $1.5 billion. By 1997, SCIMED's over-the-wire NC Bandit and rapid exchange Viva catheter were among the leading angioplasty products sold worldwide.[15] The Bandit balloon catheter was used in an angioplasty procedure performed on Mother Teresa in Calcutta, India.

Heart Technology

Beginning with SCIMED, companies were added in rapid-fire succession. Yet for all the speed that Boston Scientific could muster, other forces were also gaining in its industry. Throughout 1995, the economic imperative for hospital mergers became more pressing. Hospital mergers were announced seemingly on a daily basis, and it sometimes appeared as if the entire hospital industry were morphing into one giant organism.

In a way, this trend helped Nicholas and his team at Boston Scientific. During the first acquisitions, Boston Scientific had been moving ahead of the general curve. By the summer of 1995, however, analysts had begun to write about the need for consolidation, and Nicholas found his offers falling on more receptive ears.

Late that summer, Boston Scientific announced an acquisition that was part product

Time Warner Inc. and Turner Broadcasting announce a merger to create the world's largest media company.

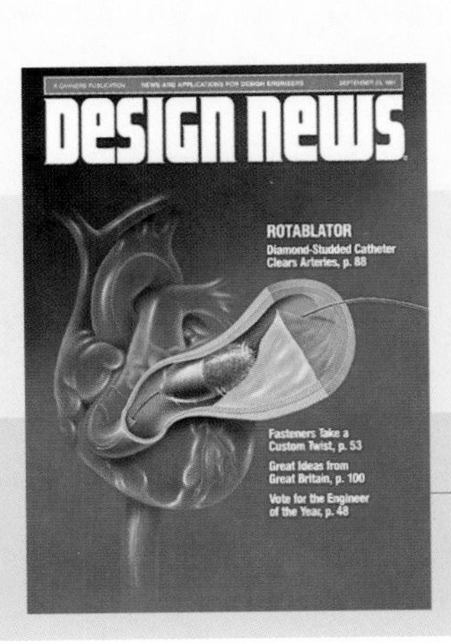

Boston Scientific acquires Heart Technology, run by David Auth, with sales around $80 million in 1995.

Moving at 100,000 revolutions per minute, the tiny Rotablator was used in cases of diffuse coronary artery disease when angioplasty and surgery would not be effective.

driven and part strategic: Heart Technology, Inc., maker of the novel Rotablator. The acquisition was structured as a tax-free, stock-for-stock transaction valued at approximately $500 million.[16] Based in Redmond, Washington, Heart employed 500 people and reported sales of $58.4 million in 1994.[17]

The Rotablator was a high-speed, diamond-tipped drill used to open clogged arteries.[18] There was no truly comparable product on the market, and the acquisition expanded Boston Scientific's cardiology franchise into cases where PTCA might not work—the Rotablator is especially effective in arteries where the plaque is highly calcified.

Like many other high-tech start-ups, Heart was run by its founder and chief visionary. David Auth, a 54-year-old physicist and successful inventor, had made the Rotablator his life's work.

Auth had worked in interventional medicine as far back as the 1970s as a physics professor at the University of Washington, where he developed the contact laser scalpel. In 1981, he began looking for ways to use lasers to clean plaque from occluded arteries but soon discovered the tissue would be susceptible to heat and light damage.

"So I looked into the use of radio frequency energy, ultrasonic energy, and mechanical energy," Auth remembered. His break came when he applied the concept of differential cutting, based on the fact that a rotating blade will not cut a soft

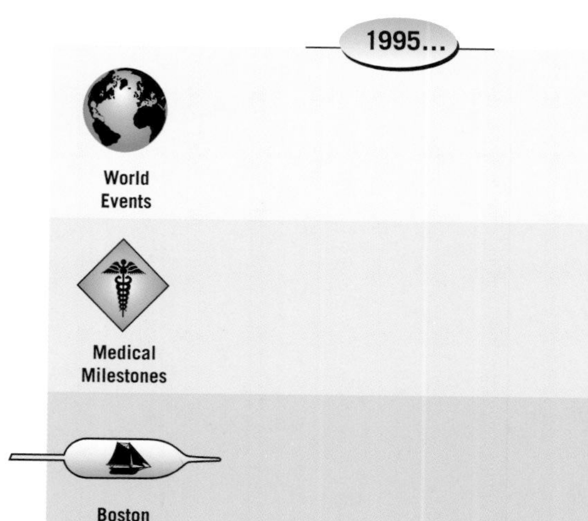

Chemical Banking Corporation and Chase Manhattan Corporation announce a merger to create largest bank in U.S.

surface (like the wall of an artery) but will easily cut hardened material (like calcific plaque). After this "eureka moment," he began looking for funding.

Auth soon cut a deal with Squibb and left the University of Washington in the early 1980s to found a small department within the pharmaceutical juggernaut and develop the arterial drill. In 1988, the device was approved for testing in humans and soon demonstrated the ability to clear arteries that were too damaged for even balloon angioplasty. The tiny air-powered drill rotated in excess of 100,000 rpm.

Then fate intervened. Squibb announced in the mid-1980s it was planning to dump the Rotablator project, leaving Auth once again on his own. In 1989, he was able to raise $14 million and buy the fledgling technology, creating Heart Technology to promote his efforts. In 1992, Auth took his company public, and the Rotablator received FDA approval for use in the coronaries a year later. When Boston Scientific acquired Heart in 1995, Auth agreed to travel and help train physicians to use the device, but he was not an employee of Boston Scientific.

Meadox

The next strategic merger added Meadox Medicals, a global leader in the emerging field of grafts for vascular surgery and endovascular therapy. As SCIMED's and Heart's had been, the acquisition was structured as a tax-free, stock-for-stock transaction, and it was valued at about $425 million.[19] Meadox posted revenues of approximately $100 million in 1995, with 53 percent from international sales.[20]

Boston Scientific had experience in stent grafts, and Meadox, with its graft expertise, was an important acquisition, putting Boston Scientific in a potential leadership position. Meadox's stent fabric was already being used by other companies to make endovascular stent grafts. Endovascular surgeons use stent grafts primarily to treat vessels that have an aneurysm.[21] A stent graft provides better sealing than a conventional stent and behaves more like the natural artery wall. It can be used in the biggest arteries in the body, including the aorta, to prevent aneurysms from rupturing.

"If you combine Meadox's vascular graft technology with Boston Scientific's stent and catheter technology, you can have a device and delivery system that is less invasive, which can lead to faster recovery times and lower costs—which is exactly

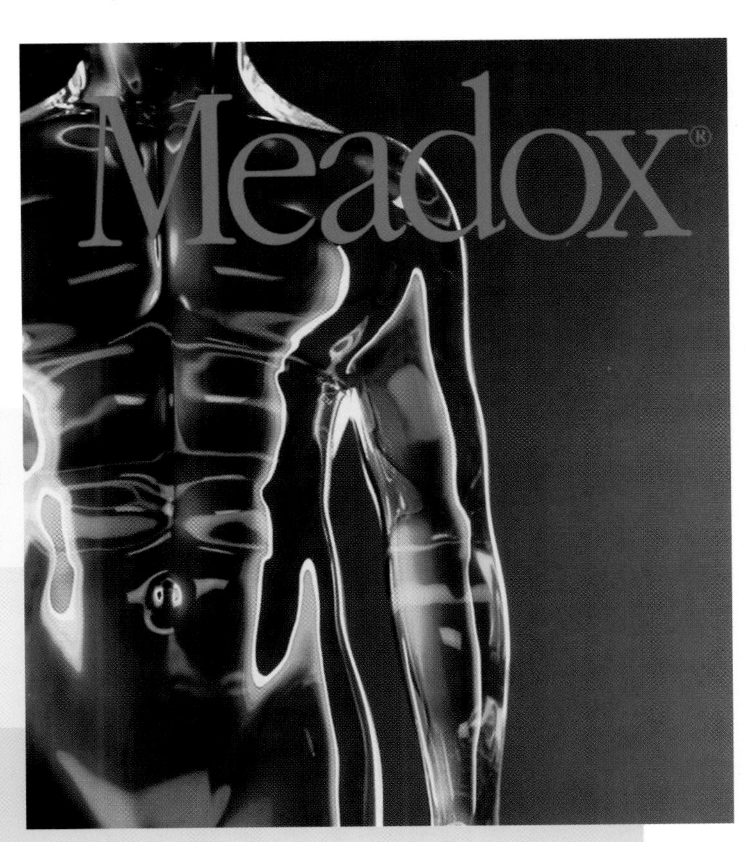

Meadox was a global leader in vascular grafts used to treat damaged arteries like the aorta.

A bomb explodes outside the Oklahoma City Federal Building, killing 168 people.

The steerable pulmonary embolectomy catheter system is featured on an episode of television's popular weekly medical drama ER.

EPTechnologies

THE FIELD OF INTERVENTIONAL ELECTROPHYSIOLOGY was already making great strides when Boston Scientific announced the 1995 acquisition of EPTechnologies. The Sunnyvale, California, company was purchased in a tax-free stock transaction valued at approximately $150 million.[1]

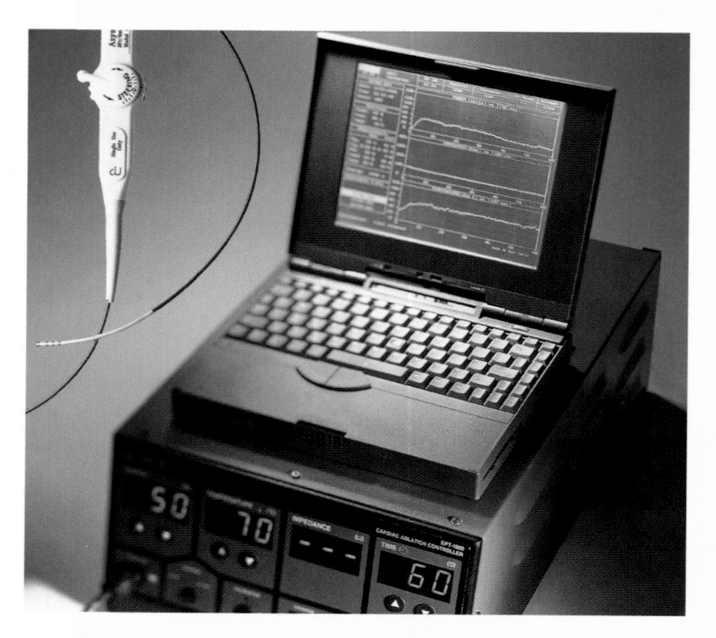

EPT, which had about 160 employees and $25 million in revenue,[2] sold electrophysiology catheters for the diagnosis and treatment of abnormally rapid heart rates called tachyarrhythmias. This condition occurs when the heart's electrical conduction system is disrupted.[3]

The company formed in the early 1990s to exploit the use of temperature-controlled radio frequency ablation to treat arrhythmias. Ironically, Boston Scientific's involvement with this technology dated much further back. In 1975, Boston Scientific's steerable catheter was used to map electrical patterns in the heart. In 1992, Mansfield EP was formed and merged with EPTechnologies at the time of the merger.

Unlike most treatments for abnormal heart rhythms, which only corrected symptoms, the therapy provided by an electrophysiologist treated the root of the disease. This approach was particularly attractive in that it would reduce the need for open-heart surgery.

An EPTechnologies cardiac ablation controller and Steerocath-T electrophysiology catheter. This acquisition added a new cardiology-targeted product line to Boston Scientific's portfolio.

1995...

World Events

Medical Milestones

Boston Scientific

Pete Nicholas and Bill von Liebig celebrate the closing of the Meadox acquisition.

what healthcare providers want to see," said Salomon Brothers analyst Eli Kammerman.[22]

Target Therapeutics

Boston Scientific announced on January 20, 1997, another major strategic acquisition, one that moved it into the fields of interventional neurology and neurosurgery. The acquired company was Target Therapeutics, which was bought in a tax-free stock swap for approximately $1.1 billion.[23] This staggering amount was more than 10 times Target's total sales, as opposed to the usual formula of ten times earnings. Yet Target was important because, like Boston Scientific, the company was engaged in market creation, bringing entirely new therapies and ways of thinking to medicine. The company had pioneered the field of interventional neuroradiology and neuroendovascular therapy.

Once again, Boston Scientific had a long association with this technology. In the 1970s, Medi-Tech had produced multilumen catheters for pioneers in this emerging and tiny field. In the 1990s, Boston Scientific was betting the devices would be a major growth area.

"Target, based in Fremont, California, makes extremely thin, supple catheters, like hollow plastic vermicelli, that can enter the blood vessels of the brain to treat pre-stroke and pre-cerebral aneurysms," reported the *New York Times*. "One of its products, the Guglielmi Detachable Coil, is the only device that has been approved by the Food and Drug Administration for treatment of inoperable or high-risk brain aneurysms."[24]

The 12-year-old company, which began as a joint venture between Collagen Corporation and ACS, was well established in Japan, where doctors readily recommended its products for cerebral aneurysms. More than 60 percent of Target's revenue of $69.8 million came from Europe and Japan. In the United States, however, fewer than 7 percent of cerebral aneurysms were treated with interventional medicine.

Pete Nicholas toasts the acquisition of Meadox with Bill von Liebig, stent graft pioneer and Meadox chairman. The acquisition of the New Jersey company was valued at $425 million.

Sales reach $1.191 billion: SCIMED, $518 million; Medi-Tech, $335 million; Microvasive Endoscopy, $164 million; Microvasive Urology, $72 million; EPT, $34 million; and Target, $62 million.

MinTec

In a move that complemented the Meadox purchase, Boston Scientific announced the purchase of MinTec, Inc., on May 3, 1996, in a cash transaction valued at approximately $72 million.[1]

MinTec, a privately held company headquartered in Freeport, Bahamas, had a leading position in the sale of endovascular stent grafts in Europe. Its devices were used to treat abdominal aortic aneurysms, peripheral aneurysms, and peripheral vascular disease. Boston Scientific planned to combine MinTec with Meadox, instantly creating a world leader in endovascular devices.[2]

"The MinTec acquisition was a shrewd move, giving Boston Scientific access to a sophisticated technology that will help it address a potentially very large market," reported the *Wall Street Journal* in 1996. "Piper Jaffray analyst Archie Smith estimates there are some 1.7 million Americans with the kind of condition MinTec stents focus on, although currently only about 45,000 people a year have surgery to treat it. Mr. Smith estimates the market at potentially $300 million a year."[3]

Prior to the merger, Target, Boston Scientific, and Cordis Endovascular Systems had been involved in three-way patent litigation. "Target claimed the other two companies were infringing its patent on a [catheter that had variable flexibility] that is able to negotiate the difficult territory of the brain," reported the *Wall Street Journal*. "Target won a preliminary injunction in U.S. District Court in San Jose, California, preventing Cordis and Boston Scientific from selling its catheters. But the U.S. Court of Appeals for the Federal Circuit in Washington, D.C., stayed the injunction."[25]

The matter was still pending when Boston Scientific bought Target. Boston Scientific CFO Larry Best said he believed his company would have prevailed in court and that the lawsuit "was not a driver in the negotiations." But, he added, "Obviously our part of the litigation will go away."[26]

That lawsuit may have disappeared, but Boston Scientific was soon threatened with more legal trouble. The company finalized its merger with Target on April 8, 1997. Three days later, Boston Scientific's shares fell $14 to $46 after company

Opposite: A brain scan showing a Target Therapeutics catheter deep inside the brain. When Boston Scientific bought Target, neurointerventional technology was an emerging and important tool for treating dangerous brain lesions.

World Events

Inflation remains low.

Medical Milestones

A study questioning the safety of heart catheters startles doctors.

Schneider Worldwide is created within Pfizer.

Boston Scientific

In January, Boston Scientific announces the 1995 acquisition of EPTechnologies in Sunnyvale.

Boston Scientific acquires Symbiosis Corporation in Miami.

Boston Scientific continues expansion of manufacturing operations in Galway, Minneapolis, San Jose, and Miami.

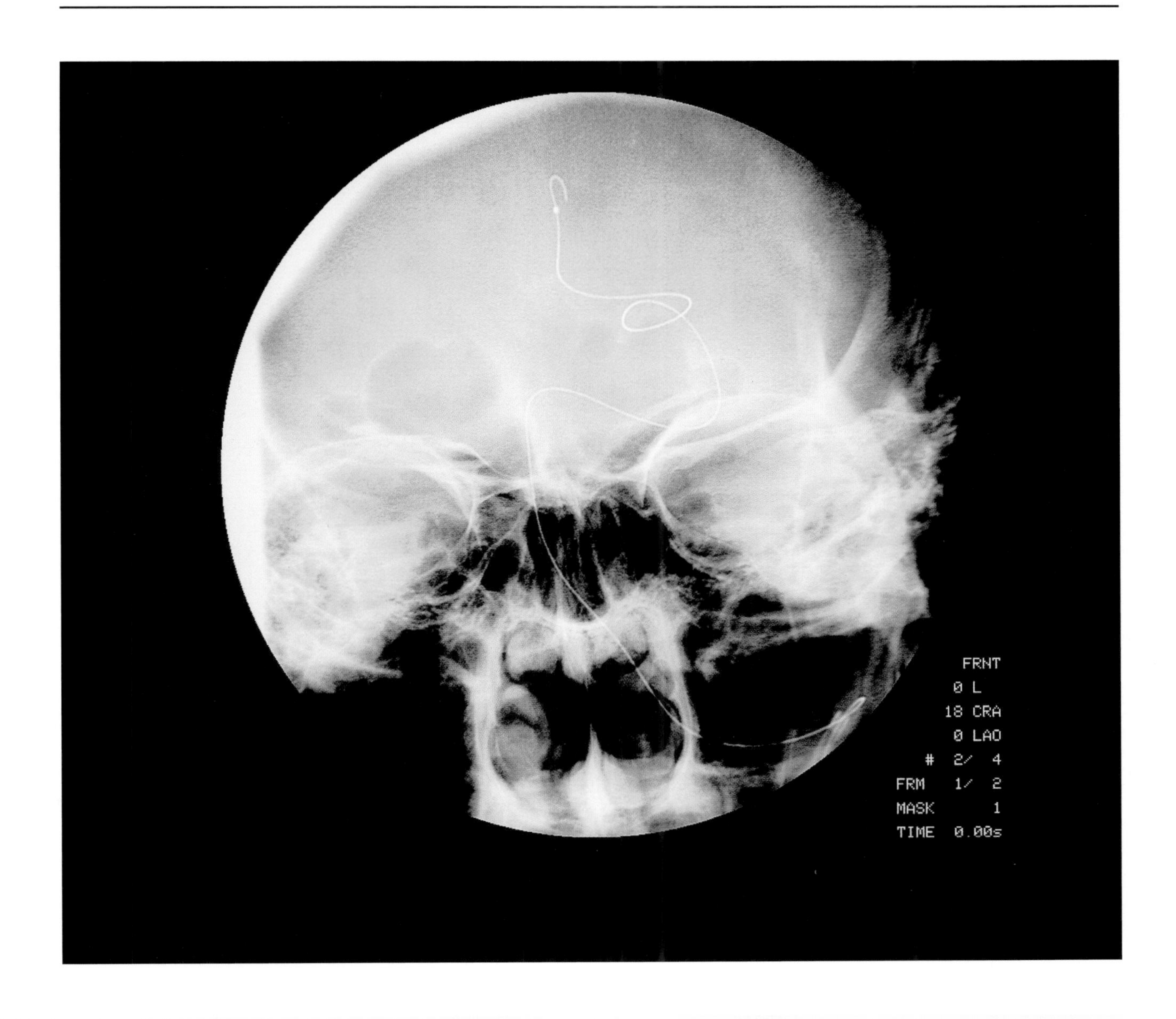

Three of Clinton's former business associates are convicted of fraud and conspiracy.

A bomb explodes at the Olympic Games in Atlanta.

J&J announces the acquisition of Cordis.

Boston Scientific creates new European distribution center in Beek, Holland.

Boston Scientific net sales increase to $1.462 billion; 78 percent of sales come from vascular business, 22 percent from nonvascular.

In March, Joe Ciffolillo retires.

The company has 9,580 employees.

officials announced first-quarter income would be significantly below estimates, partially because of inventory buildup and partially because of currency problems. When former directors of Target saw their stock value drop nearly 25 percent, they threatened to file a shareholder lawsuit.[27]

The issue subsided without litigation.

The Medinol Stent

In the midst of all the acquisitions, Boston Scientific made another important strategic move when it established an alliance with a private Israeli company called Medinol. Medinol was a leading developer of coronary stents—a technology that

Boston Scientific created an alliance with Medinol, a Jerusalem-based stent and cardiology company. Stent technology was rapidly advancing, and Boston Scientific was hoping Medinol's NIR stent, in close-ups on right, would gain early market share in the United States.

1996...

World Events

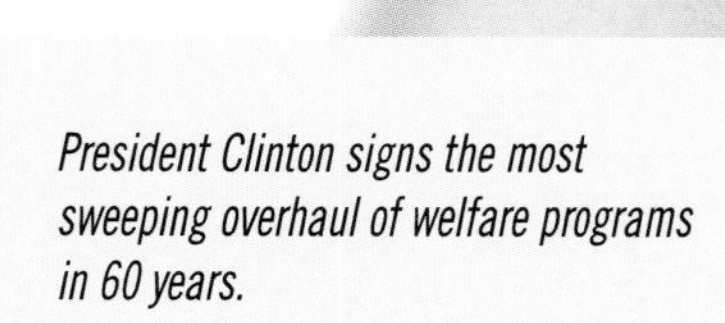

President Clinton signs the most sweeping overhaul of welfare programs in 60 years.

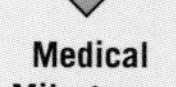

Medical Milestones

Massachusetts medical device companies form their own trade association.

Joachim Burhenne dies of Lou Gehrig's disease.

Schneider Worldwide, with 2,200 employees, celebrates 20 years of PTCA.

Boston Scientific

Boston Scientific implements regional management organizations in Asia/Pacific, India, Latin America, and Central Europe.

On May 3, Boston Scientific acquires assets of MinTec in a cash transaction valued at approximately $72 million.

Boston Scientific announces plan to close Milford manufacturing facility.

was rapidly becoming crucial to success in the cardiology market.[28]

Since their introduction in the early 1990s, coronary stents had been rapidly changing the use of PTCA, in many cases augmenting coronary balloon angioplasty.

Although conventional PTCA was enormously helpful for tens of thousands of patients every year, the problem of restenosis had yet to be solved in the coronary arteries. Patients who underwent PTCA were often dismayed to learn their arteriosclerosis had returned in a couple years and the arteries had narrowed again, or restenosed. This often meant another PTCA, and sometimes open heart surgery was required.

Coronary stents were the first step toward improving the restenosis rate. Through Medinol, Boston Scientific (which already had coronary stents on the market but had not gained significant market share) hoped to establish itself as a leader in the emerging stent market. Medinol was founded by Dr. Jacob "Kobi" Richter, chairman, and Dr. Judith Richter, CEO. Boston Scientific was licensed to market and distribute a broad range of the company's stents.[29]

The NIR Coronary Stent was the first product to come out of the alliance. It was introduced in March 1996 in Europe, where it quickly became a leading product.[30] By late 1996, Boston Scientific was looking forward to securing FDA approval for the NIR stent and jumping into the chaotic U.S. stent market.

Its approval was delayed, however, and Boston Scientific found itself the only major catheter company in the United States without a stent on the market—a predicament it had to work hard to remedy.

Strategic Mass Achieved

Throughout this period of great change, Boston Scientific continued its traditional critical self-examination, recognizing that the influx of new companies and technologies would change its carefully developed culture. Hopefully, said Nicholas, for the better.

"We were going to be adding organizations together and looking for synergies to ensure that one plus one is three or four," he said.

> *The compelling first and most important ground rule as we went forward was that as we merge the companies and integrate the businesses and rationalize the operations, we select the best of the best.*
>
> *There were no sacred cows, no protected people. Now that meant that people at BSC were just as vulnerable as the people in the company being acquired. In the case of SCIMED, for example, we looked at the equity of its brand name and their organization versus the equity of Mansfield, and we determined their brand name was far more valuable, so we abandoned our Mansfield division.*
>
> *The second requirement for the acquisitions was that we were going to at all costs try to do these consolidations or acquisitions in a way that was seamless to our customer. We were going to preserve at all costs the customer relationship.*[31]

FBI arrests Ted Kaczynski as a suspect in the Unabomber bombing case.

FDA Commissioner David Kessler resigns.

Boston Scientific forms alliance with CorTrak Medical, maker of drug delivery systems.

Boston Scientific purchases the 1.3-million-square-foot Jordan Marsh warehouse in Quincy, Massachusetts, for U.S. distribution center.

Worldwide trials of angioplasty versus surgery are completed and analyzed; angioplasty remains a viable alternative to surgery, but not the preferred treatment until restenosis problem is solved.

A 248,000-square-foot building is erected at SCIMED's Maple Grove facility.

In a very significant way, especially in an era of consolidation, this translated into better leveraging of technologies and ideas across Boston Scientific. Even before the acquisitions began, Boston Scientific had hired its first full-time corporate strategist. Don Hovey was given the job of helping each division develop its growth strategy without offending people in the separate organizations, who "are very empowered," as John Abele once put it.

"The typical strategic plan is a top-down kind of thing," Hovey said. "I quickly learned that wouldn't work at Boston Scientific. My job really was to understand where the businesses were and to take that as a starting point. It really was, at the beginning, a very bottom-up process."[32]

True to form, Boston Scientific pushed its operating duties deep into the divisions, hoping that good ideas would percolate up through the organization. As the acquisitions were added in steady succession, however, there was no question it would be harder for

Carotid
Tracheobronchial
Coronary
Esophageal
Biliary
Renal
Colonic
Aortic
Ureteral
Iliac
Prostatic
Urethral

This 1997 diagram was produced by Boston Scientific to show the many parts of the body its products were designed for. No other company in the world was as focused on interventional medicine exclusively and, at the same time, offered expertise across the same breadth of specialties.

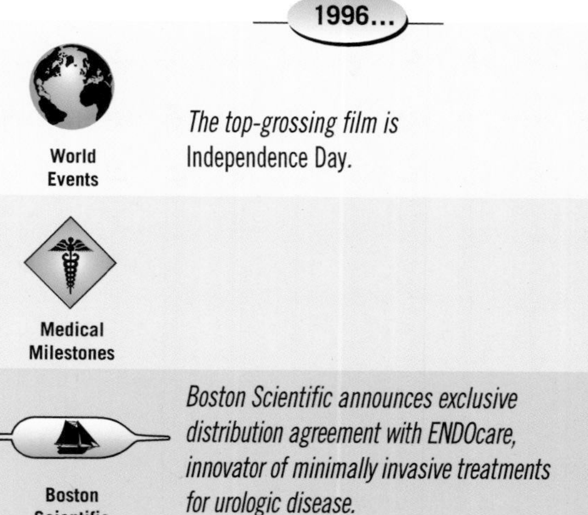

EPTechnologies and IVUS are consolidated into one 160,000-square-foot leased site in San Jose.

Peter Nicholas's string of acquisitions had grown Boston Scientific to 8,000 employees and more than $1 billion in revenue by 1995.

Boston Scientific to react as a single organization. Not only had it inherited a group of fiefdoms in its divisions, it was now the largest enterprise in the world devoted solely to minimally invasive medicine. The challenge had shifted from honing Boston Scientific's existing culture to merging many different cultures across a far-flung organization.

In fact, Boston Scientific had become a large company. By 1995, it had increased the number of its employees to 8,000, expanded its facilities by more than 1 million square feet, and expanded its product line from slightly more than 3,000 product codes in 1994 to 8,500[33] and its stable of issued patents from 190 to 600.[34] Likewise, sales jumped enormously, breaking the $1 billion mark in 1995 and reaching $1.1 billion. From a production point of view, the company had 14 direct sales operations overseas, with 1,500 employees outside the United States. Considering the sudden, burgeoning growth and the complexity of it, Peter Nicholas was frequently heard to comment that Boston Scientific was a "billion-dollar start-up."

Behind the significant cultural challenge the company faced, however, lay a singular success. Nicholas had achieved his goal of strategic mass and positioned Boston Scientific as the world leader in minimally invasive medicine. It was the realization of decades of planning.

According to a Form 10-K filed with the Securities and Exchange Commission in 1996, "The acquisitions have helped the company to reach a certain strategic mass which should enable it to compete more effectively in, and better absorb the pressures of, the current health care environment of cost containment, managed-care, large buying groups, and hospital consolidations."

Reorganization

Throughout the acquisitions, Boston Scientific leadership worked feverishly to reorganize the company. It was a time of upheaval and uncertainty, yet there were certain cultural similarities across all the acquisitions. All of the new organizations were medical device companies. Many still had founders working for them, and they often thrived in a loose, fast-moving, and nonhierarchical environment. There were some bruises throughout the two-year effort to integrate the new companies, but many employees of both

Bill Clinton is reelected president.

At Symbiosis, Boston Scientific leases a 140,000-square-foot building already under construction adjacent to its existing 200,000-square-foot facility.

EPT division launches the Constellation, a diagnostic mapping basket catheter, the Big-Tip Blazer catheter for diagnosing/treating cardiac abnormalities, and the ICE ultrasound catheter.

Year-end revenue is $1.5 billion: SCIMED, $727 million; Medi-Tech, $378 million; Microvasive Endoscopy, $200 million; Microvasive Urology, $100 million; Target, $89 million; EPT, $35 million.

SYMBIOSIS CORPORATION

ON JANUARY 26, 1996, BOSTON SCIENTIFIC announced it would purchase Symbiosis Corporation, a subsidiary of American Home Products, for approximately $153 million in a cash transaction.[1] The acquisition had the effect of "bringing home" a major outside supplier.

Miami-based Symbiosis developed and manufactured specialty medical devices, including the popular reusable biopsy forceps sold by Microvasive Endoscopy.[2] Its largest customer was, in fact, Boston Scientific. Symbiosis owned about 150 patents and was a winner in *Industry Week*'s annual search for America's ten best plants. By 1995, the company employed about 700 people and reported revenues of approximately $60 million.

Commenting on the merger, Pete Nicholas said, "We have worked closely with the people of Symbiosis since its inception, and we share a remarkably similar spirit of innovation, speed, and growth. In this case, merging a market leader with its low-cost supplier makes great sense."[3]

The relationship between Symbiosis and Boston Scientific was very entrenched; without

World Events

Medical Milestones

Boston Scientific

Boston Scientific is ranked No. 2 on the Boston Globe's *Top 100 list.*

Boston Scientific debuts on the Internet.

Boston Scientific announces stent technology alliance with Medinol.

help from Boston Scientific, it is possible there would never have been a Symbiosis. Four Cordis Corporation engineers founded it in 1989. Kevin Smith, one of the partners, had dropped out of the Massachusetts Institute of Technology in 1981, calling it a "colossal waste of time." Four years later, he and a friend named Charlie Slater, also an engineer, founded S Squared Engineering in Slater's garage.[4] They worked at it part-time and kept their jobs at Cordis.

In 1988, Smith received a patent on a disposable cardiology syringe.[5] In 1989, after quitting their jobs, Smith, Slater, and two other engineers, Bill Box and Tom Bales, founded Symbiosis to sell the disposable syringe.[6] Soon after production started, Smith approached John Abele at an American Heart Association meeting and asked if Boston Scientific would be interested in buying a cardiology forceps. "No," Abele said, "I don't want cardiology biopsy forceps, but I do want ones for the GI market."[7]

According to an article in *New Miami* magazine, "Symbiosis started making a low-cost, disposable, gastrointestinal biopsy forceps. This changed the market from reusable to a disposable market."[8]

In its first three years, sales at Symbiosis went from zero to $15 million. "No ordinary star, this company is a supernova, a collection of bright ideas that suddenly seem brilliant together," said *New Miami*. That year, the 33-year-old Smith said, "To be quite honest, the real corporate goal here is to make Symbiosis the coolest place in the world to work."[9]

Cool indeed. As one article noted, Smith fostered a working environment at Symbiosis that some say was "more akin to that in the movie 'Animal House' than to an executive suite.... [Smith] had snow skis propped against the wall and a glass desk so cluttered you couldn't see the top of it. Among the company's top brass, memos were out, blue jeans were in. Smith's employees were an unusual bunch, too. Several used to work as 'roadies,' or stagehands, for touring rock groups. Some kept guitars in their offices." The company also had a firing range in its building and several employees who were into juggling. It wasn't uncommon, Abele remembered, to walk through the halls and pass people juggling bowling pins, tennis balls, or even fruit.

In 1992, American Home Products acquired Symbiosis, netting Smith and his three partners about $37 million each. About 50 employees split an additional $26 million.[10] However, there were cultural differences between the pharmaceutical company and Symbiosis, leading Boston Scientific to buy the company in 1995. In this way, Boston Scientific guaranteed its source of the highly profitable biopsy forceps and helped reward a long-time supplier and partner.

The company opens a regional headquarters in Singapore.

Sales award winners celebrate in Boston Scientific's Japanese division, one of its largest overseas operations.

Boston Scientific and the new companies reported that for the most part the integrations worked themselves out very well.

Of the eight acquisitions, the two hardest in terms of cultural blending were probably Meadox and SCIMED.

With SCIMED, there were subtle differences. At Boston Scientific, the company had fairly specific ideas about how its people should dress and favored a more professional, East Coast approach toward business attire. At SCIMED, the dress code was more relaxed, remembered Jim Corbett, then president of SCIMED International. "I remember we had a big sales meeting the day of the merger," Corbett said.

> *It was the awards banquet for Boston Scientific, and all the SCIMED guys were there. There were a thousand people in the ballroom, and I wore tan slacks, a sport coat, blue striped shirt, and a tie. I was later told by some of the guys who work for me who were from the original Boston Scientific, "We thought you were out of your mind. What were you thinking?"*[35]

Beyond these superficial discrepancies, however, almost everyone involved realized that the whole is greater than the sum of its many parts, and Boston Scientific moved quickly during the reorganization effort. In the middle of 1995, the company split into two broad halves: vascular and nonvascular.

Not coincidentally, this first restructuring was timed in conjunction with the retirement of one of Boston Scientific's highest-ranking executives. On March 31, 1996, Joe Ciffolillo left the company to pursue a more personal ambition: since the day he graduated college, Ciffolillo had planned to retire at age 55. When he announced his official retirement, he was only three years late.

"To me, the definition of a successful career is you work hard, you accomplish what you can accomplish, you accumulate some wealth, and you move on to make room for other people," Ciffolillo said.[36]

Ciffolillo's contribution to Boston Scientific had been immense, and the team he created and the enthusiasm he brought to the sales forces reverberated through the company for years to come.

"No words of thanks can adequately convey our feelings of deep gratitude to Joe for his numerous contributions to Boston Scientific," wrote Nicholas. "Joe was an early employee of Boston Scientific, and his extraordinary leadership, vision, and belief in the dignity and value of every single employee at BSC provided the basis for BSC's remarkable past success. Joe will be missed at BSC as a friend, counselor, and mentor."[37]

After his retirement, his duties were split. The fast-growing vascular businesses were put under the control of Dan Cole, former president of SCIMED. With this move, Boston Scientific confirmed that Cole was being groomed as the probable successor to Pete Nicholas.

The nonvascular operations were headed by Paul LaViolette, former head of Boston Scientific International. Within these two broad product categories, Boston Scientific addressed five main markets: interventional cardiology, interventional radiology,

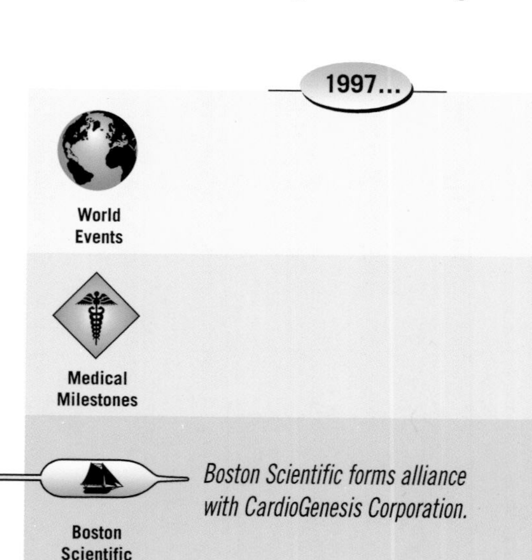

World markets are roiled by Asian economic problems.

Boston Scientific closes its manufacturing facilities in Belgium and Denmark and moves production to Ireland.

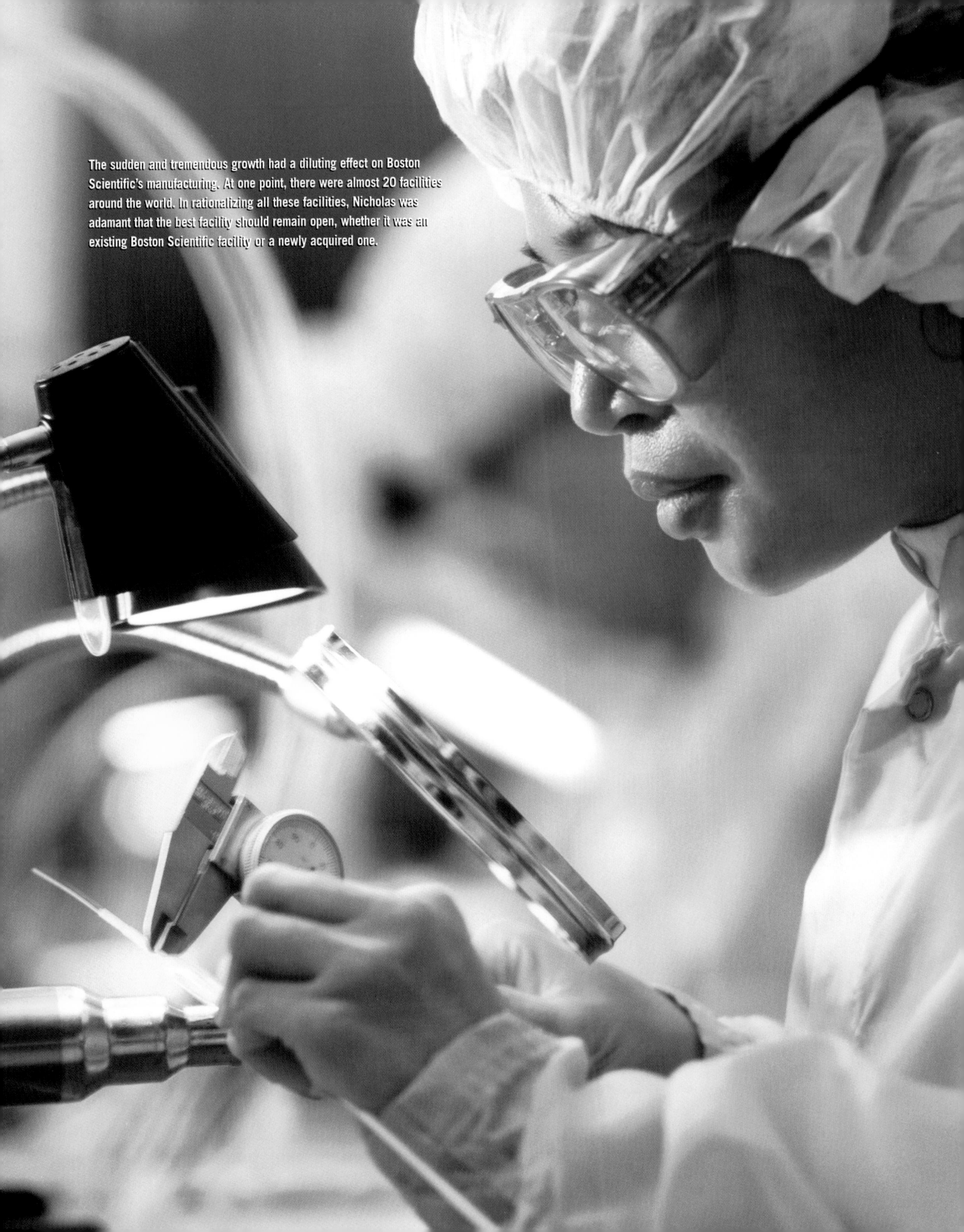

The sudden and tremendous growth had a diluting effect on Boston Scientific's manufacturing. At one point, there were almost 20 facilities around the world. In rationalizing all these facilities, Nicholas was adamant that the best facility should remain open, whether it was an existing Boston Scientific facility or a newly acquired one.

interventional gastroenterology, vascular surgery, and urology. Boston Scientific was either the market leader or second in every category.

Later, when Target added an emphasis on interventional neurology, the company was again reorganized. Target was grouped with Medi-Tech and Meadox to make a third division devoted to noncardiology vascular specialties. Cardiology, with Mike Berman running it and anchored by SCIMED, became a stand-alone division.

Domestic Consolidation

The reorganization entailed more than shuffling specialties across the company to make sure the sales forces were focused and the technology was leveraged. There was also the very real task of rationalizing the many new manufacturing facilities, which experienced significant overlap.

In addition to its own Natick headquarters, Boston Scientific had inherited new headquarters in Maple Grove, Minnesota; San Jose, California; and Oakland, New Jersey, in addition to one started in Paris, France. It had seven research facilities, including one in Ireland, and six distribution centers, with operations in Beek, the Netherlands; Tokyo; and Singapore. (A regional headquarters was later added there.)[38] The company's manufacturing was spread among many major facilities—10 in the United States and one each in Ireland, France, Denmark, and the Bahamas.[39] At one point during the acquisitions, said Mike Mabrey, vice president of manufacturing, the company had as many as 18 manufacturing sites, a situation management worked to remedy as it sought greater efficiencies.

By 1997, the manufacturing plant in Galway had outgrown its capacity, prompting expansion into Cork, Ireland. Pictured is ultrathin catheter manufacturing in Galway.

"I was part of the group that tried to rationalize all these acquisitions from a manufacturing perspec-

1997...

World Events

China peacefully regains sovereignty over Hong Kong.

Medical Milestones

Medtronic becomes third company marketing a cardiac stent; until now J&J and Cook controlled the $750 million annual market.

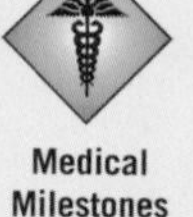

Boston Scientific

Boston Scientific and Cook form alliance with Angiotech (technology to reduce restenosis).

A $60 million expansion is announced in Galway, Ireland.

Boston Scientific launches the Symphony stent in Europe.

tive," he said. "We started out with 18 and ended up taking that down to nine. That changed with the Target acquisition, and we went back up to 10."[40]

As the burden of work shifted from many facilities to a few, Boston Scientific rapidly expanded its existing plants.

Green Pastures in Ireland

Overseas, the acquisitions had added two manufacturing and distribution facilities, in addition to the existing Galway, Ireland, plant. SCIMED had a facility in Petit Rechain, Belgium, and Meadox had a production center in Stenlose, Denmark. Both were closed and their production moved to Galway.

To take the pressure off Galway, Boston Scientific planned a second manufacturing facility, this one near Cork, Ireland.

According to a November 1997 article in the *Irish Times*, "The investment is the largest to date by a healthcare company in Ireland, and the biggest project sponsored this year by the Irish Development Agency. Sources in the IDA say they are particularly happy with the development because the company is now the world leader in the manufacture of interventional medical instruments, a booming area in an otherwise consolidating healthcare industry."[41]

The Nonvascular Groups

Within the company, the acquisitions changed Boston Scientific's revenue picture as vascular and cardiology became huge contributors to the bottom line. Yet the company's nonvascular businesses were still growing quickly, representing a traditional Boston Scientific strength and a major element of the company strategy to lead at every level in interventional medicine.

When Paul LaViolette took over the nonvascular business, Microvasive Urology was anchored by stone management technology and dilatation catheters, and its salespeople had penetrated deep into the operating room. Yet the franchise remained narrowly focused and limited mainly to the United States. By quickly moving into new markets with new technologies and leveraging existing strengths into new areas, he restored urology to rapid growth. In two years, the franchise grew from about $65 million to $150 million, with $30 million in overseas sales.

But urology was quickly becoming a crowded field; many companies were developing interventional urology devices. "The public is starting to become more aware, or less concerned about talking about their urologic diseases," remarked John Carnuccio, manager of Microvasive Urology at the time.[42]

As with previous growth in interventional medicine, this development opened up both challenge and opportunity for Boston Scientific. LaViolette hoped to be able to grow the business into interventions for incontinence, prostate disease, and bladder disease.

In Microvasive Endoscopy, the situation was subtly different. Prior to the Symbiosis acquisition, Microvasive Endoscopy had basically reached its domestic market potential with the popular biopsy

Princess Diana is killed in Paris car crash.

Boston Scientific completes the acquisition of Target Therapeutics, Inc., in a tax-free stock swap valued at approximately $1.1 billion.

forceps and had virtually no sales overseas because of a European cultural bias against disposable products. Moreover, the company relied heavily on outside suppliers. After it bought Symbiosis, however, Boston Scientific was able to globalize its endoscopy franchise, growing it from about $100 million in 1994 to about $300 million in 1998, with approximately one-third of its sales coming from overseas.[43] Its sales force was second in size only to SCIMED's.

Although Boston Scientific continued to look at targets for acquisition in endoscopy, it soon found that few solid candidates existed. As a result, Microvasive Endoscopy generated an internal growth plan, although it still maintained outside relationships with Josh Tolkoff, the Medi-Tech engineer who helped design the original angioplasty balloon. Tolkoff founded his own company, ACT Medical, which served as a kind of unofficial research and manufacturing facility for Microvasive Endoscopy.

Microvasive Endoscopy also offered biliary stone removal baskets, gastrointestinal dilatation balloons, and stents for esophageal cancer therapy. "In 1989, we really had only two product lines, including the biopsy forceps," said long-time Vice President of Microvasive Endoscopy Stephen Moreci. "Now we have eight different franchises, and we still have those two. There's a very balanced product line. We're taking the line and moving it around the world, introducing it into Japan and Europe and new emerging markets."[44]

The next step for Microvasive Endoscopy, according to Moreci, was "inside/outside" surgery. In this novel technique, a flexible endoscope would be inserted through natural body openings and used to perform minor internal surgeries without breaking the skin. "We're finding that you can certainly treat the organs you're in—the stomach, the esophagus, the colon," Moreci said. "But we're also finding that you can get to other organs from the inside. We're looking at futuristic versions of that concept. For instance, if you can exit the wall of the esophagus, you find yourself in the heart. Since you're inside the body, there's no real pain and no skin incisions."[45]

Throughout all this growth and acquisition, Boston Scientific had maintained its quiet position in nonvascular specialties. Even to analysts who followed the medical device industry, the nonvascular businesses were difficult to understand and wildly varied. Yet the two Microvasive divisions contributed a significant portion to the company's revenues. (It's hard to tell exactly how much because even in 1996, Boston Scientific still wasn't providing detailed market information, and analysts hadn't yet started heavy coverage of the company.)

International Growth

In 1995, as LaViolette moved over to the nonvascular businesses, Jim Corbett from SCIMED was put in charge of Boston Scientific International Corporation, which handled both vascular and nonvascular businesses. Before arriving at Boston Scientific, Corbett had built one of the industry's best overseas sales organizations for SCIMED, including a $100 million operation in Japan.

At the time of the acquisition, SCIMED's overseas business was almost twice as large as Boston

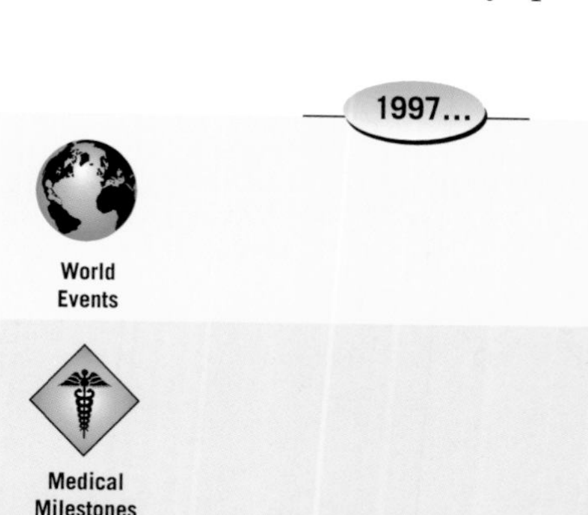

Former Target directors threaten to sue Boston Scientific when their shares plunge just days after the April acquisition.

Michel Darnaud is named president of Boston Scientific Europe.

Scientific's. SCIMED's international business model was unique in the medical device industry. Instead of concentrating on individual countries, as Boston Scientific had done, SCIMED had set up regional distribution across Europe. The challenge was to merge the organizations while keeping a business that was united across all of Europe and paying attention to cultural variations among the different countries. One way to do this was to hire people from many different countries. Although the headquarters of the organization were in Paris, a majority of the employees were non-French.

Merging Boston Scientific's international business into SCIMED's had other interesting ramifications. SCIMED was basically a one-technology company, whereas Boston Scientific had a depth of technology in interventional radiology, endoscopy, and urology. So to some degree, the overseas operation covered territory that Boston Scientific had already been through in the 1980s. The new operation was asking sales forces to sell many products to many different specialties.

The Boston Scientific headquarters in Paris were located in this building. To keep the company connected to local markets throughout Europe, this facility was staffed by people from many countries. In addition to its large operation in Europe, Boston Scientific had also become a major player in the large Asian market.

Left: Mike Mabrey was put in charge of manufacturing consolidation. His team reduced the number of facilities to 10 and reorganized the whole production side of the company.

Right: The company also reorganized its operating units and split into vascular and nonvascular groups. Paul LaViolette was put in charge of the nonvascular divisions, including urology and endoscopy.

"It's history repeating itself," commented Doug Daniels, who moved from Microvasive Endoscopy to manage a joint endoscopy/urology group in the international division.[46]

A New Team Forms

The executive team throughout this period of upheaval was also fluid. Dan Cole, who inherited the vascular organization from Joe Ciffolillo and ran the cardiology division, left the company. His departure left Nicholas without a successor, and a search began for new upper-executive talent.

Before long, Philip LeGoff was named group president, vascular businesses, while Mike Berman continued to run the cardiology business. LeGoff, who would also leave the company before long, assumed responsibility for the three noncardiology divisions. Like other outsiders, LeGoff remembered being a little taken aback by his hiring process and how it came to typify his experience at Boston Scientific. "The first trip to the company, I met three people but not Pete," he said.

> *I was invited for a second round of interviews, and Pete wasn't around. I was a bit upset, wondering what all this was about because I was supposed to report to him. But that was the process, and I'm not sure it was intentional. I think it translates to the speed at which things are happening at Boston Scientific such that it's very difficult to have everybody around the same day. After I got the job, two weeks before joining the company, I was given a telephone line with a voice mail. I wasn't even with the company yet, and every day I had an average of 15 voice mails. That's strong acceleration.*[47]

Within the vascular group, Medi-Tech and Meadox each averaged about 20 percent annual growth. Once Target's products, which reported 47 percent growth from 1996 to 1997, were added to the established sales network, the vascular group

World Events

Scientists in Scotland create Dolly the lamb, the first genetic clone of an adult animal.

WorldCom Inc. acquires MCI Communications.

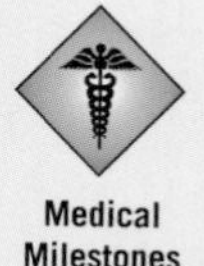

Medical Milestones

Boston Scientific

At the end of 1997, the company has 9,000 employees.

as a whole was expected to expand somewhere between 20 percent and 30 percent every year.

The End Run

Less than 18 months after the first acquisition was announced, Boston Scientific posted numbers that would have seemed like fantasy a short time before. At the end of 1997, the company had $1.8 billion in revenue and 9,000 employees. The whirlwind of expansion and acquisition had changed Boston Scientific forever, and the next several years would be spent rediscovering the new company that had been created. Boston Scientific had seemingly come from nowhere and transformed itself into a world player in coronary angioplasty and the undisputed leader in nonvascular interventional medicine. Externally, the challenge remained finding or developing a U.S. stent, while the internal challenge was to hold the center firm as Boston Scientific sprawled around the world.

"Management believes it has developed a sound plan for continuing the integration process," read the 1997 annual report.

> *However, in view of the number of major transactions undertaken by the Company, the dramatic changes in the size of the Company, and the complexity of its organization resulting from these transactions, management also believes that the successful implementation of its plan presents a significant degree of difficulty. The failure to integrate these businesses effectively could adversely affect the Company's operating results in the near term and could impair the Company's ability to realize the strategic and financial objectives of these transactions.*[48]

The initial financial results troubled analysts (the company reported lower-than-expected earnings throughout the first half of the year), but it was the strategic and cultural issues that bothered Boston Scientific on a deeper level. The company had been built on the loyalty of its people and their belief in its overall mission. According to the *New York Times*,

> *[Pete Nicholas's] biggest worry was losing the "richness and crispness" of Boston Scientific's culture, a culture characterized by risk-taking, highly devoted employees, many of whom hold large financial stakes in the company's future through generous stock options. Mr. Nicholas is optimistic that the integration of the new companies will be smooth. And analysts, though wary, say if any company can pull it off, Boston Scientific can.*[49]

The top-grossing film is Men in Black.

In October, shares plunge; the company is hurt by launch of Guidant stent, decreased health care spending in Europe, and uncertainties over Japanese approval for Rotablator.

Year-end revenue is $1.8 billion: SCIMED, $818 million; Medi-Tech, $446 million; Microvasive Endoscopy, $246 million; Microvasive Urology, $132 million; Target, $123 million; EPT, $44 million.

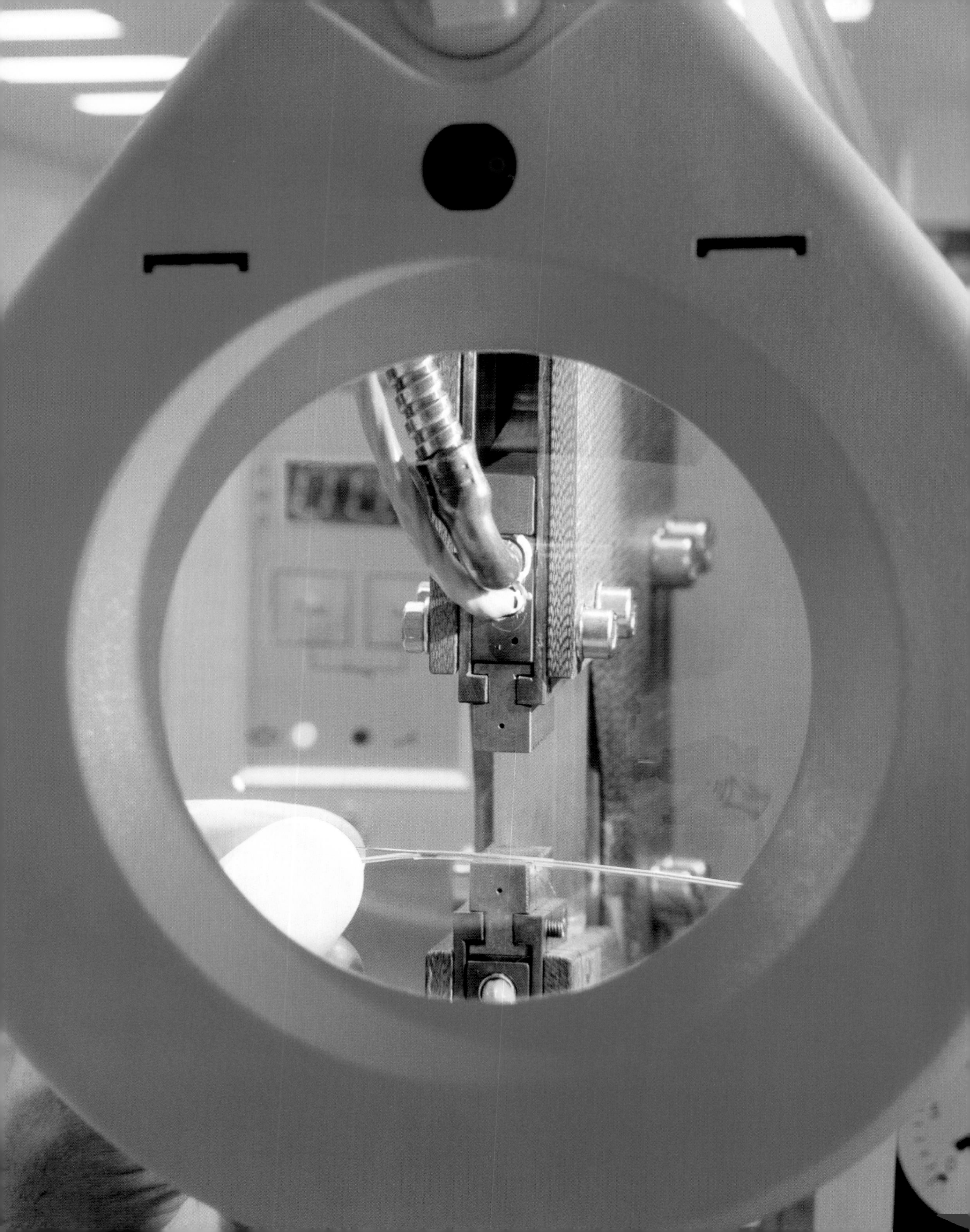

CHAPTER EIGHT

WALKING THE TALK

1998–2000

Companies do have souls. They do, in fact, respect relationships. They do have honor and walk like they talk.

—Peter Nicholas, 1998

IN THE MIDST OF ALL THE UPHEAVAL—the changing nature of health care, the integration of disparate companies and cultures—minimally invasive medicine itself was in the midst of yet another revolution. In the early 1990s, an Italian physician named Antonio Colombo dramatically simplified the process by which cardiologists could place a stent in the coronary arteries after balloon angioplasty.

Previous to Colombo's work, stents were associated with a risk of thrombosis that sometimes resulted in a postprocedural acute coronary event, often a fatal heart attack. Because of Colombo, this risk dropped by a ratio of about 10:1. The successful application of coronary stents, similar in structure and function to stents used elsewhere in the body, represented a major leap forward for minimally invasive cardiology.

Although many people think Johnson & Johnson had the first coronary stent in the United States, that honor actually went to Cook Inc., which introduced a first-generation coronary stent in 1993. Immediately after the approval, however, the company became embroiled in a patent war with Johnson & Johnson over the Palmaz patent on the concept of a balloon-expandable coronary stent.

Despite the uncertainty, stents caught on very quickly; the market grew at least 50 percent each year after 1993. Within a few years, cardiologists were using stents in about two-thirds of angioplasties, and the market was expected to reach almost $2 billion by the turn of the millennium.[1] By 1996, the stent market was still dominated by relatively few brands, such as the Johnson & Johnson Palmaz-Schatz stent.

In 1995, hoping to bundle its stent with a catheter delivery system, J&J leaders had again discussed the idea of a merger with Peter Nicholas at Boston Scientific. Shortly after Nicholas refused the offer, J&J launched an unfriendly takeover of Cordis Corporation, a maker of angioplasty balloons and related equipment.

"J&J's stent is proving so successful that it's redefining treatment for the disease," reported the *Wall Street Journal* at the time of the acquisition, adding, "'Cordis's angioplasty line will bolster the stent against future competition,' said Daniel T. LeMaitre, analyst at Cowen & Co. 'This deal will dramatically change the rules of the game in the minimally invasive cardiology market.'"[2]

One year later, J&J settled its patent litigation case against Cook Inc. The move was strategic for J&J because it gave Cook access to the patent but for products that no longer had value. At the same time, it established a precedent: J&J had forced a competitor to acknowledge its patent.

Opposite: Cardiac catheter manufacture, pictured in the Galway, Ireland, plant. After its string of acquisitions, Boston Scientific faced the task of rationalizing manufacturing for thousands of new product codes in many new facilities, even as technology changed again.

Meanwhile, stent technology continued its advance and Johnson & Johnson continued to solidify its hold over the market. By 1997, the big company commanded 95 percent of the U.S. stent market. That year, Medtronic became the third company to market a cardiac stent in the United States, but like Cook's stent, it was considered an early-generation product and never grabbed significant market share. It was followed by next-generation stents offered by Guidant (formerly ACS) and Arterial Vascular Engineering (AVE).[3]

In the space of a few years, the AVE stent also fell by the wayside (new versions were later recovered under Medtronic), but the Guidant product proved how fast-moving and fickle the medical technology business can be. Seemingly overnight, the Guidant stent knocked Johnson & Johnson off its perch and grabbed about 90 percent of the U.S. stent market. Regarding the ongoing patent issue, Guidant and Johnson & Johnson settled, with Guidant giving Johnson & Johnson money and access to a new rapid-exchange technology.

At least some of Guidant's success had to do with the method it used to introduce its product. Gone were the early days when a couple doctors tried a technique with a minimally invasive product, published a paper, and championed it to other doctors. Guidant's stent was brought to market in a rush of trials, training, and teams of paid doctors promoting it.

The idea of a doctor being paid to promote a medical device was not exactly new in the industry and had always occupied a murky ethical position at the crossroads of technology, patient care, and profit. "Periodically, medicine would sort of get out of hand," said John Abele. "It happens in cycles that enthusiasm for technology and moneymaking opportunities would cause physicians to lose sight of their Hippocratic oath."[4]

In fact, throughout the 1990s, the issue received new attention as cost issues and competitive pressures became more urgent. In his provocative 2000 book, *Saving the Heart*, author Stephen Klaidman examined the $90 billion a year cardiology industry. Perhaps more important for the questions it raises rather than answers, Klaidman's book talks about the "new breed of business-oriented physician-researcher" and the tremendously complicated relationship between medical innovation, profit, patient care, and prudence.[5]

As a recent development, stents were a particularly good example of this conundrum, and Klaidman noted that during their incredibly rapid introduction "commerce was driving the pace."

Stephen Klaidman, writing about the development of cardiac care, shed light on the modern relationship between money and health care.

1998...

World Events

President Bill Clinton is impeached by the House of Representatives.

Medical Milestones

Boston Scientific

Rotablator is approved by national health care programs in Japan.

The stent promotions had a new twist, however, because not only were doctors promoting the stents to other doctors, but patients were aggressively seeking information on their own conditions. This represented a sea change in medicine and was largely due to the rapid introduction and acceptance of the Internet, which released a flood of information to the public, allowing average patients to become overnight experts on their conditions. Physicians began to report seeing patients who brought in reams of articles on stenting that they had printed from Internet research.

Boston Scientific watched these early years of coronary stent development and acceptance from the sidelines. As with coronary angioplasty balloons before, the company was missing a competitive stent in the U.S. market and spent 1997 developing a new stent delivery system and preparing an application for U.S. approval of its NIR stent, which had already gained market leadership in Europe, and awaiting approval of the Radius stent. Boston Scientific had expected the NIR stent to be approved significantly before Radius and now found itself in the position of potentially releasing two stents simultaneously.

Once approved, these stents were expected to establish Boston Scientific as a world force in the coronary stent market, by then the largest segment of the medical device industry.

It was a closely watched competition. USAA Investment Management analyst Tim Reynolds told one reporter that "Success in the company and the stock is going to hinge on getting the NIR stent through." With FDA approval, he noted, Boston Scientific would be able to sell the stent in combination with catheters and balloons, offering the

The Beek Customer Fulfillment Center, where thousands of orders are processed. Over the years, Boston Scientific had made great strides forward in its ability to control inventory and shift production among its various manufacturing facilities.

Boston Scientific has a total of 10 manufacturing sites, down from a high of 18.

complete delivery system that Johnson & Johnson had tried to build through hostile takeover.[6]

Wall Street Has a Heart Attack

Toward the end of 1997, however, it became apparent that the long-awaited Boston Scientific stent would not be approved that year. In its annual report, the company pushed back the expected date into the last half of 1998:

> *The NIR stent, a product that has received high marks from our European physician customers and currently enjoys a leading market share position there, is expected to launch in the second half of 1998. The NIR is a highly flexible, highly conformable, balloon-expandable stent. We will also launch Radius this year, our first self-expanding, nitinol stent.*[7]

At the same time, another generation of stents entered the U.S. market, with Guidant again leading the way with a single-user rapid-exchange catheter system. The rapid-exchange catheter, which was based on a patent held by Schneider Worldwide in Switzerland, was the standard in Europe. It was little used by U.S. doctors, who had become accustomed to Johnson & Johnson's over-the-wire technology. (In fact, Johnson & Johnson and Boston Scientific both promoted over-the-wire systems in the United States, and the patent battle that had weakened SCIMED was over SCIMED's use of a rapid-exchange delivery system that infringed the Schneider patent.)

As the new stents were introduced, Boston Scientific found itself surrounded by doubters. The company's earnings were still depressed because of inventory buildup and currency fluctuation, and rumors began to fly that its stent would again not be approved on time.

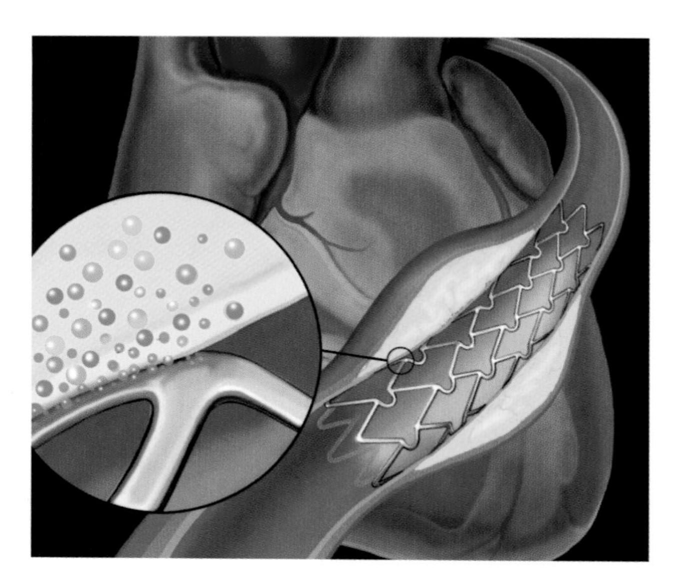

Boston Scientific continued to pursue new technologies aimed at reducing restenosis. This 1999 illustration shows the NIR coronary stent delivering the antirestenosis drug Paclitaxel into a blood vessel (inset). Coated stents improved upon already significant gains in combating this common side effect of PTCA.

World Events

Exxon announces acquisition of Mobil Corporation, the largest corporate merger ever.

Medical Milestones

The FDA approves Viagra for impotence.

Boston Scientific

BSC buys Schneider Worldwide from Pfizer and makes play for market leadership in cardiology.

FDA approves BSC's NIR and Radius stents.

"The concerns range from the timing of and likely commercial prospects for the company's NIR coronary stent to debates about whether the current levels of inventories and receivables are dangerously high and may prompt a large write down," wrote PaineWebber analyst David Lothson. Yet paradoxically Lothson recommended the company as a "buy" stock even as he reported on the market's fears:

> *Boston Scientific has established market leadership in nearly every important market niche in which it competes in vascular and nonvascular catheter markets.... A secretive and extremely proud company, Boston Scientific has not played Wall Street's game like most other public companies, providing neither detailed sales and profit data about its operations nor guidance regarding its ability to successfully identify and exploit new market opportunities.*[8]

This calm remark later proved rather prescient. For the moment, however, Boston Scientific had put itself in a position that made analysts nervous, and its stock had been swinging wildly all year. As one newspaper reporter noted, "Boston Scientific gave Wall Street a heart attack in 1997."[9] The stock lost nearly a quarter of its value in April, after officials warned that first quarter profits wouldn't meet analyst expectations.[10] By August, it had not only recovered but reached a 52-week high of $78.44. It was pummeled two months later when officials again announced that earnings would fall below estimates.[11]

Throughout all these ups and downs, analysts continued to recommend Boston Scientific as a good buy—even if the company was famously uncooperative. One investor, whose firm owned one million shares in Boston Scientific, told the *Wall Street Journal* that "few management teams have the nerve to say to brokerage houses, 'We're not going to give you guidance in the next few months, we're going to manage for the long term.' "[12]

In January 1998, Montgomery Securities analyst Kurt Kruger encouraged investors to build positions in Boston Scientific.[13]

A Bold Play

Nicholas was satisfied with Boston Scientific's relationship with analysts. He wouldn't have had it any other way, in fact. "We have always said to ourselves that we wanted to be measured on the basis of our deeds, our actions, not speculation on what others thought we might do or could do or would do," said Nicholas.[14]

What the company did do, however, took observers by surprise. On June 17, 1998, only months before it expected to get FDA approval for its coronary stent, Boston Scientific announced it would buy Schneider Worldwide for $2.1 billion. The deal was set to close in November.

The acquisition had been prompted by a phone call from Ed Pratt, the retired CEO and chairman of Pfizer Inc, to Peter Nicholas. Pfizer had bought Schneider in 1986 as part of a wave of acquisitions in the medical device business. Large

John Glenn returns to space on Discovery mission.

Cardiologists use stents in two-thirds of angioplasties to prevent restenosis of coronary arteries.

BSC recalls NIR Sox stent six weeks after U.S. launch when doctors report difficulties using the device.

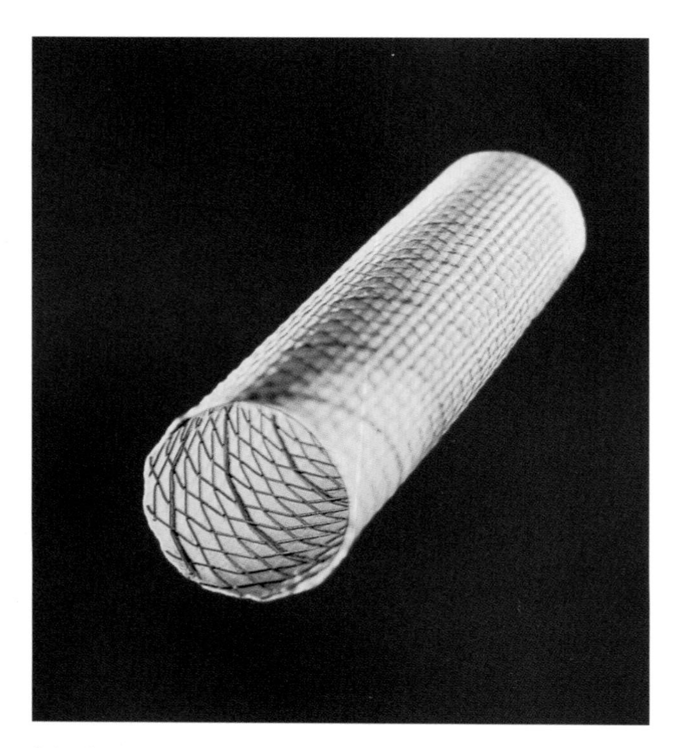

Schneider, a company that Boston Scientific had known about for 30 years, added invaluable stent technology to the company's cardiology division. The Schneider Wallgraft stent was deployed into peripheral vessels and nonvascular applications.

medical companies like Pfizer and Johnson & Johnson were anxious about missing out on a valuable opportunity and rapidly scaled up their device businesses.

By the middle 1990s, however, pharmaceutical companies in particular realized they weren't suited for the much faster device business and didn't like the thin profit margins. They began to shed device subsidiaries. In 1997, Pfizer was looking to sell Schneider, leading Pratt to call the Boston Scientific CEO and say, "Pete, do you still want Schneider?"

"Of course we do," Nicholas answered, so Pratt talked to William Steere, CEO and chairman of Pfizer. A couple days later, Pratt reported back that Steere was ready to sell and instructed Nicholas to call Pfizer President Henry McKinnell.

"I called him and he said yes, they were ready to sell, and yes, they were open to discussion with me," Nicholas remembered. "He took the concept to the board, and eventually the board rejected that idea and wanted to just have an auction. It ended up being an auction with the bankers."[15]

With sales of $330 million at Schneider, Boston Scientific agreed to pay a "relatively stiff" price by offering $2.1 billion, according to the *Wall Street Journal*.[16] But Schneider held valuable patents that made it worth far more than a standard multiple of annual sales. The company was one of only two in the United States (including Guidant) with rights to make the rapid-exchange angioplasty balloon. It also had patents to the popular Wallstent, which held a market-commanding position for treating peripheral vascular disease.

With its own NIR stent quickly approaching the U.S. market, Boston Scientific was making a bold play for market leadership in cardiology.

World Events

U.S. Justice Department and 20 states file antitrust lawsuits against Microsoft Corporation.

Bombings at the U.S. embassies in Kenya and Tanzania kill nearly 200.

Medical Milestones

Scientists read the genetic code of the bacterium that causes tuberculosis.

Boston Scientific

BSC's Japanese subsidiary improperly books millions in sales during first nine months of the year.

But Boston Scientific was not the only company seeking a position in the stent market through acquisition.

In early 1999, after the Schneider/Boston Scientific deal had closed, Medtronic announced that it was buying Arterial Vascular Engineering (AVE) for about $4.3 billion. This acquisition was important to both Medtronic, which needed a solid stent, and AVE, which realized that once Boston Scientific's stent was approved, AVE wouldn't have the critical mass to compete with both Guidant and Boston Scientific.

Boston Scientific employees listen to Pete Nicholas's presentation about the Schneider acquisition. The strategically important acquisition was valued at $2.1 billion and brought valuable stent technology to Boston Scientific.

Dr. Jack Kevorkian is charged with murder for doctor-assisted suicide.

Medtronic announces it will buy AVE, adding stents to its heart device lineup. The acquisition is completed in 1999.

SEC challenges BSC's 3rd quarter $524 million charge taken to write off R&D from its Schneider Worldwide purchase.

NIR Approval

While the Schneider acquisition was still in the works, Boston Scientific spent summer 1998 preparing the medical community for the NIR stent with a major advertising and marketing push centered on the slogan "Nothing Comes NIR."

The NIR stent offered several advantages over our competitors' stents, according to Mike Berman, SCIMED president. Its design incorporated both longitudinal flexibility and radial strength, properties that were usually at odds with each other.[17] Flexibility allowed doctors to navigate tortuous blood vessels. The NIR's design enabled it to become stronger as it expanded, providing superior support to the vessel wall.[18] The stent profile, or the cross-sectional area of the device, was smaller than any other's, said Berman. And, unlike other stents, the NIR had a uniform pattern without gaps for tissue to escape into the artery.[19]

True to prediction, the FDA approved the NIR and Radius stents in summer 1998. With these approvals, Boston Scientific became the only company to offer stents in every area of minimally invasive medicine, including peripheral vascular stents, urinary stents, aortic stents, biliary stents, and finally coronary stents. Coupled with Schneider's Magic Wallstent, which was approved for coronary application in October, it was the only company to offer three heart stents (including the one that resulted from the Medinol partnership).

The NIR Stumbles

With the NIR approval and the pending Schneider acquisition about to close, it appeared things couldn't get any better. Boston Scientific would soon own a leading position in interventional cardiology and stenting technology, and NIR sales were climbing steadily. For a period of several weeks, the NIR stent was the market leader.

"They are constantly pushing the edge of the envelope," remarked analyst H. Axel Schulpf, president of H. A. Schulpf & Company, in the middle of 1998. "They have the broadest product line, thousands of products and product categories, and a large if not the largest market share in everything that they compete in. I see them being the dominant firm."[20]

In the middle of 1998, David Lothson, a PaineWebber analyst who had followed Boston Scientific since its 1992 IPO, released a report entitled *Cardiovascular Device Companies: Emerging Oligopolies*. "In it, I tried to look at what they did that made them so successful," Lothson said in an interview.

> *If you had to tick them off, they bought businesses at the right price in almost every case. They bought businesses that they were very familiar with in terms of the industry. They almost always retained the management and integrated them as part of Boston Scientific. And they focused their acquisitions in areas that made them a major player in minimally invasive cardiology. About*

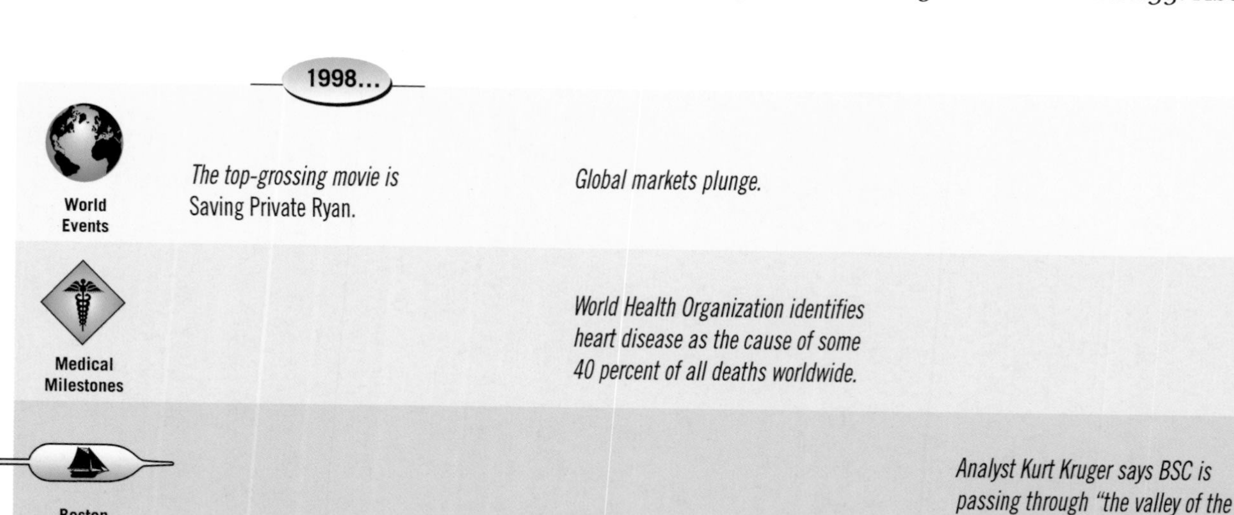

two-thirds of their acquisitions were focused in that area.[21]

The first sign that something was about to go wrong came that fall—and the observation that things couldn't get better turned out to be only too accurate. The coming months would test Boston Scientific in a way the company had never been tested. It faced a series of internal challenges that painfully pinpointed any weakness in its organizational structure, its approach to its industry, and, most importantly, its relationship to its own employees.

It began with the Schneider acquisition. Previously, Boston Scientific and Pfizer had agreed to close the acquisition in November, but Pfizer surprised Boston Scientific by insisting the acquisition closing date be moved to September. Boston Scientific agreed, knowing it would take a tremendous amount of energy and management resources to close a $2.1 billion acquisition two months ahead of schedule.

While Boston Scientific was consumed with this work, the first reports began to trickle in that there was a problem with balloon leakages in the NIR on Ranger with Sox delivery system. Problems with medical devices weren't new. The market-leading Guidant stent, for instance, had the unnerving tendency to fall off the catheter. But Guidant had studied the issue and concluded it was due to operator error rather than a flaw in the product's design and protected itself with sophisticated damage control. Boston Scientific, with no formal public relations department and no formal damage control, had no way of countering any criticism of its stent system.

According to news reports, Ranger balloons equipped with Sox, thin cuffs that attach the stent to the balloon, were perforating. This meant the balloon couldn't expand to its full size, although in all but a tiny fraction of cases the stents were delivered successfully. In October, Boston Scientific elected to pull this particular delivery system from the market but still offered the NIR stent on the Ranger balloon without the Sox adaptation. The company predicted that its supply of NIR stents to the market would not be disrupted.

The Trials Continue

Only a month later, Boston Scientific received a devastating but completely unrelated piece of news. Accounting irregularities were discovered in the company's Japanese subsidiary, which had improperly booked about $100 million in sales. The problem had first been discovered through unrelenting pressure from Larry Best in Boston, and once it had begun to come to light, Boston Scientific launched a full-scale investigation into what was going on.

"We in the United States were curious about different phenomena and going over auditing results," Nicholas said. "When it finally began to crack and the floodgates opened, we were all over it. We had an investigation that was absolutely thorough and take-no-prisoners, and we satisfied ourselves that

U.S. government posts first budget surplus since 1969.

this was something that had been hatched, orchestrated, and executed in Japan without the knowledge of anybody."[22]

This included Jim Corbett, who was running the operation. Yet although Corbett's innocence was without question, he remained ultimately responsible. "I met with Jim, and I told him it was unthinkable to me that a manager, an executive in our company at his level, could be so removed from his business as to not know or prevent this kind of thing from ever happening," Nicholas said.

> *I said, "You have an option. You can leave today, or if you believe in your innocence and you think this is a matter of oversight, you can stay with the company until the conclusions are reached. At that point, if you're exonerated, you can leave on your own volition."*
>
> *He believed in his innocence. He believed that he would be vindicated, and he chose to take the leave of absence but stay in the company and face the music. There was no music. There was no finger pointing to him. There was no implication of Jim Corbett, and when he became satisfied with that, he resigned.*[23]

Boston Scientific reported a $79 million charge to cover the discrepancy, and Corbett's responsibilities were delegated to Paul LaViolette, president of Boston Scientific International. After International's years of rapid and sometimes chaotic growth, LaViolette professionalized the overseas operation.

Alone, the discrepancy in Japan might not have attracted an avalanche of attention, but Boston Scientific was already several weeks late with its third-quarter financial report because of accounting and valuation questions associated with the Schneider acquisition. Just before the acquisition, the Securities and Exchange Commission had changed the rules for allocating acquisition costs to research and development. Boston Scientific, which had expected to allocate much of the Schneider acquisition to research and development, suddenly found it wasn't allowed to and had to refigure its financial statement, delaying the release of third-quarter results.

Considering the situation in Japan and the NIR recall, the timing couldn't have been worse. From the outside, these elements—which in reality had no bearing on one another—somehow appeared to be connected. Analysts openly speculated that Boston Scientific was suffering through some kind of cultural and financial meltdown. Moreover, the very public problems were beginning to put stress on the important Medinol relationship.

In a November article titled "Wall St. wants word with Boston Scientific," the *Boston Globe* conducted a rare and extensive interview with CEO Pete Nicholas and noted that the market value of the entire company had been cut in half since late August. This tremendous drop, the newspaper said, had a lot to do with the way Boston Scientific had structured its relationships with the outside world.

1999...

World Events

Serbian forces kill Kosovo civilians.

Medical Milestones

Massachusetts Gov. Paul Cellucci undergoes coronary angioplasty.

Boston Scientific

The *Globe* quoted Bear, Stearns analyst Frederick Wise: "One of the raps against this company is that management hasn't fully made the transition to acting like a public company. They are not a small, stealth, private company anymore."[24]

The article went on to say that "weak corporate communication may have magnified the series of problems and complications that have beset Boston Scientific in the last month."[25] Larry Best in particular was singled out to "shoulder the blame for the company's problems. Most analysts said Best is spread thin in a lean organization."[26]

Best himself, who before joining Boston Scientific had authored a book on taking companies public, understood this misperception. "When we decided to embark on an aggressive building of strategic mass through acquisition, I was very aware that we were deciding to enter a period in which the challenge was going to be managing through chaos," Best said.

> *Managing chaos, if you prepare for it, is something you can successfully do. When you're in that state of elaboration and you're adding thousands of thousands of employees, you are obviously not spending as much time as you otherwise would on the normal day-to-day running of the business. Therefore, you are creating some chaos, and it is a high-risk model to embark on. The reason we felt comfortable embarking on it was because of the quality of people that we have at Boston Scientific.*[27]

Nicholas also disagreed with the media's slant on the story. Nicholas pointed out that Boston Scientific wasn't acting any differently than it

The *Commonwealth*, pictured in Boston Harbor. This poster was produced by the Japanese staff to help employees there understand the parent company.

always had. The company had historically preferred to let its deeds speak for themselves instead of mounting lavish public and investor relations campaigns. The company was still getting used to dealing with the public and, unfortunately, was experiencing a baptism by fire.

The troubles had yet to run their course. In late November, the company became aware of an investigation by the U.S. Justice Department that appeared to have arisen from the recall of the NIR stent. Although the Justice Department did not divulge the reason for the inquiry, it demanded documents relating to the stent's approval and testing.

This investigation was particularly troubling to leaders at Boston Scientific because it raised the possibility that the company was breaking laws. For a company that had always counted on its "reputational assets," as Peter Nicholas referred to it, this was devastating.

"No one had accused us of wrongdoing, but the implicit purpose of the Department of Justice is to try to understand what happened because of some concern about criminal actions or intent," Nicholas said. "That goes to our integrity as people, as business people, as human beings, and that was very difficult for me personally. If there was any redeeming aspect in that, it was that our customers did not lose faith."[28]

Neither did the financial community. Despite a dropping stock price, a third quarter loss of $509.4 million (due to Schneider), and at least 10 shareholder lawsuits, most major analysts continued to recommend Boston Scientific as a "buy." And in the midst of its problems, Boston Scientific was named one of "America's Most Admired Companies" by *Fortune* magazine.[29]

The Year End

As December ended, Boston Scientific closed the books on perhaps the roughest year in its history. This period, nicknamed "the Year of Job" inside the company, had a profound effect on Boston Scientific. "The year just completed was also a year of reckoning," wrote Pete Nicholas in the annual report.

> *We are cooperating fully with the Department of Justice investigation begun in the wake of [NIR] recall, and believe the government will agree the company acted appropriately. The discovery of business irregularities in our Japanese operation makes us realize that, as we grow, we must develop better safeguards to prevent such occurrences. And we must do a better job of communicating and instilling our corporate values, including personal integrity and accountability, throughout the global organization.*[30]

Although Boston Scientific successfully resolved the SEC inquiry and the Justice Department investigation would drag on, it was a much changed company. It reported $2.23 billion in sales for the year and had 12,000 employees and 2,000 patents. It was truly a global company and, despite the challenges

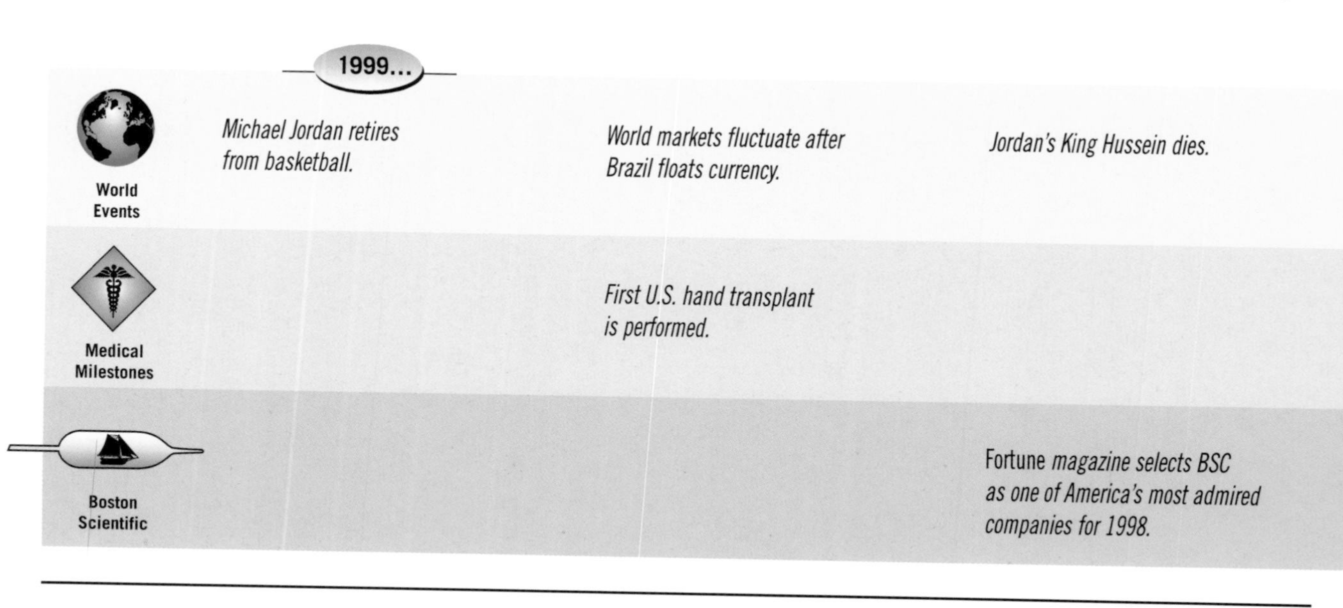

posed in the year, either led its major markets or was somewhere near the top. It was the largest minimally invasive medical device company in the world and expected rapid growth in every business. Boston Scientific was either first or second in the markets of minimally invasive cardiology, urology, neurology, endoscopy, and radiology.

Yet it had to work to rectify the image and communication problems springing from the year's events. "For a long time, we'd been fortunate to manage in good times and in an environment of high growth," said Jamie Rubin, vice president of human relations.

> *In our case, we probably didn't have the systems in place that we needed to carry us through some of these things. There wasn't a steady stream of formal communication from the senior managers in the company. Informal communication is one thing in good times, but it isn't going to carry the day in bad times because it becomes rumor and speculation.*[31]

Throughout the last half of the year, there had been some attempts at communicating to employees, but it was too late to stave off a major blow to morale. At one point, Pete Nicholas even did a live interview with CNN, which was recorded and distributed throughout the company. Yet, as Nicholas himself said, these efforts were after the fact and couldn't protect the employees from an avalanche of bad surprises.

In the future, Rubin said, Boston Scientific would take a more proactive role in communicating bad news to its employees and good news outside the company. "There is no lack of willingness for the leadership of the company to get up in front of our employees, and no lack of consistency in terms of walking our own talk and admitting things went wrong," she said.

> *I think this was a good wake-up call and an acknowledgment and experience because we now have embraced tools that will carry us through these events.*
>
> *Also, people have said to me, "Why can't we read about the good things, as well as the bad things?" That goes back to the communication tools we didn't have in place. Our people are very bright, so I think they understood intellectually, but emo-*

BSC Europe Magazine. Because of the company's rapid growth, communication was an even more pressing issue. Throughout the late 1990s, Boston Scientific worked on its process of internal communication, both formally and informally.

tionally it hurts because they have such a sense of pride in their company.[32]

Restructuring

Early in the next year, Boston Scientific would indeed call upon its commitment to better communication. In 1999, the company announced it was restructuring as a result of the Schneider acquisition and would displace about 2,000 jobs, including 250 at Watertown. Like many acquiring companies, Boston Scientific was growing faster than its resources allowed. Over the previous three years, it had acquired companies with similar technologies and was still rationalizing its manufacturing and eliminating duplication.

This time, Pete Nicholas sent out a personal letter to the more than 12,000 employees explaining the move. "As we enter 1999 and continue the process of improving all components of our company and establishing the right global structure to achieve strong growth, we will continue to implement initiatives begun last year aimed at streamlining worldwide operations and concluding the integration of Schneider," wrote Nicholas.

Regrettably, [these initiatives] will result in the displacement of an estimated 2,000 persons worldwide.

We have made every effort to plan these initiatives with great sensitivity for those employees who may be affected.... Many of you will have questions. Your managers have been fully briefed on this announcement and will be conducting meetings today and in the future to discuss it further. They will be available to hear your concerns and get answers to questions. We are committed to keeping the lines of communication open.[33]

1999...

World Events

Medical Milestones

Boston Scientific

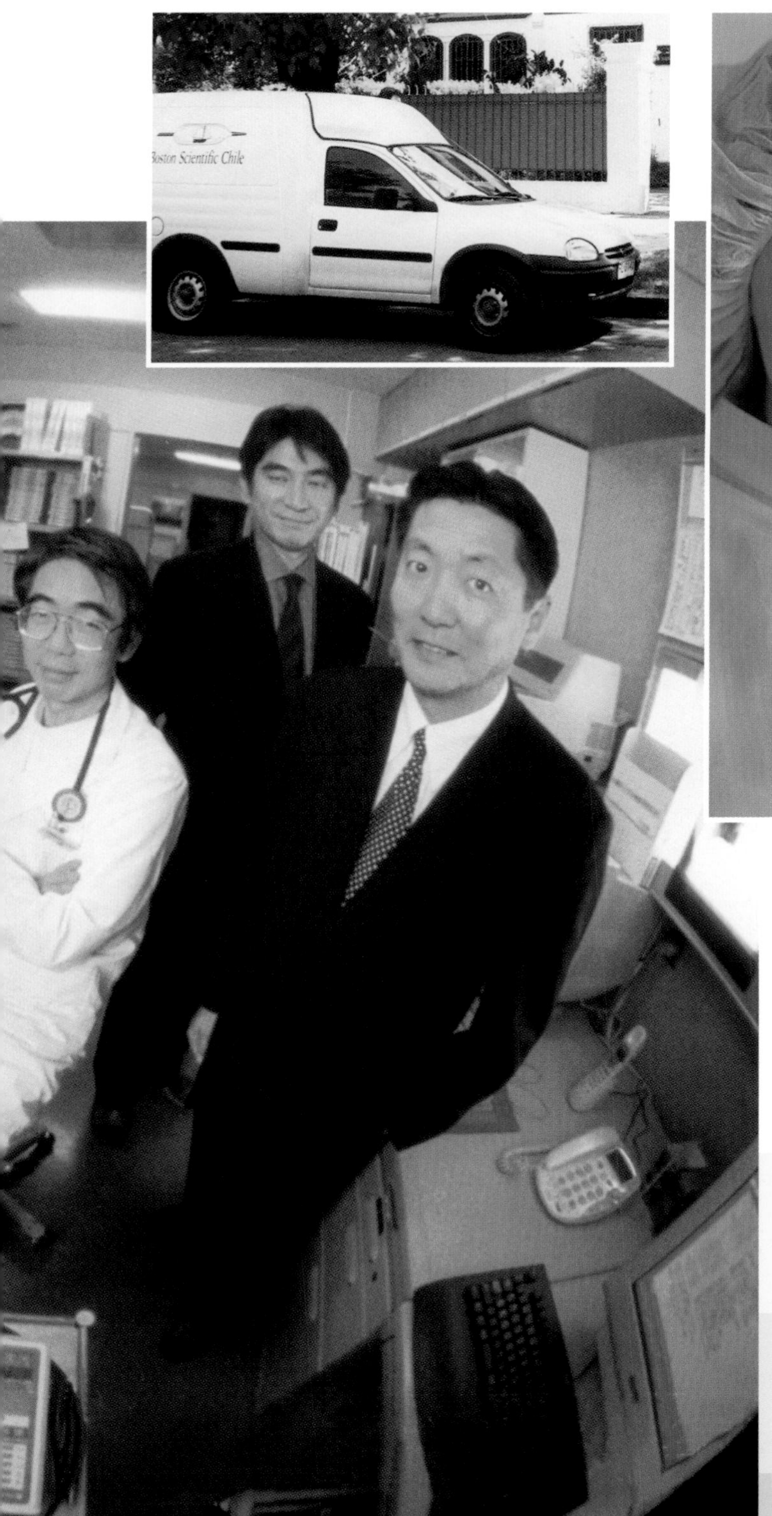

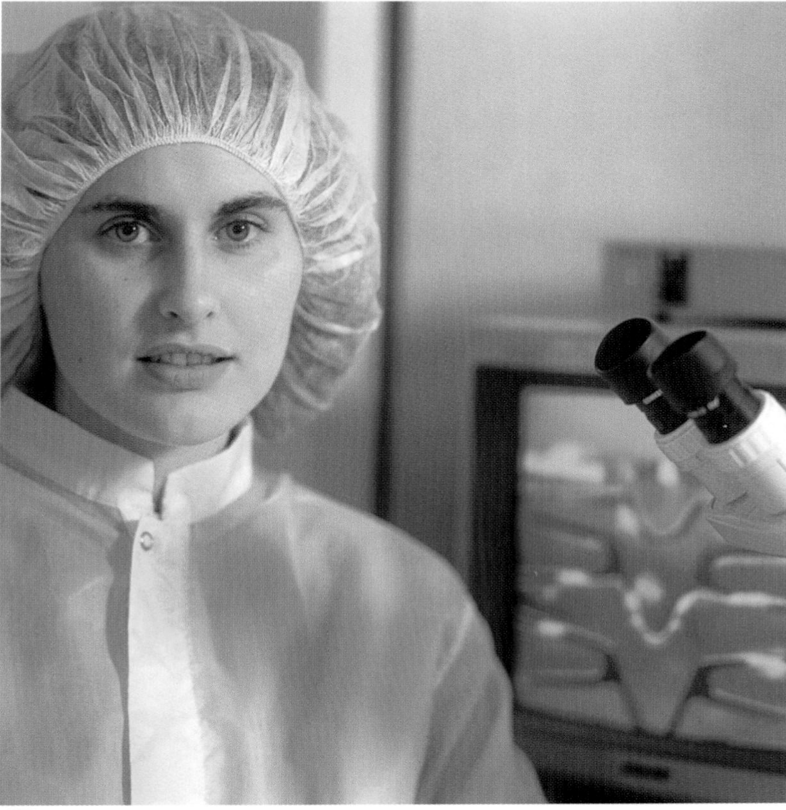

As an international company, Boston Scientific had dedicated staffs and facilities in Japan, left, South America, top left, and the huge manufacturing plant in Galway, above. By 1997, before the "Year of Job" began and after the acquisitions were over, Peter Nicholas had begun looking for a successor to lead the company. This hunt would take almost two years and be suspended by the Schneider acquisition and the raft of challenges in 1998.

Serbia agrees to NATO peace plan requiring military withdrawal from Kosovo.

As part of this promise, Boston Scientific appointed teams of people to travel and talk to every single member of the company in every single facility. The entire senior staff was on these teams and spent weeks shuttling among facilities talking to the company's thousands of employees.

Although it would take time, Boston Scientific had begun the task of coming to terms with its new role as a multinational corporation with thousands of employees, billions of dollars in sales, and multiple product lines. This coming of age promised to touch every facet of the corporation, from the ability to make decisions to the very concept of leadership at Boston Scientific. "I think if you went out and asked people at some of the acquired companies what life is like after being acquired, I believe the perception is that decision making has become more encumbered," Rubin said.

> *I think that's a real sore spot in the organization, and I think frankly the lack of clarity around decision making and decision makers has inhibited our results and our ability to execute. Again, it goes back to other things like a lack of formal, streamlined, consistent communication. It's the lack of wanting to define roles and responsibilities. We've never wanted to ratchet people roles down too tightly. On the other hand, in order to effectively drive business, you do need a reasonable level of defined roles and responsibility. We're not talking about giving way to bureaucracy, but we're recognizing that we need a different set of tools in our tool bag to manage effectively, given size, scope, and complexity.*[34]

Nicholas Steps Down

As part of Boston Scientific's transition, Peter Nicholas felt it was time for him to take an important step. In 1997, he had announced to the board of directors that he was beginning to search for a successor. Nicholas had been CEO since 1979, and he and John Abele felt it was time for the founders to step aside. So, in 1997, Nicholas employed an executive search firm and called through some of the best medical companies in America looking for candidates. The search was interrupted, however, by word that Schneider was in play, leading Nicholas to "put the search on ice" until the acquisition could be wrapped up.

In 1999, Nicholas was once again ready to step aside, and he resumed the search in earnest. Before the Schneider deal, Nicholas had been court-

World Events

International Olympic Committee recommends expulsion of members involved in bribery scandal.

Medical Milestones

Boston Scientific

Mike Mabrey retires.

ing Jim Tobin, president of BioGen. Tobin was perfect for the job. He was a strategic thinker, similar to Nicholas, but he was also an operations expert and could get control of the operational side of the company.

Tobin wasn't receptive. He had joined BioGen with the understanding that he would assume control as CEO in the near future. By late 1998, the situation at BioGen had changed, and Tobin watched his hopes fade. In January 1999, he resigned from BioGen and decided to head out West into an early retirement.

"I called him up and we chatted," Nicholas said.

> *He said he was planning on retiring. I said, "Jim, I understand what you're saying, but in two or three or four weeks, you're going to start getting restless, and you're going to want to get your brain back in gear, and I think we should talk."*
>
> *In February we talked, and we had several marathon sessions together, and by March 10, we had concluded that we were soul mates and this had to be. I told the board of my decision. They were wildly enthusiastic, needless to say.*[35]

Opposite: In 1999, a successor was finally found, and the two founders agreed that it was time to step away and let new management steer Boston Scientific into the future. Pictured from left to right are Peter Nicholas, who had been CEO for 20 years; John Abele, who as founder-chairman had worked to establish the principles of Boston Scientific; and Jim Tobin, who in 1999 was named CEO.

Although Tobin was taking day-to-day control of the company, Nicholas said he would still be actively involved in strategic planning and long-range vision.[36] The news was greeted happily on Wall Street, where Boston Scientific shares were upgraded.

Before Nicholas stepped down, there were two other important moves in the upper executive ranks. Phil LeGoff was given responsibility for both vascular and nonvascular operations, although he would leave the company shortly, and Michael Mabrey, vice president of manufacturing, announced his retirement. During his 12 years with Boston Scientific, Mabrey was an integral part of the effort to organize Boston Scientific manufacturing during the flurry of acquisitions. To commemorate his retirement, the company printed a plaque of gratitude that read in part:

> *C. Michael Mabrey has, since joining Boston Scientific Corporation in 1987, exerted his brand of quiet leadership throughout the Operations organization…*
>
> *C. Michael Mabrey has been the architect of Boston Scientific's facilities program and strategies, demonstrating creativity and firmness…*
>
> *C. Michael Mabrey has been a selfless and collegial team player, an unfailing source of discerning business judgement, and a model of steadiness and reliability.*[37]

Into History

By 2000, it was safe to say that Boston Scientific's early history was drawing to a close.

Astronomers find evidence of other solar systems in the universe.

Senate votes to acquit President Clinton of impeachment charges in the Monica Lewinsky scandal.

The Dow Jones industrial average rises above 11,000.

BSC announces 2,000 job displacements due to integration of Schneider Worldwide and streamlining of manufacturing operations.

Whatever the company faced in the future, it was comfortably secure in its past accomplishments. It had helped pioneer minimally invasive medicine and was one of the pioneering companies in physician education. It had helped found medical societies and helped doctors build practices focused on minimally invasive therapy. In some fields, like endoscopic accessories, Boston Scientific had basically invented the field, helping to contribute to the welfare of untold thousands of patients.

Later, after the inherent risk in managed care became apparent, Boston Scientific became a major driver of change across its industry. In 1995, after it kicked off its string of acquisitions and competitors realized what was happening, the leading four or five companies in the industry made almost 50 acquisitions and strategic investments between them in an effort to keep pace.

Why Boston Scientific was so successful where others failed could be traced to the original series of conversations between Pete Nicholas and John Abele in 1979. They built a company based on teamwork and a relentless drive for leadership free from ego. Instead of crushing its acquisitions, the company drew strength from them and integrated them into the Boston Scientific team. SCIMED, an independent-minded, fast-moving market leader, was a perfect example.

"Everybody here brings value to the discussion," said Art Rosenthal, who joined in 1994 as the chief technical officer. "Everybody here is connected to the business. 'Yes' is not a word that we come by without challenge. It's very common at Boston Scientific to have anybody and everybody asking questions, even if it appears we shouldn't be asking those kinds of questions or if someone doesn't have the title to ask those questions. Everybody's business card says the same thing: 'BSC.' Your name is really your business card, not your title."[38]

Boston Scientific is a company driven by new technologies, so naturally it seeks inspiration from all corners of American industry, and it seeks to use new medical technologies to their fullest potential. Its central purpose is to find engineering solutions to biological problems. This creates the interesting phenomenon that a solution in one part of the body can sometimes be moved to another, giving rise to the ingrained Boston Scientific principle of leveraging technology across its divisions.

"We have done huge pieces of business with our SCIMED business, for example," said Dale Jackson, retired vice president of operations and former head of the Spencer, Indiana, plant. "We've been able to take some of the balloon manufacturing technology that they had—along with Medi-Tech balloon manufacturing technology, which was totally different—and create whole new franchises."[39]

Rosenthal used a medical analogy to describe the way Boston Scientific works:

Look at all the lumens in the body—whether they have fluid in them or not—as roadways, conduits to other parts of the body. We can deal with the lumen itself or we can use it as a path-

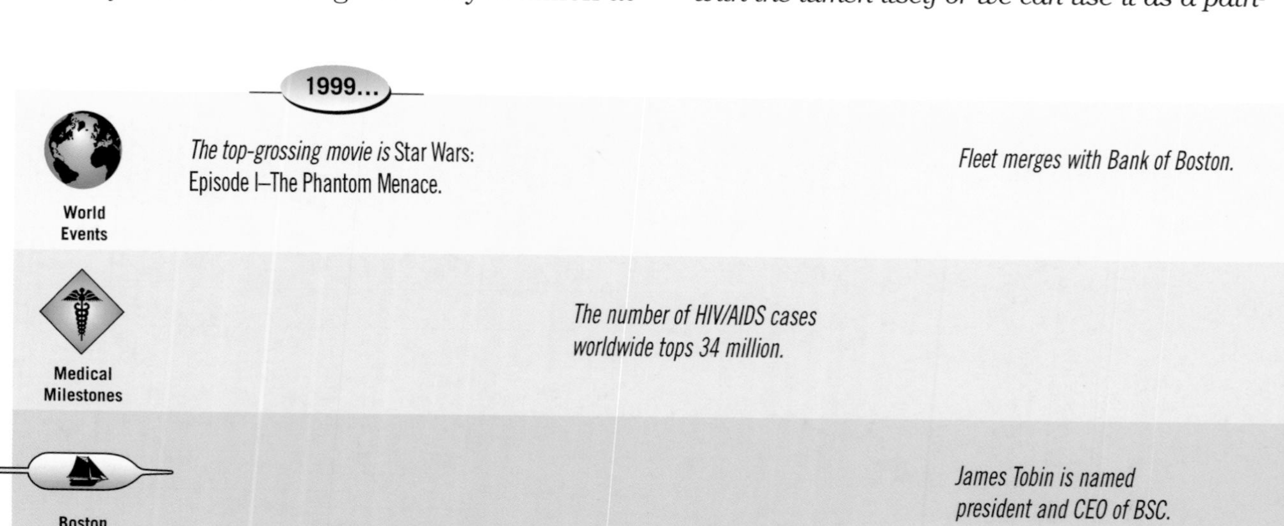

The ship-in-a-balloon symbol remained central to Boston Scientific's core mission: to make medicine less painful, less traumatic, less expensive, and less time consuming for patients. This mission was still as paramount as it was at the founding of the company.

way. We've always looked at fixing the road only, but now we're seeing that the road can probably get you somewhere, and there's no reason why you can't "inside-out" everything.[40]

When asked why Boston Scientific was able to emerge at the top of the industry, employees consistently gave the same answer. It was not the concept of a stealth company that hid its success from the market, or the theory of strategic mass. While those concepts were inextricably linked to the company's leading position, they were only the tools of its success. Instead, the employees talked about the partnership between John Abele and Pete Nicholas, the Boston Scientific team, and the company's focus on patient care.

"The partners have always fostered within Boston Scientific a very entrepreneurial, innovative environment," said Lisa Lamb, the director of employee communications and a Boston Scientific employee since before the IPO.

They very much encourage us to push the envelope. They themselves get involved on a regular basis. You see them throughout the building. They're very much interested in what's happening. They've created an enthusiasm in Boston Scientific that I would say is unique. I think the thing that really keeps people going at Boston Scientific is the fact that the products that we make actually help

Scientists raise mouse intelligence by manipulating a gene.

people, and they help society. We've had wonderful, wonderful customer testimonials, letters from patients about how they've benefited from our technology. It makes it all worthwhile. You get the sense that the company is in it to help further the capabilities of less-invasive medicine not only for itself, but for everybody—for the patients, for our physicians, even for our competitors.[41]

The Boston Scientific board of directors, pictured in 2000. Pictured from left to right are Lawrence L. Horsch, Sen. Warren B. Rudman, Ray J. Groves, James R. Tobin, Joel L. Fleishman, Peter M. Nicholas, John E. Abele, Joseph A. Ciffolillo, and N. J. Nicholas.

Boston Scientific headed into the millennium as a new creation. The company began corporate marketing campaigns designed to promote the Boston Scientific name and create a common language across its many divisions. They would be united by common computer systems, many of the same products, and the same mission and values.

Yet there was also a sense of evolution because, despite Boston Scientific's efforts to deal with its challenges of the previous years, the turmoil continued in the company, in the medical device industry, and in health care in general. Boston Scientific existed in an environment defined by rapid change.

Technology would undoubtedly be a major influence in Boston Scientific's future, as it would change daily life across America. With the rise of Internet-based medical advice Web sites and the ability to move and store huge amounts of information for almost nothing, businesses like Boston Scientific had the opportunity to grow larger while digging even more deeply into specific medical specialties, much like the common image of outer space growing in every direction all at once. One natural consequence of Boston Scientific's dual movement to grow larger as a corporation and move deeper into specific specialties was the strengthening of the company's divisions. The Internet will likely accelerate this trend.

As the company evolved, so had the partnership between Abele and Nicholas. By late 1999, Nicholas held the titles of chairman and CEO, and he had run the day-to-day operations of the company for 20 years. John Abele held the title of founder-chairman and was something of a mystery to outsiders. Over the years, he had disengaged from many of the business decisions, but he still remained involved in the company's mission. "I'm sort of a corporate philosopher about the company vision, goals, and values," he said. "And I'm the corporate historian."[42]

Regarding his partner's seemingly dual focus on Boston Scientific as a corporation and Boston Scientific as a crusade, Peter Nicholas was a firm believer in its success:

> *You can have it both ways. That philosophy was sort of the holy grail of our enterprise. That's what he wanted, and so did I. Eventually, he got enamored of the business process even though, in the beginning, he kept disdaining his involvement because he didn't really want to be up to his neck in business issues. He wanted to be up to his neck in the things he'd always been up to his neck in, which were then and still are very integral to our success. These are not just pedantic, peripheral, unimportant issues. These are critical issues. Without what he could do, we wouldn't have succeeded.*
>
> *Companies do have souls. They do, in fact, respect relationships. They do have honor and walk like they talk. John has been apprehensive, a reluctant participant, an acclimated participant, an embracer of it, enthusiastic, and finally an advocate. He's gone through this whole cycle, and it's only because he and I have walked like we talk as partners. What we said to each other in the beginning is what we really meant.*[43]

Behind everything that had been done to create Boston Scientific lay a powerful motivator: the patients themselves. Minimally invasive medicine had been a grassroots revolution, driven in large part by patients who wanted alternatives to major surgery. Boston Scientific had been a tireless advocate, educating the public, the government, and doctors about the benefits of minimally invasive medicine. And even as the company doubled in size every two years, underneath its chaotic daily life it stood on a solid foundation. As Nicholas wrote:

> *As Boston Scientific has grown, it has changed. Our much larger global enterprise demands different processes from those that served us well in the past. Employees who have joined the company in the last year or two may not have fully internalized the values that guide our organization. This is normal. Growth is organic. It means change. It means constantly redefining who we are, what we stand for, what we want to accomplish and how we will do so. Our strength lies in our vision ... and in our ability to execute it. It lies in the spirit of innovation which permeates our culture and in having people who can translate that vision and spirit into reality.*[44]

EPILOGUE

THERE IS NOT A "LOGICAL SPOT" FOR THE story of Boston Scientific, or of less-invasive medicine, to end. Cataclysmic changes in public perceptions and expectations of health care, acceleration in technology development, and significant changes in business culture, financing, politics, and regulatory and social conditions all continue.

Technological changes in fields as diverse as molecular biology, imaging, nanotechnology, and information technology have made it easier to diagnose and treat more diseases faster and more definitively. This success continues to increase demands on a health care system that is struggling to survive and respond in ways that are more "high tech and high touch," more efficient as well as more personal.

The traditional organizational structure of medicine, with its compartmentation (or "siloization") of knowledge by anatomy (cardiology, neurology, urology, gastroenterology, orthopedics) and technology (anesthesiology, radiology, and clinical chemistry) is being assaulted by new technologies and expanding medical understanding, requiring new and different skills to understand and apply.

The effort to respond to these disruptive technologies is tearing at the heart of medicine. The need to be more efficient and productive requires not only new sets of skills but a totally different systemic organization, different methods and topics of education, different processes and sites for delivery of health care, and different methods of funding health care that motivate and support collaboration and teamwork across previously competitive fields.

The evolution of technology is not the only factor affecting the environment. Technology, and a new willingness to take risk, have changed the organization and strategy of all businesses, including those outside of medicine. Even the computer and media industries are vulnerable to disruptive technologies that could trivialize their current products overnight. Many once-strong businesses, such as companies like Xerox, Chrysler-Daimler, and Proctor & Gamble, are struggling to find the right way to continually reinvent themselves to remain relevant to their changing marketplaces.

One seemingly logical tool of reinvention is consolidation. The pressure to consolidate in order to achieve economies of scale is enormous, but this approach is rife with downsides and dangers. Large consolidations are often accompanied by an increase in bureaucracy and the inability to change quickly. Perhaps worse still, these new megacompanies have difficulty supporting an entrepreneurial "let's do it" mind-set among employees.

Nevertheless, many industries have experienced waves of supermergers, creating gigantic new entities. Their long-term viability remains to be seen, but as the buying public has demonstrated time and time again, consumers don't necessarily respond as much to a monopoly driven by a single organization as to how a particular marketplace should be developed.

Also, despite the emergence of these huge industry behemoths, entrepreneurialism, in its forms both good and cynical, has never been stronger. The affluence of the last several decades has produced a surplus of investment capital that is funding tens of thousands of start-up companies. Too much money chasing too few good ideas creates market values that can't be justified on the basis of earnings, only on the basis of "strategic value" and dreams of being bought by a large company or going public. The idea of creating benefit for customers (or patients) gets stretched pretty thin. The media, the public, and just about everyone else grow increasingly cynical at commercial efforts to create the "good life."

In this tumultuous climate, Boston Scientific has taken many steps, including leading an industrywide consolidation, to remain viable. And even as it tried to stay abreast of change, the company experienced several of its hardest years during the late 1990s. From a productivity and quality point of view, the company reengineered a number of processes. From a personnel point of view, it developed a more attractive recruiting and retaining strategy to keep good employees. To foster entrepreneurialism, it has created internal opportunities for development. And to address the ongoing challenge of communicating with itself and the outside world, a communication department was established and its new director was made a member of the executive committee.

But Boston Scientific's main competitive strength does not lie with its internal reorganizations or any one company initiative. In this environment of vulnerability, Boston Scientific is perhaps less vulnerable than it might seem because it is "driven as it started out." The company was founded as an entity that tried to develop technology that led to products that led to procedures that reduce patient risk, trauma, cost, and time. As simple, and perhaps as obvious, as this sounds, it is a mission that is easy to understand, can be measured without much difficulty, and stays relevant to health care systems anyplace in the world.

The implication of this guiding philosophy, which remains as current in 2001 as it was in 1969, is that the specific technology doesn't matter. Boston Scientific is not a technology company or a stent company or a metals company. It is a company whose primary asset is an understanding of medical and health care–system needs. Its goal is to be an intellectually innovative company, not a company that is defined by its products.

As a consequence, Boston Scientific is in a constant state of flux, evolving to meet the expectations of a public whose health care demands will always be ahead of what any corporation or government could supply. This state of constant evolution takes place within an ethical framework that, as medical technology becomes increasingly sophisticated, extends even beyond improved patient care. The ability to address disease states has improved to the point that society must ask itself who should receive the newest treatments and how much these treatments should be worth. A perfect example can be found in the AIDS scourge in Africa: the progression of this dreaded disease can be checked by drugs that the countries cannot afford. Where does the ethical solution lie? Where is the appropriate balance between humanity and the incentive for continued medical innovation?

Even more entangling, the technological component of medicine has very nearly reached a point at which people can be artificially enhanced, physically and mentally. The ramifications of this ability will reach far beyond any debate we can imagine today.

Boston Scientific is in the middle of this revolution, a dealer in disruptive technologies, a forerunner of the future, an organization that cares about doing what is appropriate, not what is possible, in a health care system that is becoming increasingly dominated by money and technology. Despite the challenges it has faced, and will undoubtedly face in the years to come, this driving philosophy has been its greatest competitive advantage. Boston Scientific has touched the lives of hundreds of thousands of people with its technology. It has helped to educate thousands upon thousands of physicians and other health care professionals and has participated in thousands of medical conferences.

Far from complete, the story of Boston Scientific will continue to be written in the years to come, but as the first stage of its development draws to a close, it has earned its place in medical history.

Notes to Sources

Chapter One

1. Leslie A. Geddes and LaNelle E. Geddes, *The Catheter Introducers* (Chicago: Mobium Press, 1993), 45–47.
2. Ibid.
3. Richard L. Mueller and Timothy A. Sanborn, "The history of interventional cardiology: Cardiac catheterization, angioplasty, and related interventions," *American Heart Journal*, 129 (1995): 147.
4. Bernard Lytton, *Perspectives in Urology* (Roche Laboratories, 1976), 119.
5. Mueller and Sanborn, "The history of interventional cardiology," 148.
6. Lytton, *Perspectives*, 119.
7. Ibid., 124.
8. Henry Plummer and Porter Vinson, "Cardiospasm: A Report of 301 Cases," *Medical Clinician North America*, 5, 355–369.
9. *Merriam Webster's Medical Dictionary* (Springfield: Merriam-Webster Incorporated, 1995), 511.
10. Geddes and Geddes, *Catheter Introducers*, 23, 25.
11. Ibid., 37.
12. Ibid., 16–17.
13. "Profile of the Cook Group Companies" (Cook Group Inc. brochure, Cook Group archives), 1987.
14. Geddes and Geddes, *Catheter Introducers*, 54.
15. "Portraits in Radiology: Charles T. Dotter, M.D.," *Applied Radiology*, 1981, 28.
16. Mueller and Sanborn, "History of Interventional Cardiology," 146.
17. Charles T. Dotter and Melvin P. Judkins, "Transluminal treatment of arteriosclerotic obstruction," *Circulation*, 30 (1964): 657, 658.
18. *Life*, 14 August 1964, 43–45.
19. "Portraits in Radiology," 29.
20. Dotter and Judkins, "Transluminal treatment," 670.
21. Frederick S. Keller and Josef Rosch, *The Father of Interventional Radiology: Charles Dotter, Highlights of His Life and Research* (Tokyo: Exerpta Medica, 1994), 7.
22. "Portraits in Radiology," 28.
23. Ibid., 28.
24. Geddes and Geddes, *Catheter Introducers*, 54.
25. Charles Dotter, "Transluminal Angioplasty," 1966, video, supported by the Oregon Heart Association. Filmed at the Department of Radiology, University of Oregon Medical School.
26. John Abele, interview by Burt Cohen, www.ptca.org/archive/inter-views, posted 15 March 1997.

Chapter One Sidebar: Forssmann's Breakthrough

1. Werner Forssmann, *Experiments on Myself: Memoirs of a Surgeon in Germany* (New York: St. Martin's Press, 1974), 81–83.
2. Ibid., 84.
3. Ibid., 85.
4. Mueller and Sanborn, "History of interventional cardiology," 155

Chapter Two

1. Geddes and Geddes, *Catheter Introducers*, 45–47.
2. Mueller and Sanborn, "History of interventional cardiology,"155.
3. Geddes and Geddes, *Catheter Introducers*, 48.
4. Ibid.
5. John Kolb, "Elastic linkage is heart of steerable catheter," *Product Engineering*, 8 September 1969, 19–20.
6. Keith Rabinov and Morris Simon, "A New Selective Catheter with Multidirectional Controlled Tip," *Radiology* (1969): 96, 172.
7. Kolb, "Elastic Linkage," 19.
8. Ibid., 20.
9. Rabinov and Simon, "New Selective Catheter," 172–173.
10. Don Davis, "He's dead, but his genius lives on," *Middlesex News*, 22 June 1980.
11. Ibid.
12. Ibid.
13. Ibid.
14. Ibid.
15. Ibid.
16. John Abele, interview by Kathy Koman, tape recording, 24 September 1997, Write Stuff Enterprises.
17. Mirtala Bentov, "Itzhak Bentov From Atoms to Cosmos," undated, Boston Scientific Corporation archive.
18. Viola Osgood, "Bentov Obituary," *Boston Globe*, 27 May 1979.
19. Davis, "He's dead, but his genius lives on."
20. Ibid.
21. Abele, interview by Koman, 24 September 1997.
22. Brigid McMenamin, "An Odd Couple," *Forbes*, 17 October 1994, 58–59.
23. John Abele's Curriculum Vitae, Boston Scientific Corporation archive.
24. "Medical Instrumentation, A Problem," *Industry*, 31 (July 1966): 7, 21.
25. John Abele, "The Role of Industry in an Accelerated National Program of Biomedicine (Instrumentation)" (presented at "Research in the Service of Man," sponsored by U.S. Senate Subcommittee on Government Research and the Oklahoma Frontiers of Science Foundation, Oklahoma City, 26 October 1966.)
26. John Abele Curriculum Vitae.
27. John Abele, interview by Kathy Koman, tape recording, 6 October 1997, Write Stuff Enterprises.
28. Ibid.
29. Ibid.
30. John Abele, interview by Kathy Koman, tape recording, 6 January 1999, Write Stuff Enterprises.
31. Ibid.
32. "How it all began," *BSC Europe Magazine*, April 1997, 5.
33. Morris Simon and Keith Rabinov, "A model of the aorta for teaching selective catheterization," *British Journal of Radiology* 43 (April 1970): 5.
34. Medi-Tech press release, 24 June 1969, Boston Scientific archive.
35. "How it all began."
36. Abele, interview by Koman, 6 January 1999.

Chapter Three

1. Elaine Pappas-Graber, "A Star in a Growing Galaxy," *Boston Business Journal*, 27 April 1981.
2. Medi-Tech employee newsletter, September 1976, Boston Scientific Corporation archive.
3. John Abele, interview by Kathy Koman, tape recording, 27 January 1999, Write Stuff Enterprises.
4. Medi-Tech employee newsletter, March 1979, Boston Scientific Corporation archive.

5. Kolb, "Elastic linkage," 20.
6. Abele, interview by Koman, 24 September 1997.
7. Sue Sawyer, interview by the author, tape recording, 8 April 1998, Write Stuff Enterprises.
8. Abele interview by Koman, 6 October 1997.
9. John Abele, interview by Kathy Koman, tape recording, 25 August 1997, Write Stuff Enterprises.
10. BSC/MTI history, Boston Scientific Corporation archive.
11. Abele, interview by Koman, 6 October 1997.
12. Bob Brown, interview by the author, tape recording, 23 December 1997, Write Stuff Enterprises.
13. Ibid.
14. Bob Arcangeli, interview by the author, tape recording, 7 April 1998, Write Stuff Enterprises.
15. Cooper Scientific Corporation, brochure for New Surgex, Boston Scientific Corporation archive.
16. John Abele to Rene Luks, 11 October 1979, Boston Scientific Corporation archive.
17. John Abele to Aaron J. Ball, 5 October 1979, Boston Scientific Corporation archive.
18. "Zavala Lung Model," Medi-Tech brochures, 1979–1980, Boston Scientific Corporation archive.
19. Josh Tolkoff, interview by the author, tape recording, 9 April 1998, Write Stuff Enterprises.
20. Lazar Greenfield, interview by the author, tape recording, 8 April 1998, Write Stuff Enterprises.
21. Ibid.
22. John Abele, interview by Jon VanZile, tape recording, 25 July 2000, Write Stuff Enterprises.
23. John Abele, "A Tribute to Dr. Joachim Burhenne," BSC Historical Perspectives, February 1997, Boston Scientific Corporation archive.
24. Ibid.
25. Ibid.
26. Ibid.
27. Abele, interview by Koman, 6 October 1997.
28. John Abele, "Defining Moments," video, 23 May 1996, Boston Scientific Corporation archive.
29. Brown, interview.
30. Abele, "Tribute to Dr. Joachim Burhenne."
31. Ibid.
32. Ibid.
33. Peter Cotton, interview by Jon VanZile, tape recording, 16 April 1998, Write Stuff Enterprises.
34. Dean Harrington, interview by the author, tape recording, 7 April 1998, Write Stuff Enterprises.
35. Brown, interview.
36. Richard Myler, interview by the author, tape recording, 9 April 1998, Write Stuff Enterprises.
37. Spencer B. King, "Angioplasty from Bench to Bedside to Bench," *Circulation* 93 (1 May 1996): 1621–1622.
38. Ibid.
39. Sheila Stavish, "Andreas Gruentzig: Cautious Innovator," *CARDIO* (February 1984).
40. Geddes and Geddes, *Catheter Introducers*, 13.
41. Ibid., 73.
42. Ibid., 74.
43. King, "Angioplasty from Bench," 1622.
44. Stavish, "Andreas Gruentzig: Cautious Innovator."
45. Abele, interview by Cohen.
46. Ibid.
47. Ibid.
48. King, "Angioplasty from Bench," 1623.
49. Abele, interview by Cohen.
50. Myler, interview.
51. King, "Angioplasty from Bench," 1624.
52. Abele, interview by Cohen.
53. Myler, interview.
54. Abele, interview by Cohen.
55. Andreas Gruentzig, "Transluminal Dilatation of Coronary Artery Stenosis," *Lancet*, (4 February 1978): 263.
56. Myler, interview.
57. Abele, interview by Cohen.
58. Ibid.
59. King, "Angioplasty from Bench," 1625.
60. Stavish, "Andreas Gruentzig: Cautious Innovator."
61. Abele, interview by Cohen.
62. Ibid.
63. John Abele, interview by Kathy Koman, tape recording, 5 January 1998, Write Stuff Enterprises.
64. John Abele, "Mansfield History," *Cardiac Chronicle*, spring 1991.
65. Cooper Scientific Long Range Plan 1977-1980, Boston Scientific Corporation archive.
66. Ibid.
67. Matt Clark with Dan Shapiro, "Substitute Scalpel," *Newsweek*, 30 October 1978.
68. John Abele, interview by Kathy Koman, tape recording, 15 October 1997, Write Stuff Enterprises.
69. Ibid.
70. McMenamin, "Odd Couple."

Chapter Three Sidebar: The Cowboy Days and the FDA

1. "Excerpts and Summary of a National Conference on Medical Devices," *Journal of the American Medical Association* (1 December 1969): 1746.
2. Cooper Scientific Long Range Plan.

Chapter Three Sidebar: Ahead of It's Time

1. Myler, interview.
2. Abele, interview by Koman, 6 October 1997.
3. Ibid.
4. Ibid.

Chapter Three Sidebar: Pete Nicholas

1. McMenamin, "Odd Couple."
2. Pete Nicholas, interview by the author, tape recording, 7 April 1998, Write Stuff Enterprises.
3. Ibid.
4. Ibid.
5. Ibid.
6. Ibid.

Chapter Three Sidebar: Clogology

1. Fleischer, David, "Clogology," *Mayo Clinic Proceedings* 65 (1990) 600-602.
2. Ibid.

Chapter Three Sidebar: Dotter's Crying Towel

1. John Abele to Charles Dotter, 19 January 1987, Boston Scientific Corporation archive.
2. John Abele to Charles Dotter, 5 April 1977, Boston Scientific Corporation archive.

Chapter Four

1. William Cook to Kenneth Nilsson, 13 April 1979, Boston Scientific Corporation archive.
2. Nicholas, interview by author, 7 April 1998.
3. John Abele to Kenneth Nilsson, 8 February 1979, Boston Scientific Corporation archive.
4. John Abele, interview by Kathy Koman, tape recording, 24 November 1997, Write Stuff Enterprises.

5. Abele, "Mansfield History."
6. McMenamin, "Odd Couple."
7. Abele, interview by Koman, 24 November 1997.
8. Pete Nicholas, interview by Kathy Koman, tape recording, 15 April 1999, Write Stuff Enterprises.
9. Ibid.
10. Nicholas, interview by author, 7 April 1998.
11. Pappas-Graber, "Star."
12. Malcolm Rowe to Medi-Tech, 31 May 1979, Boston Scientific Corporation archive.
13. Ibid.
14. Ibid.
15. Wilfredo Casteneda, interview by the author, tape recording, 31 August 1998, Write Stuff Enterprises.
16. Harold Coons, interview by the author, tape recording, 8 April 1998, Write Stuff Enterpises.
17. Tolkoff interview.
18. Ibid.
19. Rowe to Medi-Tech.
20. Dave Budreau, interview by the author, tape recording, 17 February 1998, Write Stuff Enterprises.
21. Terrence Deal and Allan Kennedy, *Corporate Cultures: The Rites and Rituals of Corporate Life* (New York: Addison-Wesley, 1982), 1.
22. Nicholas, interview by Koman, 15 April 1999.
23. Ibid.
24. Brown, interview.
25. John Carnuccio, interview by the author, tape recording, 17 February 1998, Write Stuff Enterprises.
26. Pete Nicholas and John Abele, interview by Kathy Koman, tape recording, 6 May 1999, Write Stuff Enterprises.
27. Abele, "Mansfield History."
28. "Boston Scientific Acquires KMA," *Catheter Chatter*, 1 April 1980, Boston Scientific Corporation archive.
29. Abele, "Mansfield History."
30. Abele, interview by Koman, 24 November 1997.
31. John Abele, interview by Kathy Koman, tape recording, 4 March 1999, Write Stuff Enterprises.
32. Abele, interview by Koman, 24 November 1997.
33. Ibid.
34. Abele, interview by Koman, 24 September 1997.
35. Cooper Scientific Long Range Plan.
36. Abele, interview by Koman, 24 September 1997.
37. "Tutorials in Percutaneous Transluminal Angioplasty," produced for Barry Katzen's course, University of Miami, 14–15 September 1981 and 12–13 October 1981.
38. Abele, "Defining Moments."
39. Peter Klaidman, *Saving the Heart* (New York: Oxford University Press, 2000).
40. Arcangeli, interview.
41. Lawrence Galton, "Operation without Surgery," *Parade Magazine*, 10 October 1982.
42. Michael Waldholz, "Long Thin Tubes Take Place of Scalpel in Some Treatments," *Wall Street Journal*, 26 November 1982.

Chapter Four Sidebar: In Search of Home

1. John Abele, interview by Kathy Koman, 13 November 1997, Write Stuff Enterprises.
2. Ibid.
3. Ibid.
4. Medi-Tech press release, 1982, Boston Scientific Corporation archive.
5. Larry Grady, "The mill by the river remembers its roots," *News-Tribune*, 15 November 1984.
6. Abele, interview by Koman, 13 November 1997.
7. Grady, "The mill by the river."
8. Abele, interview by Koman, 13 November 1997.
9. Ibid.
10. Mike Mabrey, interview by Kathy Koman, tape recording, 8 December 1997, Write Stuff Enterprises.

Chapter Five

1. Pete Nicholas, interview by Kathy Koman, tape recording, 5 January 1998, Write Stuff Enterprises.
2. Abele, interview by Koman, 5 January 1998.
3. Ibid.
4. Chuck Aschauer, interview by the author, tape recording, 7 April 1998, Write Stuff Enterprises.
5. Nicholas, interview by Koman, 5 January 1998.
6. McMenamin, "Odd Couple."
7. Abele, interview by Koman, 5 January 1998.
8. Ibid.
9. Peter Nicholas, interview by the author, tape recording, 7 July 1999, Write Stuff Enterprises.
10. Peter Nicholas, interview by the author, tape recording, 27 July 1999, Write Stuff Enterprises.
11. John Abele to Chuck Aschauer, 15 November 1984.
12. Aschauer interview.
13. Abele, interview by Koman, 5 January 1998.
14. Al Couvillon, interview by the author, tape recording, 17 February 1998, Write Stuff Enterprises.
15. Joe Ciffolillo, interview by the author, tape recording, 8 April 1998, Write Stuff Enterprises.
16. Ibid.
17. Ibid.
18. Ibid.
19. Ibid.
20. "Dick Chenoweth set high standards at BSC," *BSC Matters*, October 1990, 6.
21. John Abele, interview by the author, tape recording, 30 July 1998, Write Stuff Enterprises.
22. Jamie Rubin, interview by the author, tape recodring, 17 February 1998, Write Stuff Enterprises.
23. Ciffolillo, interview.
24. Nicholas, interview.
25. Bob Krajeski, interview by the author, tape recording, 8 April 1998, Write Stuff Enterprises.
26. Ciffolillo, interview.
27. Ibid.
28. Jim Vance, interview by Jon VanZile, tape recording, 21 September 1998, Write Stuff Enterprises.
29. Hal Mardis, interview by Jon VanZile, tape recording, 27 August 1998, Write Stuff Enterprises.
30. Dale Jackson, interview by Jon VanZile, tape recording, 27 May 1998, Write Stuff Enterprises.
31. Ibid.
32. Joe Dowd, interview by the author, tape recording, 8 April 1998, Write Stuff Enterprises.
33. Ibid.
34. Ibid.
35. Joe Lacman, interview by the author, tape recording, 18 February 1998, Write Stuff Enterprises.

36. Janet Sullivan, interview by the author, tape recording, 9 April 1998, Write Stuff Enterprises.
37. William O'Neil, "Seminar on Balloon Aortic Valvuloplasty—Introduction," *American College of Cardiology*, 1991.
38. "Balloons can open narrowed valves," *Heartbeat* (Mansfield newsletter), October 1987, 2.
39. Nicholas, interview.
40. Ibid.
41. Brown, interview.
42. Jerry Lacey, interview by Jon VanZile, tape recording, 5 July 1998, Write Stuff Enterprises.
43. "An Overview of Boston Scientific International," *BSC Matters*, May 1989, 1–2.
44. John Abele, interview by the author, tape recording, 7 February 1998, Write Stuff Enterprises.
45. "BSC's international business flourishes," *BSC Matters*, July 1990, 3.
46. Lacey, interview.
47. "Metals on the Move!" *Tech-Gazette*, August 1987, 1.
48. Alan Milinazzo, interview by the author, tape recording, 9 April 1998, Write Stuff Enterprises.
49. Josh Hyatt, "Reluctant Millionaires," *Boston Globe*, 9 August 1992.
50. Abele, interivew by Koman, 5 January 1998.
51. "BSC Forms Single Operating Company," *BSC Matters*, March 1989, 1–2.
52. Ibid.
53. Abele, interivew by Koman, 5 January 1998.
54. Rubin, interview.
55. Larry Jasinski, interview by Jon VanZile, tape recording, 19 May 1998, Write Stuff Enterprises.
56. Abele, interview by Koman, 5 January 1998.
57. *20/20*, 13 November 1986.
58. John Abele, "Promoting Interventional Radiology," *Cardiovascular and Interventional Radiology* 10 (1987): 245–246.
59. King, 1626.
60. Richard Myler et al, "Coronary Angioplasty: Indications, Contraindications, and Limitations," *Journal of Interventional Cardiology* 2 (1989): 181.

Chapter Five Sidebar: Nicholas and the Banks

1. Nicholas, interview by author, 7 April 1998.
2. Ibid.
3. Abele, interview by Koman, 7 February 1998.
4. Tom Piper, *Harvard Business School Case Study*, copyright 1896 by the President and Fellows of Harvard College.
5. Nicholas, interview by author, 7 April 1998.

Chapter Five Sidebar: Seven Stages in the Evolution of an Idea

1. Richard K. Myler, "Coronary Angioplasty: Balloons and New Devices. How Big is a Niche, How Much is it Worth...and to Whom?" *Journal of Invasive Cardiology*, 4 (1992): 65.

Chapter Five Sidebar: The Long Flight Home

1. Mark Whitaker and Harry Anderson, "An Odyssey of Terror," *Newsweek*, 24 June 1985, 45.
2. Brown, interview.
3. Ibid.
4. Ibid.
5. Ibid.
6. Ibid.

Chapter Six

1. Boston Scientific Corporation, 1993 annual report, 2.
2. Ibid., cover.
3. Nicholas, interview by author, 7 July 1999.
4. Nicholas, interview by author, 27 July 1999.
5. Ibid.
6. Nicholas, interview by author, 7 April 1998.
7. Ibid.
8. Abbott Laboratories, "BSC Assessment: A Preliminary Report," August 1991, Boston Scientific Corporation archive.
9. Ibid.
10. Ibid.
11. Ibid.
12. Ciffolillo, interview.
13. Pete Nicholas and John Abele, letter to employees, 19 February 1992, Boston Scientific Corporation archive.
14. Hyatt, "Reluctant Millionaires."
15. PaineWebber, analyst report, 17 June 1992, 1.
16. John Abele, interview by Kathy Koman, tape recording, 15 August 1997, Write Stuff Enterprises.
17. Hyatt, "Reluctant Millionaires."
18. John Abele, interview by Jon VanZile, tape recording, 1 September 2000, Write Stuff Enterprises.
19. Hyatt, "Reluctant Millionaires."
20. Ciffolillo, interview.
21. Gavin Anderson & Company, press release, New York, 19 May 1992, Boston Scientific Corporation archive.
22. Vanessa Parks, "The Boston Scientific Bonanza," *Middlesex News*, 30 May 1993.
23. Pete Nicholas, interview by the author, tape recording, 4 April 1998, Write Stuff Enterprises
24. Boston Scientific Corporation, 1992 annual report, cover.
25. Ibid., 4.
26. Ibid.
27. Boston Scientific, Form 10-K, 1992, 13.
28. Press release, 26 May 1992, Boston Scientific Corporation archive.
29. Press release, 29 June 1992, Boston Scientific Corporation archive.
30. Parks, "Boston Scientific Bonanza."
31. Joseph Painter to Pete Nicholas, 13 July 1992, Boston Scientific Corporation archive.
32. Taylor McNeil, "Zoning board comes under scrutiny," *Watertown Sun*, 5 August 1992.
33. Joe Clements, "Boston Scientific set to buy Carling Park," *Boston Business Journal*, 21–27 May 1992.
34. Josh Hyatt, "Watertown firm spreads out," *Boston Globe*, 21 July 1992, 39.
35. Ibid.
36. David Tyler, "That was the year that was," *Natick Tab*, 28 December 1992.
37. Jerry Ackerman, "High-tech firm may leave Mass.," *Boston Globe*, 11 February 1993.
38. David Tyler, "Boston Scientific buys office park for $22 million," *Natick Tab*, 25 May 1993.
39. Michael Knell, "Boston Scientific completes deal to buy ex-Prime site," *Boston Herald*, 21 May 1993.
40. Jamie Rubin, interview by Kathy Koman, tape recording, 25 March 1999, Write Stuff Enterprises.
41. "BSC's international business flourishes," *BSC Matters*, July 1990, 4.
42. Ibid.
43. Mike Mabrey, interview by the author, tape recording, 18 February 1998, Write Stuff Enterprises.
44. "Boston Scientific Corporation Announces Plans for Ireland Manufacturing Facility," press release, Boston Scientific Corporation archive, 2 February 1994.
45. "Letter to Shareholders," Boston Scientific Corporation, 1994 Annual Report, 7.

46. Press release, 7 January 1994, Boston Scientific Corporation archive.
47. Paul LaViolette, interview by the author, tape recording, 17 February 1998, Write Stuff Enterprises.
48. "BSC Forms New Division: Mansfield EP," *BSC Matters*, fall 1992, 5–6.
49. Bob Arcangeli, interview by the author, tape recording, 18 February 1998, Write Stuff Enterprises.
50. Dolores Kong, "Use of latest artery tests faulted," *Boston Globe*, 11 November 1992.
51. Gina Kolata, "When doctors say yes and insurers no," *New York Times*, 16 August 1992.
52. "Letter to Shareholders," 1994, 4.

Chapter Seven

1. John Abele, interview by Jon VanZile, 27 September 2000, tape recording, Write Stuff Enterprises.
2. Nicholas, interview by author, 27 July 1999.
3. Abele, interview by VanZile, 27 September 2000.
4. "Boston Scientific Corp., Seasoned Skipper, Choppy Seas," Merrill Lynch analyst report, 5 November 1997, 4.
5. Larry Best, interview by the author, tape recording, 3 August 1999, Write Stuff Enterprises.
6. Milt Freudenheim, "Two Medical Companies to Merge," *New York Times*, 9 November 1994.
7. Boston Scientific Corporation, 1995 annual report.
8. Dale Spencer, interview by the author, tape recording, 9 April 1998, Write Stuff Enterprises.
9. Ibid.
10. Nicholas, interview by author, 27 July 1999.
11. "SCIMED loses bid to overturn $68m ruling," *Boston Globe*, 28 November 1995.
12. Freudenheim, "Two Medical Companies to Merge."
13. Boston Scientific Corporation, 1995 annual report, 4.
14. "Boston Scientific and SCIMED Announce Agreement to Merge," press release, 8 November 1994, 1–3, Boston Scientific Corporation archive.
15. Vector Securities International, analyst report, 18 September 1997, 7.
16. "Boston Scientific and SCIMED Announce Agreement to Merge," press release.
17. "Boston Scientific to buy Heart Technology," *Boston Herald*, 31 August 1995, 32–35.
18. Press release, Boston Scientific Corporation, 30 August 1995.
19. Boston Scientific Corporation, 1995 annual report, F-3.
20. Marie Gendron, "Boston Scientific in new buy," *Boston Herald*, 9 September 1995.
21. "Boston Scientific and Meadox Medicals Announce Agreement to Merge," press release, 29 September 1995, Boston Scientific Corporation archive.
22. Audrey Choi, "Boston Scientific Agrees to Buy Meadox for $425 Million in Stock Transaction," *Wall Street Journal*, 2 October 1995.
23. "Boston Scientific and Target Therapeutics Announce Agreement to Merge," press release, 20 January 1997, Boston Scientific Corporation archive.
24. Lawrence Fisher, "Boston Scientific to acquire specialized catheter maker," *New York Times*, 21 January 1997.
25. Laura Johannes, "Boston Scientific Inc. Agrees to acquire Target Therapeutics for $1.1 billion," *Wall Street Journal*, 21 January 1997.
26. Ibid.
27. Eric Convey, "Boston Scientific may face legal action in Target deal," *Boston Herald*, 16 April 1997.
28. BSC 1996 10-K report, 4.
29. "Boston Scientific Corporation Announces Stent Technology Alliance," press release, 13 November 1995, Boston Scientific Corporation archive.
30. Eckhard Lachenauer, interview by the author, tape recording, 8 April 1998, Write Stuff Enterprises.
31. Nicholas interview, 27 July 1999.
32. Don Hovey, interview by Jon VanZile, tape recording, 21 May 1998, Write Stuff Enterprises.
33. Boston Scientific Corporation, 1995 annual report, 2, 5.
34. "Leveraging New Technology," *Industry Week*, 1 July 1996, 24.
35. Jim Corbett, interview by the author, tape recording, 9 April 1998, Write Stuff Enterprises.
36. Ciffolillo, interview.
37. Boston Scientific Corporation, 1995 annual report, 4.
38. "Boston Scientific Opens Regional HQ in Singapore," *Dow Jones Business News*, 20 January 1997.
39. BSC 1996 10-K report, 18.
40. Mabrey, interview.
41. "US healthcare firm to create 2,050 jobs with 40m investment in Cork and Galway," *Irish Times*, 10 November 1997.
42. Carnuccio, interview.
43. LaViolette, interview.
44. Stephen Moreci, interview by the author, tape recording, 7 April 1998, Write Stuff Enterprises.
45. Ibid.
46. Doug Daniels, interview by the author, tape recording, 18 February 1998, Write Stuff Enterprises.
47. Philip LeGoff, interview by the author, tape recording, 8 September 1998, Write Stuff Enterprises.
48. Boston Scientific Corporation, 1997 annual report, F-2.
49. Glenn Rifkin, "Boston Scientific grows fast and wall street applauds," *New York Times*, 28 December 1995.

Chapter Seven Sidebar: Cardiovascular Imaging Systems

1. "Development of Ultrasound Imaging Technology Expected to Accelerate as Boston Scientific Corp. and Cardiovascular Imaging Systems Agree to Merge," press release, 31 August 1994, Boston Scientific Corporation archive.
2. Press release, 31 August 1994, Boston Scientific Corporation archive.
3. "FTC challenged Boston Scientific's $100 million deal," *Boston Globe*, 20 January 1995.
4. "Boston Scientific Corp. and Cardiovascular Imaging Systems, Inc. announce FTC litigation," press release, 19 January 1995, Boston Scientific Corporation archive.
5. BSC 1995 10-K report, 6, 22.
6. John Abele, interview by Jon VanZile, tape recording, 1 September 2000, Write Stuff Enterprises.

Chapter Seven Sidebar: Vesica Medical

1. BSC 1995 10-K report, 6.
2. "Boston Scientific Announces Expansion of Urology Business Through Acquisition of Vesica Medical, Inc.," press release, 23 March 1995, Boston Scientific Corporation archive.

Chapter Seven Sidebar: EPTechonologies

1. "Boston Scientific and EP Technologies Announce Agreement to Merge," press release, 9 October 1995, Boston Scientific Corporation archive.
2. Aaron Zitner, "Natick firm continues buying spree," *Boston Globe*, 10 October 1995.
3. Press release, 9 October 1995, Boston Scientific Corporation archive.

Chapter Seven Sidebar: Symbiosis Corporation

1. "Boston Scientific Announces Acquisition of Symbiosis," press release, 26 January 1996, Boston Scientific Corporation archive.
2. Michele Chandler, "Symbiosis will be sold for $153 million," *Miami Herald*, 27 January 1996, 1C–3C.
3. Press release, 26 January 1996, Boston Scientific Corporation archive.
4. Rosalind Resnick, "What To Do With $30 Million?" *Florida Trend*, June 1993, 46.
5. David Villano, "Team Symbiosis," *New Miami*, July 1991, 14.
6. Ted Reed, "Life After Merger," *Herald*, 29 October 1995, 1K–2K.
7. Abele, interview by VanZile, 1 September 2000.
8. Villano, "Team Symbiosis."
9. Ibid.
10. Reed, "Life After Merger."

Chapter Seven Sidebar: MinTec

1. Boston Scientific Corporation, 1996 annual report, F-12.
2. "Boston Scientific Corporation Announces Acquisition of MinTec," press release, 3 May 1996, Boston Scientific Corporation archive.
3. Audrey Choi, "Boston Scientific Buys MinTec, a Maker of Stent Devices for About $70 Million," *Wall Street Journal*, 6 May 1996.

Chapter Eight

1. Scott Hensley, "Cardiac Relief: Stent Prices Could Drop With FDA Approvals Ahead," *Modern Healthcare*, 14 July 1997, 86.
2. Ron Winslow, "J&J to Proceed with Purchase of Cordis Corp.," *Wall Street Journal*, 23 January 1996.
3. David Lothson, interview by the author, tape recording, 8 September 1998, Write Stuff Enterprises.
4. John Abele, interview by Jon VanZile, tape recording, 3 September 1999, Write Stuff Enterprises.
5. Klaidman, *Saving the Heart*.
6. "Boston Scientific Rises on Hopes for Late 1998 Sales," press release, 16 January 1998, Boston Scientific Corporation archive.
7. Boston Scientific Corporation, 1997 annual report, 12.
8. David Lothson, "Investors, carpe diem!" Paine Webber analyst report, 1 December 1997, 2.
9. John Hechinger, "Some Managers Contend Analysts Treat Boston Scientific Unfairly," *Wall Street Journal*, 7 January 1998.
10. Eric Convey, "Boston Scientific shares dive on revenue news," *Boston Herald*, 12 April 1997.
11. Hechinger, "Some Managers Contend."
12. Ibid.
13. Kurt Kruger, analysis of BSC, NationsBanc Montgomery Securities,16 January 1998, 1.
14. Nicholas, interview by author, 7 April 1998.
15. Nicholas, interview by author, 27 July 2000.
16. Joseph Pereira, Laura Johannes and Robert Langrath, "Boston Scientific to Pay $2.1 Billion to Acquire Pfizer's Schneider Unit," *Wall Street Journal*, 17 June 1998.
17. Mike Berman, interview by the author, tape recording, 24 January 1998, Write Stuff Enterprises.
18. "Nothing comes NIR," SCIMED brochure, December 1997, 1, 4.
19. Berman, interview.
20. H. Axel Schulpf, interview by Jon VanZile, tape recording, 9 September 1998, Write Stuff Enterprises.
21. Lothson, interview.
22. Nicholas, interview by author, 27 July 1999.
23. Ibid.
24. Bailey, Steve, "Wall St. Wants word with Boston Scientific," *Boston Globe*, 13 November 1998, C:4.
25. Ibid.
26. Ibid.
27. Best, interview.
28. Nicholas, interview by author, 27 July 1999.
29. "America's Most Admired Companies," *Fortune*, 1 March 1999, F-6.
30. Boston Scientific Corporation, 1998 annual report, 1.
31. Rubin, interview by Koman, 25 March 1999.
32. Ibid.
33. Pete Nicholas to the employees, 11 February 1999, Boston Scientific Corporation archive.
34. Rubin, interview by Koman, 25 March 1999.
35. Nicholas, interview by author, 27 July 2000.
36. Rosenberg, Ronald, "Tobin lands at Boston Scientific," *Boston Globe*, 19 March 1999.
37. Plaque to C. Michael Mabrey, 1999, Boston Scientific Corporation archive.
38. Art Rosenthal, interview by the author, tape recording, 17 February 1998, Write Stuff Enterprises.
39. Jackson, interview.
40. Rosenthal, interview.
41. Lisa Lamb, interview by the author, tape recording, 18 February 1998, Write Stuff Enterprises.
42. John Abele, interview by the author, tape recording, 8 April 1998, Write Stuff Enterprises.
43. Nicholas, interview by author, 7 April 1998.
44. Boston Scientific Corporation, 1998 annual report, 5.

INDEX